TO BE FAIR

TO BE FAIR

BEN FENTON

MENSCH PUBLISHING

Mensch Publishing
51 Northchurch Road, London N1 4EE, United Kingdom

First published in Great Britain 2021

A catalogue record for this book is available from the British Library

ISBN: HB: 978-1-912914-24-1; eBook: 978-1-912914-25-8

2 4 6 8 10 9 7 5 3 1

Typeset by Newgen KnowledgeWorks Pvt. Ltd., Chennai, India
Printed and bound in Great Britain by CPI Group (UK) Ltd, Croydon CR0 4YY

To Lila, Alex, Sophie and Julius, who have all lived with fairness longer than is really fair

Contents

Foreword

LAW 42 – THE ULTIMATE ANSWER

Some years ago, I learned that Law 42 of the Laws of Cricket was 'Fair and Unfair Play'. In *The Hitchhiker's Guide to the Galaxy* one of my favourite authors, Douglas Adams, chose the number 42 as the elusive answer to the Ultimate Question of Life, the Universe and Everything. All Adams himself ever said about his choice was that it was entirely random, though Adams was a devotee of the strange cult of cricket.

I choose to believe, regardless of any evidence, that the association of the number 42 with both the Law of Fair Play and the fictional answer to all the problems of our Universe is not coincidental. Over time (especially after a reordering of the Laws of Cricket in 2017 meant that Fair Play became Law 41.7), I came to the conclusion that it really doesn't matter anyway. The idea of fairness is as good a place as any, and considerably better than most, to look for an answer.

Here was my logic: human society is built on and thrives most effectively – one might say solely – on cooperation; cooperation is built on trust; trust is built on fairness. Thus, fairness is the foundation of everything we are and do.

Some people, including some very near and dear to me, regard this view as naive, unrealistic and simplistic, but frankly I think they are wrong. Life *is* simple. It is only its functions that are complex. At the end of every moment and the beginning of the next, each one of us either dies or continues living. The second option is far more likely and also is presumed to be the preferred choice.

If we live, it is also to be presumed that to be happy is preferable. Happiness generally consists of feelings in some combination of: security, satisfaction, kindness received and given, companionship, achievement, experience of beauty, experience of love. Of these characteristics, most if not all are more likely to be achieved within a community of other people rather than through a solitary existence– as Covid-19 has made painfully clear. Conditions conducive to human social happiness usually thrive in orderly rather than chaotic circumstances because tacitly or explicitly agreed rules of behaviour are held in common. Those rules create habits that, in turn, create cultures. The cultures that create the most likely foundation for happiness are those in which the shared rules are founded on a fair exchange of interest – that list of human feelings and characteristics of which happiness consists.

The earliest record that we have of a written ethical code for life is, perhaps ironically, intended as an ethical code for the *after*life. The Egyptians created a list of questions that a dead human's soul must answer before being allowed to pass into a desirable afterlife – in effect, a list of rules for living a good life. The code is called *Ma'at*.

The Egyptians were much closer in time to the early foundations of human civilisation than we are. That means two things: first, that the memory was much fresher for them of what it really means to shift from a loose collection of basic settlements into something that resembles modern society; second, that the code of *Ma'at* was a practical one. It was a manual for cooperative human life. The questions asked of the soul wishing to pass through to the afterlife are obvious enough to contain their own answers.

You may wonder how many questions there are in the code of *Ma'at*.

There are 42.

Why Should We Try To Be Fair?

The phrase 'to be fair' is one of those throat-clearing exercises people use when they are about to challenge or disagree with whomever they are talking to. It means 'wait, we should also consider this,' or, 'have you thought about the following?'

But it means so much more than that. In whatever part of whatever sentence you use the phrase, 'to be fair' is an alert. It tells us to apply our critical faculties, use our minds, exercise our judgement, draw on our memory, balance our opinions on this matter, calculate; in short, it tells us to do the things that make us the most powerful creature on this planet.

To be fair is part of your genetic make-up. It's engrained in your history and that of every person you know. It governs your life in ways you take for granted. But it hasn't always been easy or even possible to be fair. Sometimes, fairness has disappeared from our collective lives and, for billions of people now and in the millennia leading up to now, fairness has never existed. But it has looked after your interests since you were born and will look after your reputation and your legacy after you die.

In the first part of this book, I aim to show you where fairness comes from, what it means and why it matters. In the second part, I will show you the ways it fits into our lives in everything from sport to taxation to social media to warfare.

And finally, I will consider what would happen to all of us if we lost the will and the capacity to be fair.

1

Why You Should Read This Book

THE ROLE OF FAIRNESS: BALANCING
COMPETITION AND COOPERATION

Has the way we all live together changed for the worse in recent years? Do you feel that you and the vast community of competing, cooperating individuals with whom you share your part of the planet could all behave better?

Being able to know how to identify what is good and what is bad about the world we live in, and about the hearts of those we share it with, is crucial. It is crucial both in achieving contentment in our own lives and in achieving a sense of security, believing that those who follow us will be able to thank us for what we left them.

There are some things in our lives that are better not known if we want to continue to value them: how sausages are made and how laws are made are two examples that people frequently cite. Fairness is not one of those things. The opposite is true: the more you know about fairness, the more you will value it. And by its nature, the more people there are that value fairness more highly, the better. For everyone.

So, what's wrong?

For the vast majority of people exposed to the speed, complexity and immediacy of this digital, technological world, our lives and minds are fuller than they've ever been, yet there is still something missing. Greater access to information, and especially to the opinions of others, has led to confusion and division. It often seems that we are separating from each other with increasing rancour and on ever more complex lines. This is a bad thing if you believe that 'society' – the concept of being associated with others – is something that you want to enjoy and will benefit you. It is also a bad thing because it swims in the opposite direction to the human tide. Since we emerged as a separate and immensely successful species, mankind has been on a more or less permanent trajectory of finding ways to live together more effectively. Simultaneously, we have each of us as individuals been using our huge minds to win battles for space and resources so as to carve out our own place in history. The most worrying aspect of the technological world we have brought upon ourselves now is that, whatever its intentions, the effect of connecting people digitally has been to diminish our cohabiting instincts and amplify our individualism.

For almost all of human history, we have been trying to find ways to benefit ourselves by cooperating with others. To do that, we have made sacrifices of our freedom and prosperity because there is a trade-off in doing so: the security, convenience and prosperity derived from gathering together with others.

The other side of our nature from cooperation is competition. In that, we are similar to most other species of life on Earth. Being competitive was crucial to our survival as a species: *Homo sapiens* won out over other hominins because of a variety of competitive advantages, among which the ability to cooperate in hunting and fighting was hugely important. After our species triumphed over others there arose some groups of *Homo sapiens* that enjoyed competitive advantages which allowed them to prosper more than others. Some groups remained the same in small, isolated, self-sufficient basic bands; others joined larger and larger groups, formed societies of ever-growing scale and sophistication and eventually became the kind of communities we all know today. Unlike our isolated hunter-gatherer cousins who still live in remote jungles, on the fringes of deserts or on ice-bound shores, our lives have become replete with technological sophistication and complex networks of relationship with each other. Yet we are not necessarily happier, nor are we any more likely to hand on our genes to whomever and whatever comes next than are those living in secluded places with only basic tools and commodities. Neither our selves nor our species seems to be served by our way of life.

Fundamental to the earliest chapters of the human story is the *balance* between cooperation and competition. This balance affects not just relationships between nations (think of the UN, or NATO or the EU), or between political parties within nations, or between corporations or any other thrown-together gatherings of the human intellect, including families. And the process for achieving that balance, whether we recognise the idea or not, requires us to engage our genetic gift: the sense of fairness.

Determining the cooperation/competition balance was largely a matter of trial and error by our predecessors, and lessons learned by earlier generations/civilisations have not been passed down intact. We are constantly having to relearn what the experience of others ought already to have taught us. We repeat their mistakes. We are an algorithm seeking a better way, but with an imperfect memory. At its most basic, biological level the parameters of that algorithm are the drive to pass on our genes (as every generation of our species has been impelled to do) and the instinct to change things so as to achieve greater satisfaction in our conditions of life – to make progress.

Some people believe that you can divide the world between those who prefer The Beatles and those who prefer the Rolling Stones, or some such random selection. But the one fundamental point of view that defines people is where they stand on this spectrum: how cooperative should human society be and how competitive should it be? How hard should I strive against my fellow humans and how earnestly should I work with them towards common aims? We used to be able to answer these questions elegantly enough. It was called politics or discourse or consensus. But something happened to our ability simply to get on. Why is it so difficult to find common ground? How has it come to pass that the loudest voices being heard are those who represent extreme ideas? What became of empathy, the hallmark of post-war Western society?

The answer to the competitive/cooperative question is perhaps the easiest to find and it points the way to all the other answers: from our earliest times, humans have been programmed by their evolutionary pathways to compete in order to progress and to cooperate in order to sustain.

The concept of two urgent forces, one chaotic and dynamic, the other stable and orderly, is so old that it forms the basis of almost every creation myth thrown up by human civilisations from the Sumerians and Egyptians onwards. It represents the idea of blending the energy of youth with the wisdom of experience. Today, our world is so chaotic and so disordered by the pace of change that it is hard to avoid concluding that we have lost this necessary balance. We are unsettled by disruption and novel threats, by uncertainty over our survival against disease, by confusion over the behaviour and beliefs of those with whom we share our society. We find ourselves craving simultaneously the freedom to be individual and the security of being part of a mass. So, it could not be more important for us to rediscover just how it was that we managed over time – as families, as clans, as nations – to reconcile these apparently conflicting urges of competition and cooperation.

I used to think I was an optimist, but I have recently learned that I am, in fact, an agathist. This word, derived from *agathos*, the ancient Greek word for good, means someone who, while not believing every individual event will turn out well, is sure that the general trend of life is towards progress and happiness. Most agathists believe that we are in a cycle of a human revolution of a kind that has shaken all societies at random intervals. That we will return to a period of quietude after this period of disruption. If you have benefitted from the era of stability post-1945, you probably welcome that idea. But if that stability has left you stranded and disadvantaged, because you cannot afford healthcare or housing or your job is under threat from technological change, then you might see continued disruption of post-1945 norms as a better option. Whichever is more like you, if we are going to experience a moment in time when we are apparently out of balance between our basic urges, then it is surely in everyone's interests for it to be over soon, so we spend more time in a new period of human progress than in a messy period of change? Whether we want the world to be as it was fifty years ago, as it was just yesterday or as it will be in a hypothetical future, how we get there will be a matter of negotiation and consensus rather than imposition. Any change or any resistance to change in a society requires a degree of consensus if it is to endure. Forced change is fleeting.

It is in an effort to find a way to reach consensus that I advocate the value of a simple virtue – that of fairness, the elixir that has allowed us simultaneously to cooperate and compete successfully; I believe that it is fairness which has gone astray and which we must now restore.

I will examine what happened to fairness and will make a simple suggestion that in order to regain our balance, we need to revive a simple idea that embodies the human algorithms of empathy, tolerance and decency: Fair Play.

SOMETHING HAPPENED TO FAIRNESS

Please judge me fairly. I am a good man.

Erroll Graham, in an unsent letter to welfare benefits staff, found near his emaciated body after bailiffs discovered him dead in his Nottingham flat in 2018.
BBC, February 28, 2020

The acquittals of three senior Barclays executives at the Old Bailey today mean that no British bankers will face prison for their actions during the 2008 financial crisis.

Financial Times, February 28, 2020

The first of these stories was broadcast on the morning after billions of dollars were wiped from the value of global companies because of fears about the effects of the Covid-19 pandemic. The second story followed a few hours later.

These events show different kinds of human helplessness in the face of unequal power: first, the death from starvation of Erroll Graham, a benefits claimant whose payments were stopped because he was too depressed and ill to attend an assessment of his worth to society; second, the failure of a nation to apportion responsibility for financial misconduct that caused a crisis of poverty and unfairness around the world; third, the wild fluctuations in the value of supposedly secure institutions caused by the spread of organisms too small for us to see and too vast for us to fight alone.

Only the first story was expressed in terms of fairness. The Barclays case and the pandemic were not. In the case of the pandemic, this was because humans know that fairness is a calculation in which a virus plays no part. Fairness is a contract between people. What we forget, though, is that fairness is just as vulnerable to unseen people exercising unrestrained powers, or to an imbalance in the contributions that humans make to a social contract. The Barclays court case, the final chance to hold an entire system responsible for the effects of complex financial markets, was not discussed by the media in terms of fairness, and I suspect that was because of fatigue. It was twelve years since the crisis; it was ten years since the beginning of a programme of austerity to fill the hole in the national economy caused by the bail out of financial institutions. Blame didn't matter anymore. We had moved on.

But for those of us (and it should be all of us) who think of life in terms of what is and isn't fair, it was a juddering day.

Fairness is a prerequisite of trust; trust is a prerequisite of trade; trade is a prerequisite of civilisation. I do not think it is unreasonable to conclude that fairness underpins civilisation.

In each of these relationships – fairness, trust and trade – there are two parties. For both to benefit, both must be prepared to surrender some advantage or some possession, or neither will gain. It is not altruism that glues us together but moderated self-interest. In most civilisations, there are two sides: governed and governors. If those who obtain advantage abuse their position by damaging those over whom they have obtained it, a contract is broken. This eventually leads either to a breakdown in the relationship between the parties to that contract, or it leads to the imposition of the will of one on the other. History suggests it is usually those who gain advantage that do the imposing, but not always. Sometimes, those who are abused find a way of resisting. It never ends well. An imbalance between people on either side of a contract is inimical to progress by both.

The two sides must be able to understand each other's position and imagine themselves in the other's shoes. That is the only way to determine the balance of relative advantage. The exercise of empathy is an essential part of fairness. Empathy alone is not fairness because most procedures or calculations of what is fair also require us to consider and argue for our own advantage. Meekly surrendering to another's point of view only builds an inequality of opportunity that leads to resentment.

Whatever other considerations come into achieving the balance that we instinctively understand as fair, one thing is obvious: reaching a state of fairness is a procedure. When the procedure fails, when the process of calculation is not possible because the underlying rules appear to have been broken or ignored, people lose faith. They lose faith in procedure, in consensus and in mutual benefit. They turn instead to faith in more absolute terms rather than procedural ones: fair and unfair are replaced by right and wrong; implicit rules are replaced by explicit prohibitions; for one person to be good, another must be bad. And fairness goes out the window, which is a very unsettling situation both for individuals and for communities overall. The reason for this discomfort is that fairness is innately understood by human beings from infancy onwards. It is wired into the human psyche (and not just the human, as we shall see) and its loss or absence evokes primeval fear and anger.

A game of children's football in a park will last longer if the sides are fairly selected to create a reasonably equal contest than if all the best players end up on the same side. Short-term one-sidedness might bring a satisfying victory to the stronger side, but before long the weaker players will simply not want to participate. The trade-off between getting a game in the first place and being predictably and soundly beaten becomes unacceptable.

The same applies to any form of human association: a group of garden-lovers; the United Nations; a Christmas savings club; a hen night; the Congress of the United States; Goldman Sachs. All may succeed or fail but, if they play fair by each other, the chances increase that all will rise. In the long term, commercial organisations that are successful in seeing the interests of their employees, shareholders and customers as a balance of interests with their own, are likely to return most to each group.

The same applies to politics. Democracy is the clearest demonstration of the delegation of responsibility and power from a large group to a smaller group. It is a trade-off. On the one hand you participate in a democratic state by consenting to be ruled by an elected group of people to achieve the benefits of collective power; on the other, you accept that you will not always be on the winning side and your own personal interests and ambitions may not always be served by those who win the democratic game at election time. The same rules apply to the democratic trade-off as they do in playground football: if one group or one individual consistently sees their interests thwarted by actions they perceive to be intolerable, they will drop out of the game. When one player drops out, it may have no effect, but when most do, the game is up.

Fairness is a mode for politicians. It is a costume they pick from the collective wardrobe when needed. The 2020 presidential election in the US was pronounced fair or unfair, depending on which result the speaker wanted. Fairness was cited in the suffering of people during Covid-19 – in the distribution of vaccines, in the apportionment of responsibility to pay the mighty bill for lockdowns – and this is the aspect that will endure the longest. Fairness was at the centre of the Black Lives Matter campaigns across the Western world, deployed by those outraged by the death of George Floyd whose windpipe was blocked by pressure from the knee of a Minneapolis police officer.

But fairness is not a mode. It is, as we shall see, as much a part of the human condition as breathing. It is as important to us as the breath used to claim victory in elections, as the breath lost by the victims of Covid-19, as the breath denied to the George Floyds of the whole world.

I would argue that you should care about all this because this is the game you are in. You should understand not only what the rules are, but how they came about and what are the signs when they are going wrong. Because I doubt you would want to be a participant in any game where it isn't even your choice whether you play or not, and you certainly are unlikely to be on the winning side in the absence of fair play.

THERE IS A LOT OF IT ABOUT

One compelling reason to learn more about fairness and to implement it is a lesson that our earliest ancestors learned the hard way as they scavenged and hunted on the savannah: when others start to look around and show signs of nervousness then it is time for you to look around too, or you will not last long.

Our capacity to cooperate is as important to our survival as our capacity to compete. We depend on each other, far beyond blood relations, to continue, to prosper, to reproduce. How we understand and respond to and relate to members of our own species determines how successful we are as individuals.[1] Part of that complex relationship of cooperation is the capacity to notice when our close neighbours are worried about their environment. Today, a lot of people are worried about our environment but, as much as that, they are worried about the state of our relationships with each other. We hear it every day — mostly, but far from exclusively, in the field of politics. People have written and spoken about binary politics – right vs left, right vs wrong, rich vs poor, haves and have nots – and defined this as an era of populism, as if populists can only express themselves in monochrome terms. And most people would agree that we are living in an Age of Anger. In his book of that title, Pankaj Mishra argued that this kind of disruption is simply an inevitable result of modernity. The product of capitalism and globalisation in countries where it has been experienced as a knock-on effect more than as an evolution or a benefit is what Mishra calls 'an intense mix of envy and a sense of humiliation and powerlessness'. He says that people in societies that once saw humans as part of an intricate weave of life and community have been 'enlightened' into seeing their *individual* roles and selves and to view

[1]Nowak, M. A. & Highfield, R., 2011. SuperCooperators: Altruism, Evolution and Why We Need Each Other to Survive. Reprint Ed ed.:Free Press.

their own existence as one of competition with others. To simplify Mishra's argument, competition has got the edge over cooperation. Anger replaces discourse and consensus. Division, inimical to cooperation, makes impossible the procedures that lead to agreement on what is and isn't fair.

We worry about issues such as climate change, quite rightly, and we worry about the supply of other resources that make our lives tolerable. But fairness, hard-wired into our minds, is a resource and we should worry about that too, not least because it was a resource that was obtained through the deaths of tens of millions of people in wars fought last century.

We have many reasons to be interested in the science of fairness and in its practice. In the past thirty years, people far cleverer than me have developed theories of fairness in closely-argued detail. Others have written about the decline of that mechanical balance between cooperation and competition for which fairness is, in my image, the fulcrum.

But nobody, it seems to me, has made a connection between a decline in consensus (a rise in anger) and a decline in fairness. Perhaps it is to do with timing. While the causes of these declines took place over a few decades after the end of the Cold War, it took a little while for the effects to become clear in the West. Perhaps the release of an oppressive global tension made us complacent and decadent about the need to balance competition and cooperation. Perhaps the generation that did not grow up with the threat of a nuclear apocalypse, something for which politicians alone could be blamed, now focus on issues such as climate change or racial intolerance, for which their fellow human beings of all kinds can be blamed. Maybe we take fairness, like breath, for granted.

One definition of the word populism is this: a search by people to find a new balance between their own interests as individuals and the collective interests of their fellow citizens as embodied in the state. In searching for that, because we had experienced a series of assaults on the concept of fairness – the Iraq War, the financial crisis, the blurring of traditional boundaries of behaviour and identity, all of which we will consider in the pages ahead – we no longer wanted to debate in terms of balance. We just wanted to be on the right side and make damn sure we – and everyone else we could influence – knew which the wrong side was.

Perhaps our problem in the West was that 'winning' the Cold War made us complacent. We no longer felt the need to find the cooperation/competition balance, we no longer felt the need to define what was fair because we had 'achieved' the end goal of fairness – Francis Fukuyama's famous End of History[2]. We just did what the Romans did and we became decadent. We forgot why we keep order and how. Throw in the catalyst of technology that 'connected the world' just at the moment we could have done with minding our own business for a while, and it wasn't the end of history. Was it, though, the end of fairness?

THE END OF FAIRNESS?

According to the placeholder that I found on the homepage of www.fairness.com the website was 'quite extensive for the years 2000–2007 but had only irregular updates later'. The site is currently peacefully dozing.

[2]Fukuyama, F., 1992. The End of History and the Last Man. 2nd ed. London: Penguin.

I cannot express how awfully poignant this discovery was. To me, fairness is one of the most important concepts in the history of mankind. The Internet usually has an active place and a website for everything, but apparently not for fairness.

The dates seem hugely significant as well. Since the financial crisis of 2007–8, fairness has been hard to find in Anglo societies where it has, to varying degrees, been part of the fabric of life for centuries. Despite protestations after the crisis from Western leaders such as David Cameron that 'we are all in this together', it is not obvious that the burden of bailing out financial institutions has fallen fairly. It also appears to many that there has been a failure to ensure one of the most important definitions of fairness: that restraints should be placed on those we have consented to let govern us or set our rules of conduct. We expect those to whom we delegate our own negotiating position in the procedure of reaching a fair society to do certain things: govern for all; act competently; tell the truth and the whole truth; protect the vulnerable and constrain the powerful; keep us safe from crime and from external threats to our security; divide resources proportionately; the list could go on.

The essence of society, particularly in Britain where the origins of this contractual negotiation between ruled and rulers can be traced back at least 800 years, is that relationships between millions of people can be positive and constructive only when their multitude of interests are balanced out in a fair way.

Fairness has been, for at least a century, a central pillar of the type of society that people vote to achieve: placing restraint on the powerful (the rule of law); enfranchising adults so that all have the same ability to influence policy choices (voting); enshrining as a duty of the state the fair exchange of financial support in sickness or old age in return for a lifetime of contribution to its cost (pensions); similarly in regard to the fair exchange of an even-handed distribution of health care services and technology in return for a contribution to its cost (health systems such as the NHS); an underlying attitude that all participants are entitled to rules of fair play so that what the majority vote for should be enacted and what they oppose displaced (democracy).

Another expression of fairness is in the proverb 'as you sow, so shall you reap'.[3] You should be rewarded with fair shares if you enrich society; you should suffer limitations on your freedoms if you damage society; you should fairly share – according to agreed proportions of taxation – the enrichment you enjoy, because that enrichment derives from and depends on there being a stable society from which to profit.

That is the social contract which is interpreted in a thousand degrees of negotiation and consensus, but depends for its flexibility and tolerance on the assumption that the central *procedures* of fairness are not abused. But now they have been. Capitalism lost its footing in fairness. Finance was rooted in procedural concepts of human interaction. The ideas of credit, trust, bond, fair value, exchange, goodwill, stock, mutuality and equity are all examples of procedures conducted under agreed, though often unwritten, rules which only relatively recently were enacted into laws. It's the fairness-underpinning-trust-and-thus-trade-and-thus-civilisation relationship.

Yet finance failed its fairness test. When the cynical manipulation of all these procedures combined with the deliberate overcomplication of financial contracts,

[3] St Paul's Letter to the Galatians, Ch VI V 7

the whole structure of radical capitalism collapsed in an insolvent heap. The procedures we relied on failed. Fairness was raped in a mockery of the social contract that saw financial manipulators escape with their swag and innocent participants in these procedures patting their pockets, wondering where their money had gone. They asked themselves not only why they lost money, but why they were now bailing out the companies to the benefit of the enormously wealthy people who owned and worked for them. Why, also, the support systems on which the innocent participants in this rigged game themselves relied – health, welfare, police, education – faced their own financial crises, counted in billions but making victims of millions.

To repeat myself if only for emphasis, fairness is a procedure. When things that are *procedural* – things that rely on human interaction, consensus and tolerance – fail, then those who suffer as a result will blame the procedure. They turn towards alternatives that are not procedures, but *absolutes*. Fair and Unfair are replaced by Right and Wrong, by Good and Bad. These are the hard currencies that supplant the soft exchange of fairness. Why, after all, would a group of people trust in systems that are supposedly based on mutual empathy if the 'other side' exhibits no understanding of the good or bad impacts on their lives?

It was particularly unfortunate that it was the world of business, which was traditionally constructed on procedure rather than absolutism, that did such damage to the reputation of fairness. People could not therefore fall back on fairness or trust to mitigate the effects of that damage. As a result of the collapse of fairness, people's search for absolute answers that are rooted in self-defined righteousness fell into rather familiar territory: isolationism, nationalism and a hankering for the illusory comforts of the past.

It was, finally, also our misfortune to live at a time when technology makes all these tendencies to damnation more obvious and more virulent. Social media is the most efficient conduit for the sharing of bad ideas that has ever been invented.

Is it also a useful way of sharing good ideas? Yes; but what does it matter if you pump all of your city's freshwater supply into a pipe that is also carrying its sewage? In order to have any fair discussion about issues it is important, if not essential, to know with whom one is arguing. Without that knowledge, you cannot know whether any sacrifice of your own interests is being matched by a sacrifice that your protagonist is offering. Online anonymity veils intention and motivation. It allows bad actors to hide while they stir up dissent and division. It also exacerbates any tendency for the worst characteristics of human discourse to prevail over the better.

The Internet, generally, and social media in particular, gave us the chance to benefit from the wisdom of a gigantic human village; tragically, it has instead offered us the mentality of the mob. James Madison, one of America's Founding Fathers, warned of the dangers of factionalism which prevented people from remembering their duty to the common good because it 'inflamed [them] with mutual animosity.'[4] Today, thanks to social media, that mutual animosity has become a spectator sport, with the flames fanned by 'likes'. Into such a volatile atmosphere

[4]Haidt, J. & Rose-Stockwell, T., 2019. The Atlantic: The Dark Psychology of Social Networks. Available at: https://www.theatlantic.com/magazine/archive/2019/12/social-media-democracy/600763/

step those who once found it hard to spread their divisive propaganda because it was a barely noticeable taint among the flow of good, clean water. Now it is a catalytic part of a great stink.

And this is why we need to restore fairness. We have to separate the pipework, restore the drinking supply of debate and ideas to something like purity. We have to rescue the procedural approach to establishing our cooperative/competitive balance, the approach that we have developed since the Enlightenment and before.

AND ONE REASON WHY YOU SHOULD NOT READ THIS BOOK

It may be the case that you don't like repetition. If that is true, then you might want to think about putting this book down. In case it wasn't already obvious, the words *fair, unfair, fairness* and *unfairness* will appear very often in this book. I can assure you it pains me as much as it might pain you, for one simple reason: I am a reporter. Journalists are taught in their infancy that repetition of words in news stories is to be avoided at all costs. It is almost as if some law of nature weakens the structure of a narrative unless the reporter thinks of a different way of expressing themselves in each sentence. This leads, of course, to painful strangulation of imagery, euphemism and descriptive nouns, but that is considered preferable to repetition.

So, when I say that the words are going to be repeated very often, it goes against all my instincts as a communicator. It seems pointless to make an apology for that, but I may just try an explanation, because it will tell you something about the nature of fairness.

The reason for all this repetition of fair, fairness etc. is that *there is no synonym for fair*. As we will discover in the next chapter, we English-speakers should consider ourselves lucky to have one single word for fair – almost no other language does – let alone to have more than one.

In a number of books I have read on the subject, authors use other nouns interchangeably with fair. Justice, especially distributive justice, is one of them. Equity, or the more mouth-numbing equitability, is another. But they are not interchangeable.

Fair is fair. And nothing else.

2

The Principles of Fairness

WHAT DOES FAIRNESS ACTUALLY MEAN?

*Common sense isn't a real thing. And its ugly cousin,
fairness, is a concept invented so dumb people could
participate in arguments. Fairness isn't a natural part of
the universe. It's purely subjective.*

Scott Adams – creator of *Dilbert*

*When two tribes of primeval man, living in the same
country, came into competition, if (other circumstances
being equal) the one tribe included a great number of
courageous, sympathetic and faithful members, who were
always ready to warn each other of danger, to aid and
defend each other, this tribe would succeed better and
conquer the other...*

*Selfish and contentious people will not cohere, and without
coherence nothing can be effected. A tribe rich in the above
qualities would spread and be victorious over other tribes; but
in the course of time it would, judging from all past history,
be in its turn overcome by some other tribe still more highly*

endowed. Thus the social and moral qualities would slowly
tend to advance and be diffused throughout the world.[5]

Charles Darwin

If fairness is so important to us, it seems equally important that we should understand what it is. The truth is that fairness is something almost ineffable; to define it is to risk losing its essence. I think that is partly because fairness is embedded in our brains and has been during millions of years of evolution. It is, in effect, an emotion; one that links satisfaction, euphoria, security, rage and fear. Emotions are easy to feel and not too hard to describe, but very difficult to define. Fairness is also immanent: in games, in trade, in governance, the state of fairness is something innately understood by the participants, by both the winners and the losers. That, in itself, is what makes it so difficult to describe: what we understand innately usually defies easy definition.

However, if we are going to confront the erosion of fairness we have described above, we must have a stab at a definition. Be warned, it may not be something you can stick on a fridge magnet.

To that end, I have borrowed heavily from the Australian linguistic philosopher Anna Wierzbicka. As a linguist, her main interest[6] is more in tracing the origins of the word fair and identifying its place within the language of English. So, I have gone beyond her own two definitions

[5]Darwin, C., 1871. *The Descent of Man: and Selection in Relation to Sex*. 1st ed. London: J.Murray. Chapter V

[6]Wierzbicka, A., 2006. *English: Meaning and Culture*. 1st ed. New York : Oxford University Press

of fair and added a third and even a fourth and a fifth. A little further on, I have also included references to John Rawls, a great modern political philosopher whose book *Justice as Fairness* is considered by many as the definitive work on how society – which he defines as 'a fair system of cooperation' – should best be regulated. The definitions and dissections of fairness written by Rawls and other contemporary philosophers such as Tim Scanlon and Christopher McMahon provide essential foundations to a philosophical understanding of the concept.

When Rawls tries to define fairness, he says this (take a deep breath):

> *(a) Social cooperation is distinct from merely socially coordinate activity—for example, activity coordinated by orders issued by an absolute central authority. Rather, social cooperation is guided by publicly recognised rules and procedures which those cooperating accept as appropriate to regulate their conduct.*
>
> *(b) The idea of cooperation includes the idea of fair terms of cooperation: these are terms each participant may reasonably accept, and sometimes should accept, provided that everyone else likewise accepts them. Fair terms of cooperation specify an idea of reciprocity, or mutuality: all who do their part as the recognised rules require are to benefit as specified by a public and agreed upon standard.*
>
> *(c) The idea of cooperation also includes the idea of each participant's rational advantage, or good. The idea of rational advantage specifies what it is that those engaged in cooperation are seeking to advance from the standpoint of their own good.*[7]

[7]Rawls, J., 2001. Justice as fairness: a restatement. 2nd ed. Cambridge, MA: Belknap Press. Page 6

Wierzbicka translates these ideas into the bare bones of language, or 'semantic components', like this:

When people want to do some things with some other people they know that they can do some kinds of things at the same time they know that they can't do some other kinds of things because if they do things like this it will be bad for these other people.

In the interests of brevity, and because I earned my living as a reporter not an academic, I have in this chapter often boiled down the intensive academic study of brilliant minds in a way that is grossly, well, unfair to their work, but it gives you an indication of how such minds approach the idea of fairness. Because for day-to-day uses of fairness, in the procedures that inform our relationships with each other, it is important to start out with definitions that allow us to debate and discuss easily what we mean by fairness. What follows as my proposed definitions – if only fairness was simple enough to have just one – are derived from Rawls and Wierzbicka, taking a combination of the philosophical and the linguistic approach to seek clear understanding of (some of) what we mean by fair. It does not pretend to be all of the meanings, because I think they are legion.

And in pursuit of that goal, I think it is probably easiest to define what fairness and unfairness are by simultaneously pointing out what they are *not*.

WHY BEING FAIR IS DIFFERENT FROM (AND MORE THAN) BEING JUST OR EQUITABLE OR GOOD OR IMPARTIAL

Fairness is a) the state which must be achieved so individuals or groups trust each other sufficiently to agree a trade-off in welfare between individuals or groups, in circumstances where one individual benefits at the expense of another. In other words, if we believe the circumstances are fair, we collectively accept that individuals do not always have to benefit *equally* from those circumstances. The division of spoils from a hunt would be *equal* if the smallest participant, whose principal role in a community was to watch over a flock of sheep, received the same amount of mammoth meat as the king-sized hunter who brought it down, but would that be fair? An imposed equality can generally be held to be unfair, while those who prize equality above all else can believe that a condition the rest of society regards as fair is inegalitarian. This is not just theoretical whimsy. In recent times, repeated psychological experiments have shown that people, even when they appear to be expressing a natural urge towards equality, are actually seeking *fair* outcomes.[8]

This is what differentiates <u>fairness from equality</u>. Fairness is not the same as equality. It is more.

Fairness is also b) the condition in which people in a community believe that limits exist constraining the degree to which some people are allowed to cost others in order to benefit themselves. Fairness in this case determines those limits by consensus (shared opinion) rather than by imposition from a constituted power i.e. the rule of law. Where definitions of fairness are laid down, they are generally described as rules i.e. limits on behaviour agreed by participants, rather than laws, which

[8]See for example Starmans, C., Sheskin, M. & Bloom, P., 2017. Why people prefer unequal societies. Nature Human Behaviour, 07 April, mentioned in Chapter 2, Section C

are limits imposed by an institution – king, parliament, junta – with authority over all. The concept of 'just' also implies an inequality between the judges and the judged which does not apply with fairness. Laws, even when constitutionally proper, can be unfair, as Rawls observed in *Justice as Fairness*. By the same token, rules agreed by individuals or groups to be fair may be unlawful according to the common authority.

This is what differentiates <u>fairness from justice</u>. Fairness is not the same as justice. It is more.

Fairness is also c) the state in which there is consensus in a community that, as far as possible, everyone has an equal chance at success in their endeavours, or at least that they should not be disbarred unreasonably from that chance. This could be called the 'level playing field' condition, although the idea of a level playing field is not really one of fairness, because it suggests that only a playing field that does not advantage one side or the other is fair. The truth is that, in sport, fair play is achieved if both sides experience identical advantages or disadvantages of pitch or conditions: when we are confronted with a sloping football pitch, we do not have to make it flat we merely have to change ends halfway through the contest. While this is a very similar point to condition a) it differs by being a positive aspiration rather than an acceptance of certain levels of inequality.

This is what differentiates <u>fairness from the idea of a level playing field</u>. Fairness is not the same as removing advantage and disadvantage. It is much more.

Fairness is also d) the state in which a person seeking to find common ground with another puts aside unnecessary prejudices and concentrates on basic principles of life, such as the rights and liberties associated with human prosperity, in order to calculate a position that will reflect the interests of all parties appropriately. It does not require people to put aside all beliefs, because rules previously agreed by the parties will not necessarily be based on neutral positions. For instance, the rules of an organisation may assume that members all belong to one religious group, political persuasion or online video-gaming community, so the interests of that organisation take for granted certain biases and preferences. But no individual or group should be disadvantaged solely by virtue of membership of that group or of any distinguishing factor: age, sex or sexuality, race, religion or nationality.

This condition is what differentiates being fair from being impartial. Fairness is not the same as impartiality. It is more.

Fairness is also e) the state in which absolute definitions of right and wrong are suspended or ignored by a community. Such absolute conditions are replaced by agreements to prioritise harmony, consensus and prosperity over ideals of rightness and wrongness. Those seeking harmony, consensus and prosperity may therefore deem unfair something which is defined as right by a religion or another doctrinally-driven institution; that same institution may hold as wrong something that society as a whole regards as fair. In a plural society, where many religions and many political points of view are tolerated, it becomes increasingly difficult to agree on *absolute* moral rules or laws. What better alternative, Rawls asks, 'than achieving agreement based on rules that are fair for all?' Whereas the concept of good is what linguists call an 'unanalysable conceptual prime', fairness is a more complex idea, requiring analysis and definition in relation to a common, rather than an absolute, good.

> This is what differentiates being <u>fair from being moral or ethical</u>. Fairness is not the same as being good. It is more.

There may be other conditions in which fairness is the prevailing state, but these five cover most situations, from running a game of park football to running a country, and they have one important factor in common. That is: such conditions where the *procedural* approach of fairness (trade-offs; freedom to act within limits; prioritisation of common welfare; prioritising agreement; adapting to existing preconditions) has replaced various *absolute* approaches (imposed equality; rule of law; religious or political doctrines of right and wrong) which have generally evolved and arrived as reactions to centuries of conflict provoked by dogma and diktat.

The consensual, procedural conditions of fairness have most often emerged in societies wracked by violence, fermented by injustice, inequality and the oppressive and often arbitrary impositions of morality. The Thirty Years' War, the English Civil War, the French Revolution, all sought to enforce (or remove) absolute conditions of right and wrong by force. Of course, there are more recent, more bloody, more totalitarian examples. To escape those conditions, people have often decided to trade-off absolute rights and freedoms with each other so that they can, through common effort, achieve a fairer society.

And so, one might go as far as to say:

- Achieving the state a) is the function of a representative democracy (or a constitutional monarchy, in its post-1689 form in Britain)
- Maintaining the states b), c) and d) are signs of a well-functioning representative democracy
- Reaching the state e) is the aspiration of a representative democracy

To repeat, there are undoubtedly other definitions of what it means to be fair than these five. That is part of what it means to be indefinable. You need only think about all the relationships in which fairness plays a part to begin to imagine how many millions of circumstances will determine whether something is fair or not fair: employer/employee; parent/child; spouse/spouse; sibling/sibling; friend/friend; teacher/student; retailer/customer; gender/gender; race/race. Those are just the obvious ones. The opportunities to be fair – and its opposite – are as many and varied as the opportunities to smile or frown.

It is also true that what it means to be fair is different in different countries and has changed over the course of history. Wierzbicka and Rawls both identify the appearance of the modern idea of fairness with the emergence of the English Enlightenment of the seventeenth and eighteenth centuries. Amid the turmoil which followed the Civil War (when the injustices associated with Charles I's vain assertion of his Divine Right of Kingship were bloodily replaced with the Puritans' equally iniquitous idea of a divinely-ordained 'common-wealth' of people), older English concepts of representation and liberty were revived and eventually enshrined in the 1689 Bill of Rights.

The following year, John Locke, a man who influenced Rousseau, Voltaire and Kant, published his *Two Treatises on Government* in which he wrote:

*The only way whereby anyone divests himself of his
Natural Liberty, and puts on the bonds of Civil Society
is by agreeing with other men to joyn and unite into a
Community, for their comfortable, safe and peaceable
living one amongst another.*

Locke saw the process of adopting social rules as a
necessary loss of rights, but done in the name of achieving
something desirable through consensus, through
negotiation. The process of coming together in a state of
fairness in 1689 traded off absolute rights of monarchy
against absolute liberties of subjects. If you could put a
date on the 'birth' of fairness, I think it would be this
one. A people decided, for the first time, to negotiate a
balance between cooperation – horizontally among each
other – and competition – vertically between governed
and government. In reality it was just a few people and it
merely set down guidelines for how a fair social consensus
might arise, guidelines which subsequent generations
refined, rejected and redrafted. But if you like the
convenience of start points, this might work. Of course,
it is like setting a date for the beginning of logic or art.
The thought processes, the instinct, the visceral drive were
all there within us. But this period of history, certainly as
far as the British were concerned, gave it breath and life.[9]

WHY IS FAIRNESS IMPORTANT TO US?

It isn't quite pain, but it's more than emotion, isn't it?
The feeling that floods into your mind and body when

[9]If this was the birth, then the conception took place decades earlier when the
first musket-shot of debate was fired on the first day of the English Civil War in,
as it happens, 1642.

you experience something that just isn't *fair*. You might be watching your child on a sports field and nobody will pass them the ball. You might be listening to a work colleague being heavily criticised for something that you know is not their fault. You might be queueing to leave the motorway and somebody drives right up to the front of the line of stationary cars and just muscles in. If you are anything like me, any one of those experiences could make your blood boil. And when I say 'anything like me' what I mean is: if you are also a *Homo sapiens*.

Because the thing is this: all of those things I have just described excite a reaction in our brains. It is not a process we have learned, like changing gear, or frying an egg. That feeling of unfairness is something else. It is innate and latent in all of us. Feeling that something is unfair requires that we have a well-developed concept of what is fair. (Whether fairness and unfairness are actually opposites is not a straightforward question, which we will deal with on a later page, but for now let's just imagine that they are at the very least co-dependent.)

Both instincts are strong, irresistible in our minds because they are cogs in a machinery of thought and reaction which define our status, our personality, our safety, our place among our fellow human beings.

The most important thing we can know about ourselves is this: where do we stand in relation to other people? This is not a trivial question, particularly when applied to our positions in reference to people with whom we do not share a common bond of blood or love.

At the beginning of human time on Earth, that question would define an individual's chances of survival and of the survival of their genes. Nothing could be more important. Could an individual live alone in a hostile environment? Possibly, but not for long and they would, of course, not be able to reproduce which, if anything, is a greater drive than survival. The existence of a lone human would, both from their own point of view and an evolutionary one, be wasted. Could humans survive as a single-family unit? Yes, but the children's opportunities for reproduction would be fatally limited. Could they survive as an extended family or small clan? Yes, more easily, but the limitations of interbreeding would put a cap on their chance of thriving as a group. Wider interaction would be needed.

Therefore, humans needed to have relationships outside their immediate family or clan groups to achieve more than basic survival and reproduction. That meant cooperation and, in the case of the hunter-gatherers that we were until only 12,000 years ago, it meant cooperation with other groups of humans with whom we were otherwise in competition for food, water, firewood and shelter.

To construct anything beyond basic societies, it follows, we needed to overcome natural instincts to compete with others in order to cooperate and, anthropologists believe, this is the reason *Homo sapiens* emerged triumphant over other species of *homo*: because of our ability to work together in larger groups unlike other hominins. By cooperating, we competed successfully against others with whom we could not cooperate.

Tens of thousands of years later, each of us still must evaluate constantly how we relate to others and make the same calculations of self-interest. Some of us are preconditioned to be highly competitive and some to be highly cooperative; most of us are a bit of both. Yet the evidence, in everything from Parliament to a game of park football, suggests that we have developed a response to the complexities of contrasting interests that are pursued both by individuals and by small, related groups. The response is such that we can successfully achieve a balance between competition and cooperation. In turn, that has allowed the construction of enormous structures of mutual benefit between strangers who will never meet or speak and who have wildly different desires and motivations. Think of the NHS or the taxation system or elections; think of Manchester United or Black Lives Matter or the building society movement or Twitter; think of any corporation that shares its ownership with anyone who can afford to buy one unit of its equity. Think of the language of business: share; equity; credit; trust; bond.

Our understanding of trade in particular developed a language based on mutual relations and governed by a simple principle: fairness. Fair trade, fair exchange, fair prices: these are not modern concepts. They come from deep within us.

From the basic principles of trade, as prosperity born of commerce bought us the luxury of spare time, we developed more systems to enhance our enjoyment of life and leisure. Those systems were based on the same principle. Think of an art gallery or museum or a public library, where collections of intellectual property are made available – in Britain, gloriously, for free apart from the payment of taxes – to people who could neither afford to buy them nor who would ever be guests of those who could.

Think of a game of football or cricket in a park, where total strangers can join and participate because they know the rules and know what is and is not tolerated behaviour – beginning with the fundamental idea that the number of participants on each side must be balanced to make the competition mutually rewarding. Think of government, where vast numbers of different opinions on a vast number of topics are resolved into a balance of views to produce laws which we are all (more or less) content to obey.

In every case, cooperation makes competition possible and competition makes cooperation necessary. What is the ingredient that allows this to happen? It is the common understanding of how we 'play' together. In its basic state, playing together – one thinks of the enormous, unstructured games of 'football' in the Middle Ages where the entire male populations of rival villages cooperated in order to compete – has a close approximation to war. Yet we know that even under the application of chivalric rules – perhaps the first code of Fair Play – war leaves no winners. Thus, over time, we sought the thrill of competition and the satisfaction of cooperation in a mutually ordered way. We introduced rules of how to play.

Our recent ancestors, the Victorians, applied the idea of fair regulation to play. Their own ancestors had used fairness to bring order (and therefore prosperity) to government after the horror of the English Civil War and then to bring order (and therefore prosperity) to business as the Industrial Revolution and international trade ignited commerce. Applying regulation to play meant agreeing rules of conduct: one of the insuperable problems of playing football or cricket in the eighteenth and nineteenth centuries was that everyone followed different rules. So, the Georgians and Victorians did what they had been doing since the Enlightenment to everything that they considered inefficient: they regulated it from central principles. They followed the same basic aims as in government and business: order from mutual agreement; trust between participants (enforced by the fear of anarchy or authority) and the sacrifice of any profound advantage that could mean that one side would never win (such as having many more participants or playing down a steep slope while the other side always had to toil up it). Then they wrote down the rules so that everyone knew how to construct that balance between cooperation and competition.

The underlying principle of all these things, the underlying principle of life in our society, is that we all conduct ourselves according to mutually agreed rules even if they don't give us an advantage, because we know that others have to feel benefit if they are to participate. If they won't cooperate, we won't have a game. That game could be football in the park; the game could also be called 'Britain', or 'the USA'.

The diversity that most of us celebrate in the mix of minds and bodies that comprise our nations drives us to act and think in divergent ways. The mix has rapidly become more diverse since the end of the Second World War, more diverse at a pace that our processes of mutual agreement and consensus-creation have not been able to keep up with. Directly as a result of this mismatch of change versus stability, the process of divergent thought and conduct, which deeply thrills many people just as profoundly discomfits others who have yet to be convinced that diversity is necessarily a good thing for them or for the world in which they live.

One thing I have learned from reading data about the way people trust each other in the spheres of politics, business and the media is that there is a simple way of expressing the contrast between those who welcome change without much thought for consequences and those who oppose change without much thought for potential. It is this: do we want to be people who ask *Can We?*; or people who ask *Should We?* Which is the dominant force in life? By now you may be able to anticipate my own conclusion: we should be both, in balance. The function of fairness in a social contract is not just a top-to-bottom guarantee that the powerful will not exploit the powerless and the powerless will not seek to overthrow the powerful. It is also a side-to-side agreement that we will take into account each other's views and preferences, our various fears and desires, when setting our common course. (It is preferable to do this without a civil war.)

Fairness is a basis for consensus and it compels and permits us to cooperate and compete within the same set of agreed rules. Whether or not we have an interest in sport, the expression of fairness in the idea of Fair Play is something which we all have in common, regardless of culture, status, sex or age.

FAIRNESS▷ TRUST▷ TRADE▷ CIVILISATION

In seeking to persuade you to read this book, I lazily asserted that fairness underpinned civilisation, because it underpins trust which underpins trade. That may be lazy, but I think it is true. Sometimes the simplest things are more important than complex ones.

What is not simple is to work out how we know what we know about fairness. In the next chapter, we will look at what recipes our brains and even our genes contain for the calculation of what is and is not fair. But here, in an effort to prove my contention from back to front, let's imagine that we live in something called civilisation.

If you live in a city or a town in a Western society, your idea of civilisation consists of an extraordinary web of interrelationships. There are connections of space, time, sound and sight. In physical terms, roads connect our homes to other homes and to the places upon which we depend for the normal conduct of our lives: to our children's schools, to the shops where we buy food, to the transport stations where we connect to a wider network of trains or buses, to the parks where we relax, to the workplaces where we don't relax, to the hospitals where we are born and where we may die. Because these are all destinations – places we do not own, but visit and use – each connection implies some kind of exchange. Most of these are easy to understand.

In a shop, for instance, or the hairdresser's, it is obvious what the exchange is: money for goods or services. At school or in the park, there may be no overt exchange, but it is still present: we have paid, or permitted to be paid on our behalf, something for that school to be built or for that park to be maintained. In exchange, we expect to be able to use it without further cost. When we travel to work the exchange is more transparently in our favour, where we obtain value for giving something that to us is 'free' – our labour or our intellect, our skill or our knowledge. Whether the exchange is fair or not is another matter. All of these exchanges count as a development of the idea of trade.

In human relationships we are also involved in myriad connections, many of which also involve trade, even if we would never think about them as such. I would count smiling or thanking you for telling me the time as a form of trade. It is an exchange of gifts with no corporeal or monetary value but which aid the life of the other party in the exchange (evolutionary psychologists call it 'indirect reciprocity').

Those sorts of interactions are limitless in number. Every day we encounter other people and exchange valueless thoughts, gestures or ideas. Such exchanges form the basis of all human relationships. The better they go, the more opportunities there are for further exchange. That is the nature of trade. Good trades encourage more trades. If today you love someone, then trade is how your love grew. Of course, it can work the other way.

However, in discussing love, we have raced ahead in the consideration of why fairness is part of everything we do and of all our motivations. Let's step back from these advanced, modern and slightly fluffy ideas of trade and mutual benefit to the far less fluffy lives that our distant ancestors lived.

In *Sapiens*, an examination of how mankind came to dominate the planet, the historian Yuval Noah Harari says that there were three concepts that first prompted people to imagine a universal order for the whole species: money; politics and religion.[10] Money was the first and relied on trust in a single myth – that there is an imagined value in an object, such as silver or cowrie shells or barley (the currency of ancient Sumer) which can represent the real practical value of other commodities that are necessary for survival or comfort e.g. grain, cloth, skins, firewood, furs, axes, perfumes etc.

Possession and use of those commodities make life possible, then tolerable, then predictable and eventually comfortable. Achieving 'possible' allows us to live and reproduce and be part of a growing related band or community; achieving 'tolerable' allows for some choices to be made that give us a particular position or status in relation to the rest of our community, so we can expect ourselves and our children to receive some benefit – a degree of nurture and protection – from that community; achieving 'predictable' allows us to develop tactics in relation to others that shift our status upwards to make the survival and prosperity of our children more likely;

[10]Harari, Y. N., 2015. *Sapiens: a Brief History of Humankind.* Reprint ed. New York : Random House.

achieving 'comfortable' allows for leisure time to develop other ways of gaining commodities, then stockpiling or converting surpluses into forms of tradeable objects (shells or coins or promissory notes) which stand for the value of the surplus we have created.

Money evolved to allow trade to become possible, tolerable, predictable and then comfortable because it is a great deal easier to carry around a bag of shells or coins or notes or a smartphone than a pile of firewood that you might want to trade for a bundle of skins.

But money in all its forms is a myth, Harari says, based on mutual trust that those who possessed money and those who possessed commodities would stick to an agreement of the hypothetical relative value of each. If there were no concept of fair terms of exchange – that I am sacrificing my ownership of a shell so you will sacrifice your ownership of a bundle of firewood – the trade could not take place. The reason we have to reach a mutually agreed, fair exchange is simple: if I were to accept a lower rate of exchange as fair, the value of my shells becomes less than if I demand a higher exchange value. If my shells, which I have exchanged for my labour in a field or the product of my own ability to work flintstones into arrowheads, are so devalued, eventually my position in the community will decline. I will expose my children to the loss of benefits of that community. As well as seeing them shiver in the cold, I will know they are less likely to live through the winter and ensure the survival of my genes.

That's why fairness mattered to our ancestors, even if it took an awfully long time for them to develop a word for it. When something is that important, everyone knows what it means. It is, after all, the biggest deal there can be if you are a participant in the game of life.

It is only relatively recently that fairness has attracted philosophical or scientific study. In the history of experiment and thinking, it has not received anywhere near as much attention as logic or reasonableness or justice, for instance. This is despite the fact that the determination of what is fair in life – either by consensus or by instinct – relies on logic, at least partly defines reasonableness and certainly underpins our attitude to justice.

The interplay of that last pairing – justice and fairness – brings us back to the man who has brought the greatest stature to the study of fairness: John Rawls, arguably the most influential political philosopher of the twentieth century.

There are two facts I would like you to know about Rawls before all others: 1) he was brought up in Maryland; 2) he fought as an infantryman in the Pacific theatre of the Second World War.

The first of these facts is important because Maryland had been a state split in two by the competing doctrines of the American Civil War – for and against the rights of all men to be equal. People became accustomed to making concessions to the views of others, even when they were extremely opposed to their own. The alternative was permanent war.[11]

The second fact is important because Rawls' experience of the closeness and randomness of death drove him to seek

---

[11]The points about Rawls' Maryland origins and military service is taken from Hackett Fisher, D., 2012. *Fairness and Freedom*. 1st ed. New York: Oxford University Press.

a world in which people were more likely to accommodate each other's interests than seek to destroy them.

The approach to philosophy that Rawls adopted was nothing if not practical. He was looking for a formula with which to solve disagreements within a society that has contracted with its members to be fair. However, Rawls considered fairness largely in the context of justice and concentrated on the role that fairness might play in the foundation of a just society. He also saw it as an integrated part of the contracts between individuals that, when collected together, produce a basis for peaceful and productive cooperation.

He was less interested in fairness in itself than in the role it played in greasing the gears of a community's interactions. He did not equate fairness with justice, nor with equality, but took it as a sort of constant in all the other calculations of his worldview. Rawls's lifelong search was for a way to balance the interests of liberty and equality, to balance the rights of people to live as they wanted to with the basic principle that all members of society should be given equal chances to succeed. A middle path between laissez-faire capitalism and distributive socialism. Between competition and cooperation.

In his first and most enduring book, *A Theory of Justice* (1971), Rawls laid out a view of how a society could establish fair rules of the game of life which would allow the game to go on in the optimal way. He saw his work as a counter blast to utilitarianism, which had dominated political philosophy since the time of its first proponents, the eighteenth century thinkers Jeremy Bentham and John Stuart Mill. Even as adapted to more modern sensibilities, utilitarianism's concentration on achieving the greatest average good for society offended Rawls because it paid almost no attention to the differences between people.

Rawls saw that the collective process of deciding what rules people will 'play by' in a society will always be distorted by their own competing interests. We cannot escape our own desire to prosper. He argued that to find those rules, it was necessary to seek an 'Original Position', a place of neutrality from which the fairest balance of interests could be reached. To do this, he invented the idea for which he is most famous: the 'veil of ignorance'. If participants know nothing about their own place in a society – how rich or poor they are when compared to others, how clever or foolish, how able or disabled – they will be compelled to choose fair rules of cooperation that will give them the best chance of prospering and which will do the same for anyone else. If you create rules which disadvantage a group that has less of some important component of good fortune (money, talent, health), you might find when you come out from behind the veil of ignorance that you are in that group and are disadvantaged. So, you will propose the least disadvantaging rules of life.

The aim of the Original Position is to establish what is fair. How? Well, Rawls was more of a fan of Immanuel Kant than Mill or Bentham. He argued that a 'rational and reasonable' group of people behind the veil of ignorance would create the principles of a fair social contract because the moral values they shared directed them towards a moral law – what Kant called the 'categorical imperative'.

The people behind the veil, charged with representing the interests of all in society, are motivated also by 'highest-order interests'. They can frame the common conception of 'goods' – by which Rawls meant not commodities, but the 'good' rules and ideas that benefit all people in that society – and pursue those goods in the most effective way. They can change their conception of goods if they need to. They can also act so as to 'do the right thing', or in other words to follow the 'categorical imperative'.

So, what does Rawls think will be the principles that emerge from this exercise of putting people in the Original Position, unburdened by the baggage of knowledge? These are what he calls the principles of Justice as Fairness.

1) The Liberty Principle: Every member of a community should have an equal right or claim to 'a fully adequate scheme of equal basic rights and liberties' to the extent that the scheme can be applied to all members of the community.

2) The Difference Principle: Social and economic inequalities are to be arranged so that they are both (a) to the greatest benefit of the least advantaged and (b) attached to offices and positions open to all under conditions of fair equality of opportunity.

The difference principle does not, as it might appear at first, lay down rules for equal distribution of resources and opportunities, because Rawls recognised that there needed to be incentives and benefits which were appropriate to the different talents and abilities that are to be found in a social group. So there would inevitably be inequality. It is, you could almost say, a question of balance. Rawls also draws fairness into his basic explanation of what constitutes the sort of social cooperation that humans, in his ideal, would strive to achieve. I quoted it before at the beginning of this chapter. To summarise it here, Rawls says that the balance people are trying to achieve under fair terms of cooperation involve reciprocity, mutual advantage and benefit as laid down by consensual rules and an individual's reasonable aspiration to be better-off as a result of that cooperation.[12]

Other philosophers have treated fairness to an even more exacting series of examinations, some philosophical, some philological and some just biological. Christopher McMahon, professor of philosophy at the University of California, Santa Barbara, has delved deep into the meaning of the concept in several books and articles, notably *Reasonableness and Fairness*. He bases fairness and reasonableness in the area of 'moral concern', which is a general interest in, and care for, the welfare of everyone in a given society. He says the two ideas are central concepts in the 'morality of reciprocal concern'.

I realised that these types of books were not really going to be for me when I read the following sentence in McMahon:

> We could then suppose that when a human whose cognitive and motivational capacities are functioning properly is in a position to make epistemic contact with the associated normative facts, and does make epistemic contact with them, the indicated response – pursuit or avoidance – will follow.[13]

To someone as simple as me, in seeking to understand something like the fairness which is embedded in my genetic make-up, this felt a bit like reading the terms and conditions attached to my smartphone. I understand that they are there and they guarantee certain truths about the

[12]Rawls, J., 2001. Justice as fairness: a restatement. 2nd ed. Cambridge, MA: Belknap Press.

[13]McMahon, C., 2016. *Reasonableness and Fairness*. 1st ed. Cambridge: Cambridge University Press Page 5

services I have bought, but I can with a degree of safety take them for granted. I am hugely grateful someone has taken the enormous time and trouble to think them through and write them down, though I remain unsure if they are to my benefit. However, in the interests of making my understanding of life better and writing what is more a journalistic and polemic approach to the subject, I am certain we will all get on a lot better if we rely on less epistemology and more gut.

IS FAIRNESS ONLY FOR THE FAIR (SKINNED)?

A couple of years ago, I was asked to present my ideas on fairness to a nascent political group. One of their number, a white man like myself, objected to the concept on the grounds that it was 'exclusionary'. He said that people who did not have fair skin could feel that it somehow did not include them. At first I thought this such an example of mental gymnastics by someone seeking offence wherever it could be found that I was tempted simply to leave the room. But however idiotic or contrived or self-serving or manipulative people might be, their ideas are not necessarily flawed because they themselves are, so I started to think more about this apparent absurdity.

Most people do not see the world from my privileged vantage point. I have had a successful career as a journalist, am relatively wealthy and had an expensive education. I had disadvantages that others do not: for instance, my father died when I was six, the worst age according to child psychologists for a male child to lose their male role model and an event from which my mother never truly recovered. Compared to the lives of poverty and violence and oppression that millions suffer daily, this is no big deal, but I do know that events can turn your comfortable expectations inside out.

Be that as it may, my initial reaction to the accusation that fairness is 'exclusionary' was wrong. It is clearly more than likely that the idea of fairness is one that has been denied to those who do not have fair skin. I see fairness as a panacea because I see the world through the eyes of a man, a white man with a comfortable home, living in one of the world's great cities in a country enriched by colonialism (and slavery), surrounded by fellow beneficiaries of a history of trade and exploitation that denied any concept of fairness to those we dealt with across the seven seas.

Perhaps you might argue that fairness is only important, only relevant, to those with the luxury of it in a free society and the security of a fair skin. Even if it is, which I do not believe, that does not mean that it should be ignored or rejected. As you will read, we are not talking about an optional extra of human life. Fairness is a part of you, me and every human that has ever breathed and thought. Fairness is such a fundamental concept to humans that it cries out for a single word to express it. While English is the only major language that has a single word that means only 'fair', the concept exists in the DNA of everyone. However much we seek to make life inclusive and comfortable for all, it would be truly nonsensical and damaging to denigrate fairness because its (now lesser) meaning is also to do with hue. That would be as foolish as to say that we should not talk of trying to 'do the right thing' because someone who identifies themselves as being from the left side of politics might be upset by it. Objections to the meaning of words are valid when they challenge prejudice and smug assumptions founded in historical oppression. But we should not allow the mere possibility of offence to stop us trying to tweak our social contract. Nor should we let it prevent us correcting trends that empower small fractions of society at the expense of common sense, nor mute the liberty to speak and think in ways that may be distasteful to a few. Everyone has a right to object when someone else does something that is bad for them, but they are not therefore allowed to retaliate by doing something bad to the offender. That is why we developed the rule of law alongside the rules of fair play.

Again, what is obvious is that we need a balance in our society between the interests of the plurality of communities within it and the interests of the society as a whole. Too much emphasis on the competitive side of our natures will see people becoming subject to prejudice and discrimination; too much emphasis on our cooperative side will suppress individual views and deprive us of the ability to debate and solve difficult moral problems.

Should we hold back discussion or expression of ideas that cause offence to a small fraction of society? Perhaps. It ought to be one choice for how we confront prejudice or repression of one group by another, but it cannot be a *principle* of social cooperation. Part of seeking a balance between the competition and cooperation innate in all of us lies in adapting to changes in attitudes and priorities. Yet we suppress – as opposed to challenge – the offensive instincts of others at the peril of backlash and division which will have far worse consequences for fairness and tolerance in the long run.

Let me be absolutely clear: all human beings require fairness. It is not just in the genetic make-up of white people, or just in men, or just in heterosexuals, or just in those over the age of forty, or just in the left-handed. It is in human DNA. Set against that, the lessons of history are clear: that a balance of fairness across a whole society will disadvantage some people. That is the point. What we have to do, as Rawls said, is find ways of protecting those who are most disadvantaged within the context of equal opportunities for all to live the best lives they can.

Fairness is not just a British concept, but there are reasons to think that it has been under consideration in Britain, and in those countries that have Britain as a cultural ancestor, for longer than in other countries and that it plays a more central role in our language and our relationships. Of course, just because Britons talk about it doesn't mean they practise any more than, or even as much as, anyone else. And British life has embraced many philosophical concepts that emanate from other cultures and countries – destiny (*karma*), for instance, or *zen*. A sensible world population would borrow from its constituent parts all the ideas that will best serve every nation and every race.

That is pretty much what we have done since we first banded together in large and unruly numbers. The oldest creation myths of our first societies – the stories told by people who were most in touch with how we had evolved as a species from egalitarian hunter-gatherers to hierarchical agrarians – were about finding the balance between dynamism and stability, order and chaos, youth and experience. Change is good, but so is being the same.

Where the idea of fair play has been included in the rule-making of societies, it has driven forward progress towards a better society for all, as long as it has been inclusive of all. A sensible world would also stop behaving like lawyers, trawling dictionary definitions to try to find reasons to reject good ideas, and behave more like teachers, sharing the best knowledge available to bring all members of all classes up to the highest level they can enjoy. We will come back to the question of fairness for all and the prevalence of white Western philosophers and scientists as students of the issue when we look at fairness in history and in particular, fairness and empire.

IS UNFAIR THE OPPOSITE OF FAIR?

It might seem a foolish question, but there is a strong case for saying that these two words are not opposites.

Neurological studies have shown that reactions to perceived unfairness light up a different part of the brain from the reward-function area that lights up when a person makes a decision that may not be positive for them, but has a positive effect on the recipient: a fair outcome. We will look at this in more detail shortly, but suffice to say for now that the *ventral striatum* and the *orbital and medial prefrontal cortex* – reward brain areas – produce fairness responses. Unfairness reactions – which fall into the delightfully-named category of 'moral disgust' reactions – live elsewhere, in the *anterior insula*.

The different locations suggest that detecting unfairness is a different calculation from judging what is fair.[14] Neuroscientists and evolutionary psychologists say that we feel unfairness so powerfully because it represents a signal to us that our place in social hierarchies would be under threat if we ignored it. The reaction of monkeys to perceptions of unfairness is one of unfettered resentment because treatment that disadvantages an animal's status in a group is a threat to their very survival.

But the warm feeling of a fair outcome is less profound because it represents part of a benefit to the balance of our life. It is not the equal and opposite

[14]Nadin, E., 2008. How Fairness is Wired in the Brain. Available at: https://www.caltech.edu/about/news/how-fairness-wired-brain-1423

force to unfairness: being unfairly treated in a small and interdependent social group affects not only survival chances, but also the likelihood of being able to find a mate. Ask any teenager or young adult. Unfair treatment is a warning sign that you are going to have not just a bad day, but a bad life.

So why do we feel unfairness in a different way from the way we feel about fair outcomes? It is more visceral, arriving before the brain can make a logical calculation about the nature or balance of an event. The feeling that something is fair may well come quickly, but still feels like a conclusion reached rather than an instinct felt. Unfairness reels in the mind. We will see in the next section just how old and deep in our evolutionary terms and conditions these feelings are.

Our use of language is another reliable indicator of a qualitative difference between fairness and unfairness. In its earliest usage, the word unfair was not used as the opposite of fair. Instead, the antonym was foul. The opposite of fair play in the early modern usage cited by lexicographers is not unfair play but foul play. It was really not until fair play became a given, something associated with the rules of a regularised activity such as football or cricket, that its opposite became unfair play. Law 42, as we have observed, is the law of Fair and Unfair Play and was only written into the rules of the game in the late twentieth century.

Of course, in older usage, fair is a word that describes the appearance or the character of a thing or a condition: a 'fair maiden' or 'fair weather'. I am struck by the fact that using the word foul as the antonym of fair puts the meaning into the same category as weather, but not in the same category as beauty. In modern times, we do not say a plain-looking person is 'foul of face' (though Shakespeare did[15]), nor indeed 'unfair of face'.

It is even possible that the opposition of these two words matches the places that they occupy in the brain: the positive, fair, in reward areas and the negative, foul, just as we might describe a smell or someone's indecent or immoral conduct, belonging to the disgust areas. Anna Wierzbicka even suggests that the use of fair – the moral sense, as opposed to weather, beauty or other meanings – may be distinct as a shortened form of 'fair play' that evolved as shorthand for the longer phrase. Fairness, under this theory, should then be properly expressed as 'fairness of play' or 'fairness of conduct'. I wonder if this is what happened in the case of the English language: perhaps when our ancestors were looking for a way to describe the antagonistic feelings of fairness and unfairness that sat distinctly in their brains, they applied existing words. The word fair implies positivity, purity and happiness – reward; the word foul implies dirt, revulsion and rejection – disgust. In other words, the vocabulary emanates from the brain areas where these ancient emotions are lodged. It may be that they were applied in English differently because the island-dwelling English (British) had for centuries had a concept of cooperation, and of contracts between cooperators, that was slightly different from other societies and that had been elemental to their survival. It's a theory.

For now, though, let's have a closer look at the brain. Finding where fairness sits and just how much influence on how we think and how we react to others as well as to circumstances in which we find ourselves, will give us a clue to just how important it is to the critical balancing of our lives.

[15]Sonnet 137 'To put faire truth upon so foule a face'.

3

The Neurology and Psychology of Fairness

DO OTHER SPECIES RECOGNISE THE CONCEPT OF FAIRNESS?

The simple answer is yes, although it may also be no. First, we have to think about grapes.

There is a well-known video[16] that very clearly demonstrates that primates understand unfairness extremely well. In the early 2000s, two primatologists working at Emory University in Georgia began to explore the nature of exchange within cooperative communities. Their test subjects were capuchin monkeys.

Dr Sarah Brosnan and Prof Frans de Waal were seeking to understand how the processes of exchange works, so they conducted a simple experiment about the nature of exchange.

Two capuchin monkeys were placed in identical see-through cages next to, but separated from, each other. Each could see the other, but not reach them. Both had

---

[16]YouTube, *Two Monkeys Were Paid Unequally: Excerpt from Frans de Waal's TED talk* available at https://www.youtube.com/watch?v=meiU6TxysCg

been trained to receive a pebble from a scientist through a hole cut in the Perspex cage and then return it through another hole. Completing this simple task lead to a small reward of food. At first, the sessions involved both monkeys receiving the same food: a piece of cucumber. The video shows the beginning of a new session: one monkey is rewarded with a piece of cucumber, but the second is rewarded for the same task with a grape, which capuchins prefer to cucumber. This act of favouritism can be seen by the first monkey. Immediately afterwards, the scientist requires the first monkey to repeat the task and rewards it with a piece of cucumber. The effect is instant. After briefly studying the cucumber, the monkey sticks its arm back through the hole in the cage and flings it back at the scientist. Then it starts to leap about, shaking the cage, reaching out its arm again and slapping the Perspex walls. It is quite clearly throwing a tantrum. Its rage is immediate and obvious. It is reacting against unfair treatment.

The period over which our primate ancestors developed this sense is hard to determine, but it is to be measured in millions, if not tens of millions, of years. The same is true of our capacity to trade.[17] Some scientists even claim that insect species have an innate tendency to trade in order to achieve advantages in mating, although nobody has yet made claims to have found fairness in invertebrates. De Waal says dogs and birds have shown signs that they detect unfair treatment, although other researchers believe these are not of the same nature as primate behaviour.

[17]'Hominins' are a subset of 'hominids' which also includes higher apes and from which *Homo sapiens* (us) derive. All hominins are hominids, but the reverse is not the case.

By studying the monkeys, it isn't hard to work out why rejecting unfairness through negative reactions is both so basic an emotion and so visceral. This is not the same as merely seeking equality of treatment. Monkeys and apes – like modern humans – live in societies where not all individuals are equal. Hierarchies develop based on age, sex and size among other characteristics. De Waal and Brosnan carefully chose capuchins of similar status within their groups for the experiments. If you are in a situation where hierarchy does not play a role in the distribution of resources vital to survival and reproduction, you have to ensure that you are going to receive the same reward for the same work. Accepting unfair treatment is to accept that you can also be unfairly treated in mate-selection or in distribution of vital resources. You have to develop what behavioural scientists call 'social inequity aversion' – rejecting an offer in the hope of getting something closer to the share others have – in order to have the best chance of extending your existence through the reproduction of your genes.[18]

And, in evolutionary terms, that is the only important thing in life.

As we saw in the last section, it would be wrong to think fairness is the opposite of unfairness. So, while it is obvious other species do recognise unfair treatment, it is a big leap to say that they therefore recognise fair treatment. If that trait is observable only in the absence of negative reactions to unfairness, it would not necessarily serve an evolutionary purpose and might not have

[18]In the film *A Beautiful Mind*, John Nash, played by Russell Crowe, develops a theory that sacrificing the individual goals of many for the success of the group ultimately benefits the individual more. It was the basis on which he was later awarded the Nobel Prize for Economics.

survived. But it did begin to make an appearance in pre-human communities, albeit at a more recent point in the genealogy of our species genealogy. While de Waal and Brosnan's experiments are famous, it is less well-known that Brosnan repeated the cucumber/grape test with chimpanzees. In a species as far distant in evolutionary terms from the capuchin monkey as we are from the chimp, there were some cases in which an individual taking part in the test would refuse to accept a grape until the other ape got one as well. It is worth noting that chimpanzees are not egalitarian in their social lives.

All this suggests that something more sophisticated than the primitive recognition of unfairness had to evolve so that primates could become better at cooperation and at taming competition. It was only when combined with other traits that we could say that fairness for its own sake began to play a role in the development of human behaviour.

Interest in this particular subject is, as I have already said, relatively new. It was only the publication of Richard Alexander's book *The Biology of Moral Systems* in 1987 that prompted the study of moral issues, such as justice and fairness, in the context of evolutionary history rather than just the much shorter history of human thought. Alexander proposed that morality evolved as a means of resolving conflicts of interest within social groups. De Waal, whose work provided a lot of the solid proof of Alexander's thesis, says the principles of morality have three pillars:

1) Prosocial tendencies − favouring actions which bind individuals in groups rather than place them in pure competition to each other

2) Empathy and consolation – understanding what others feel, desire and fear and knowing how to resolve those emotions in others

3) Reciprocity and fairness – the capacity to commit acts which do not benefit one party solely or at least beyond the tolerance of the others; the ability to judge when that balance of effects has been reached

Many mammals – and indeed fish, birds and insects such as bees or ants – have prosocial tendencies, but few have empathy. Fewer still, in fact hardly any other species[19] than *Homo sapiens,* as far as we know, has the same kind of forward-looking (psychologists call it 'indirect') reciprocity.

Studies on the cooperation of primates by scientists such as Robert Yerkes show that chimps can understand the benefits of reciprocity and resolve conflicts of interest to achieve it. In his most famous experiment, Yerkes filmed chimps who had to work in tandem to pull a box of food towards a point where they could reach it.[20]

Their understanding is immediate and adjacent. They can see who, literally in this instance, is pulling their weight. Each member of a group can see whose account is in credit for their participation in joint enterprise. For greater levels of sophistication, a capacity to 'invest' in future enterprises which is also fundamental to trade and

[19]One of the very few other species of animal which appears to have the same reciprocal instinct that humans have is the vampire bat. They have been observed to regurgitate blood gathered on hunting trips for others who have not been successful, without any apparent reward. Make of that what you will.

[20]Yerkes incidentally is an example of someone whose own 'evolutionary path' of exploring ideas took him into dangerous territory, as his work became associated with eugenics and other ideas with perilous outcomes)

capitalism, you have to project forward to those who you believe *will* repay your beneficial behaviour with reciprocity. That is an act of trust – as my former boss Richard Edelman always says, trust is a forward-looking mark of human value – and to have trust, you must have the capacity to detect fairness or at least unfairness.

It was for de Waal and Brosnan to show that monkeys have an idea of fairness, or to be more accurate, unfairness. Once combined with the intellectual development of which chimps and their (our) close cousins, bonobos, are capable, the capacity for reacting against unfairness became part of reciprocal behaviour and began the journey to being what we call fairness.

Darwin had already pre-empted these observations in his theoretical analysis of how human nature would have evolved. In the *Descent of Man*, he suggested that as early man's powers of reason and foresight improved (the arrival of language must have played its part, too), it would become obvious that the act of helping a fellow human would lead to being helped in return. When benevolence became a habit, it would add to existing feelings of sympathy with others. On top of that, receiving praise for helping (or blame for not helping) would strongly motivate people to help 'and this instinct no doubt was originally acquired, as other social instincts, through natural selection'.

As we will see in the next chapter, the further along the evolutionary path we travel, the more sophisticated that idea – and the human capacity to exercise it – becomes. And all that might make us ask this: why on earth have we stopped trying to develop something that has been at the core of what distinguishes us, and has always distinguished our ancestor-species, from the mass of animals?*

*It goes without saying that the subjects I have skated over here have been studied and written about in far greater detail and with much greater scientific rigour than I aspire to. There are excellent summaries of the science in Lixing Sun's *The Fairness Instinct*. Sun, a professor of biology at Central Washington University in the US, has done huge amounts of research on fairness and believes what he calls the 'Robin Hood Mentality' is basic to human nature. Personally, I would prefer not to found the concept of fairness in a semi-mythical medieval mind so dominated by ideas of right and wrong and good and evil that it would barely dwell for a second on the human or evolutionary role of its contribution to the species. If, indeed, dear Robin had the remotest idea of what we call a species. There is so much more to fairness than denuding one group to alleviate the suffering of another. But Sun's scholarship is profound and his book much to be recommended.

WHERE DOES FAIRNESS SIT IN THE HUMAN (AND MONKEY) BRAIN?

Scientists now attribute details of human behaviour to precise sections of the brain in the same way as we can say which part of an orchestra is producing which notes in the thundering crescendo of a Beethoven symphony.

Where does fairness sit? When answering the question of whether unfairness is the opposite of fairness, I pointed out that the reactions to the two conditions occupy different parts of the brain. It only really occurred to scientists to try to identify the position of these reactions at the turn of this century. In 2008, researchers at the California Institute of Technology linked volunteers to an MRI scanner as they were making decisions on how to apportion a (hypothetical) food supply to individual orphans in an African school. The volunteers had studied biographies and pictures of the sixty children, but could only distribute food to a few. Having to make choices to feed some and starve others triggered empathetic reactions in different parts of the volunteers' brains which the researchers described as fairness and unfairness responses. The results provided the evidence I referred to earlier in discussing whether fairness and unfairness are opposites: positive reactions when volunteers were able to deliver food came in the orbital frontal cortex, which for shorthand purposes scientists call the 'reward' centre of the brain; negative reactions were found in the region called the insula, particularly the anterior insula, which is connected to emotional responses.

But this was just the beginning in the scientific pursuit of fairness. The extensive use of something called the Ultimatum Game, by Matthew Lieberman and colleagues at UCLA, gave researchers a scale of measurement. It is a scale against which they can judge what peculiarities of the brain or even the effect of hormones at different moments in time can have on our tolerance of unfairness or our positive reception of fairness. This scale and the Caltech study encouraged other researchers to seek more precise locations for these reactions.

Lixing Sun explains how our brains have different reactions to fairness even in its application to the two major forms of justice: procedural and distributive. The first is about the construction and conduct of ways in which justice is brought about and the fairness of those *procedures*; the second is about the proceeds of justice and the fairness of *outcomes*.

The first reaction is in areas of the brain associated with social cognition.[21] This very basic part of our

[21]The ventrolateral prefrontal cortex and the superior temporal sulcus. See Sun, L., 2013. *The Fairness Instinct: The Robin Hood mentality and our biological nature.* 1st ed. New York: Prometheus Books. pp 60–61

thought processes determines how we assess ourselves in the context of relation to others, which I asserted earlier was about the most important part of thinking we can do. Prof. Sun says that this shows that people need to be convinced that a process which is, on its surface, unfair is actually necessary for the collective benefit of a well-functioning society. The imposition of restrictions on freedom of movement to counter the effects of the coronavirus, Covid-19, is an example. Mass rejection of lockdown restrictions often occurred because of poor communications by government. Failing to convince people that limits on their liberty were justified to protect the wellbeing of others and preserve fragile health systems to continue functioning had dire consequences.

The second brain reaction, to outcomes, sits in other parts of the brain.[22] These are areas associated with emotional responses. Sun suggests this means some people have more visceral reactions to outcomes than to process issues, i.e. when they actually see or perceive the degree of inequality in distribution they are getting compared to others. If, as is the case in all other areas of mental activity, different people have different levels of reaction and different sensitivities to stimuli, this explains why it is not always easy to reconcile those who are driven by the visceral reaction to outcomes with those who focus more on the process. To put it another way, as you may have always believed, there are people who care more about law and people who care more about justice. They are pre-programmed to do so. As with the coronavirus, in all cases it is vital in achieving a broad acceptance of fairness

[22]Anterior cingulate cortex, anterior insula and dorsolateral prefrontal cortex. See Sun *ibid*

to communicate to as many people as possible the social necessity of procedures and, therefore, the social benefit of what may be perceived as unfair outcomes.

It's also worth repeating that the part of the brain which reacts to unfairness in outcomes also governs our disgust and pain reactions. In 2016, a group of scientists set out to discover whether this was governed by one simple set of neural signals, or whether they were customised to each type of reaction. After studying under MRI analysis the reaction of nineteen volunteers, they concluded that they were all part of the same function. Unfairness has not been separated out by the increasing evolutionary complexity of *Homo sapiens*, but has been there for a very, very, very long time. It's just that we have only recently had a word for it.

The location of these reactions in parts of the brain that are so fundamental to our ability to function within a social group explains a lot about who we are as a species and why we struggle so much with moral questions. This is especially true at times of stress when our brains are being required to make frequent and urgent fight or flight calculations that go back, in evolutionary terms, far beyond the relative sophistication of fairness equations. As Sun points out, gathering together in large groups is not much good to any animal if their behaviour is not cooperative. He cites wildebeest or other species which gather in large numbers. The moment their gathering has achieved its purpose – for instance, safely reaching a waterhole– they make no effort to protect or aid each other. From that point of view, the bee is more advanced than the gnu.

It isn't surprising that the last few years have produced a lot of study of how human beings relate to each other and particularly searching for the sunny side of our collective personality. Using detailed scientific data, authors such as Michael McCullough of the University of California, San Diego, as well as Brian Hare and Vanessa Woods of Duke University, have shown how the co-operative and altruistic side of human nature is baked into us. They describe how kindness and friendliness have not detracted from, but caused, our advancement as a species. Is that the same as fairness? Many of the brain reactions cited by McCullough, Hare, Woods and others come from the same parts of the mind, particularly the medial prefrontal cortex. But while it is of course "nice" to think that kindness is a more essential part of us than nastiness, it is different from fairness. It is not kind to be fair. It is just fair. You are not kind to a person when you exchange something you value for something they value; you are not kind to someone by giving them what they deserve. I would argue that you cannot be kind unless you are fair, but you can be fair without being kind.[23]

In the interests of concision, I have skipped reams of detail about how and where fairness and unfairness are processed in the great calculator within our skulls. A deeper look for those of you with a scientific appetite would take us into the world of dopamine neurons and spindle cells, pathways and messengers in the labyrinth of consciousness that teach us the difference between reward and punishment, attraction and aversion, good outcomes and bad outcomes. Prof Sun's book will take you there.[24]

For now, let's just concentrate on the fact that fairness has its origins, just as humans do as a whole, in some very

[23]This is semantics, of course. Perhaps, like any good ape-descendant, I am just defending my turf.

[24]Also see Nowak, M. A. & Highfield, R., 2011. SuperCooperators, Free Press.

ancient stages of evolution. Whether fairness evolved in us as we became more sophisticated in our interactions as social animals, or whether it was the cause of our evolution, we can be sure of one thing: there is a causative link between human progress and our sense of fair play.

In a moment, we will look at some of the games and tests scientists use to map the detail of these correlations and causations, but for now we can just remember how deep fairness is within us. It precedes divisive processes such as intellectually-based prejudices towards others based on race, religion or conduct. It is probably not deeper than the tribalism – the need to distinguish friend from foe and fight alongside one and against the other – that creates and foments those prejudices. However, I want to show you that fairness can be the lubricant in our minds that allows us to overcome our baser instincts.

Fairness, as a precursor to trust and trade, provides a means of crossing boundaries of suspicion.

THE TESTS AND GAMES THAT ALLOW PSYCHOLOGISTS TO MEASURE FAIRNESS

Who needs monkeys? You can easily test fairness on people – all sorts of people, from students at expensive American universities to hunter-gatherers in the scrublands of Namibia or the jungles of Papua New Guinea. Welcome to the extensive world of the Ultimatum Game.

The Ultimatum Game is about the most common and popular game among psychologists, ever. Mostly, that is, because it is really easy, comes up with lots of numbers in its results and can be used to measure and compare many of the infinite varieties of human nature that there are.

How does it work? Well, you take two people. One is called the proposer and you give him or her some money[25] and sit them next to the other person, who is called the recipient. The proposer has to make an offer to the other person of how they might share the money. Both people know that if the person being offered a share doesn't accept it, then the money will be taken away again and neither will get a penny. Therefore, the person making the offer has an incentive to make an acceptable (fair) offer and the person receiving the offer has an incentive not to refuse an offer that is fair, or at least not intolerably unfair.

Quite where the line is drawn on what is fair and what is unfair is the point at which the fun begins for the scientists. Think of all the likely outcomes in this game. You, the proposer, could offer the recipient £1 out of the £10 you have been given by the scientist, arguing that before this moment, neither of you had any money, so the £1 is an unexpected boon. According to a psychological theory called rational choice theory, that is exactly what should happen and by the same token the recipient should think, well, I had nothing a moment ago and for no work or effort I will now get £1.

But that is not how, in practice, either party thinks. The recipient may well think – 'No, that isn't fair: I am essential to the proposer getting anything, so I should be fairly rewarded for that.' And the proposer should be able to work the same thing out for themselves by being sufficiently empathetic to wonder what level they would set as fair if they were the recipient.

---

[25]Behavioural scientists say that this game produces reasonable results if you use play money or hypothetical sums, but to really get accurate and revealing results, nothing beats cold, hard cash that the players get to take home.

Thus we have a pure and beautiful test of fairness. What is the least sacrifice that the person who has the most resource (£10) should make to the person who has less – or in this case no – resource, so that both may benefit? What restraint should be placed on the person with the power in order that the weaker person is not disadvantaged?

All sorts of other considerations come into play. What does your offer say about you as a person? What does the refusal of an offer of, say, 50:50 say about you as a person? One of the things that researchers have discovered in the myriad variations of the game is that reputation can play a big part in it. When one person knows a little about the previous history of the other person when playing the game, it vastly alters their willingness to make a higher or lower offer or to settle for a higher or lower share, depending on the reputation of their protagonist.

The single most amazing finding for all researchers studying the Ultimatum Game since it was invented by the German economist Werner Güth and his colleagues at the University of Cologne in 1982, is that people making the offer are amazingly generous, whether or not they have ever played or heard of the game before. Very few proposers try to lowball the recipient.

The collation of thousands of Ultimatum Game results by Prof Colin Camerer at Princeton show that the median offers are £4 to £5, and the level at which a recipient is more than 50% likely to reject an offer is £2.

We should not, in any case, be drawn into thinking that the Game is about seeking equality. In fact, far more games end with an unequal split than an equal one. It is as if this vast survey of human attitudes has confirmed that what is equal is not necessarily fair and what is fair is not necessarily equal.

You might think that the position of the proposer is determined by the need to play safe and make sure his one-time offer is accepted for fear of losing everything. That would be the obvious conclusion but for one thing: the Dictator Game. In a fiendish version of the game, the recipient is denied the opportunity even to refuse. The proposer can offer £1 or even less; but they do not. In one version of the Dictator Game, where the proposer is only allowed to make one of two offers: £1 for you, £9 for me; or £5 for you and £5 for me, about 75% of proposers chose the equal split. Whether that is caused by the thought of receiving a bad reputation (although the players are strangers and will have no further interaction), or just that their mutual empathy makes them see the other person's point of view, nobody knows.

The game has been used to discover all sorts of things about the brain. One example: a South Korean study of people aged between nine and twenty-three was able to prove that the increasing likelihood of the recipient accepting less than half of the money on offer was linked to the thickness of a part of the brain that had not previously been connected with 'social cognition'.

Another study in 2014 concluded that the more alcohol recipients were given to drink, the less likely they were to accept an offer less favourable than a 50:50 split. There is a lesson for all of us in that.

Other studies have shown that younger children are less willing to share something they have received as a gift, but become more generous with age. Adults are harder to pigeonhole. Societies are harder to predict. The anthropologist Joseph Henrich teamed up with Prof Camerer to take the game to the most isolated and *sui generis* societies left on the planet, tribes from the Peruvian jungle to the Arctic Circle. Average offers ranged from

£2.70 to £5.80; average rejection amounts varied from £4 to zero. The scientists concluded that culture and local community habits have a huge effect on what people regard as fair. But everyone has a limit. But there is more to the study of limits than the Ultimatum Game. In my view, the most important area of study, still in its infancy, is the work of psychologists such as Professor Christina Starmans of Yale University.[26] She looked at the mass of data from laboratory experiments which seemed to show that humans have an in-built 'inequality aversion' from an early age. But the key word in all this huge body of research, Starmans says, is 'laboratory'. In theoretical tests, similar to the Ultimatum Game and involving sharing, whether the subjects are children as young as eighteen months or adults of all ages, left-leaning or right-leaning, men or women, black or brown or white, everyone shows a strong preference to equal distribution. They also show a preference for other people who act as equal distributors. But everyone is also thoroughly ignorant about inequality, as first noticed by Professors Dan Ariely of Duke University and Michael Norton of the Harvard Business School, who discovered[27] that Americans, regardless of sex, race or class, massively underestimate the unequal distribution of wealth in their country.

However, the real crux of Starmans' research is that, when they are asked what an *ideal* distribution of wealth should be, *nobody suggests an even split*. Even people on the left of politics, poorer people and women – all the

[26]Starmans, C., Sheskin, M. & Bloom, P., 2017. Why people prefer unequal societies. Nature Human Behaviour, 07 April.

[27]Norton, M., 2015. *The data shows we want to end inequality. Here's how to start...* Available at: https://ideas.ted.com/the-data-shows-we-want-to-end-inequality-heres-how-to-start/

sectors who most deride inequality – veer towards a split in which the richer you are, the bigger share you have and the poorer you are, the smaller share. The differential between the poorest share and the richest share in this ideal world are vastly smaller than in real life (at the time Starmans was writing, in 2016, an average American CEO was earning 354 times what an average worker was earning compared with a 20:1 ration in the 1960s) but in every case, people look to *fairness not equality*. This applies even when people are operating behind Rawls' veil of ignorance and do not know where they themselves might fit into such an allocation.

In lab conditions, we look to be equal but in the real world, we seek fair outcomes; in our hearts we are pure communists, in our heads we are enlightened capitalists. The Yale research could not discover any evidence that human beings are averse to inequality as such because, according to Starmans, tests of sharing that seem to show that outcome have actually been loaded to do so: what is revealed as the equal outcome in one of these tests also happens to be the fair outcome. Inequality without an opportunity to change your own position on the ladder of success-distribution – what we call social mobility – is unfair and objectionable to all. But we are still conjecturing as to why fairness and unfairness are so intrinsic to the nature of *Homo sapiens*.

It is a reasonable summary of all the Ultimatum Games that these scientists do not actually know why human beings do not conform to the expected pattern of behaviour based on the game's premise: that the proposer will offer the least they can get away with and the recipient will accept it because otherwise they will have nothing. This is what 'rational choice theory' would lead us to believe. That theory suggests that an idealised (though unattractive) form of humanity, usually referred to as *homo economicus*, would always choose the maximum 'utility' – that is the value to them – in any exchange. That, as we have seen here, does not happen. In even the meanest of cases, offers of 15% of the total are about as low as it goes.

Something tells us that we need to shun unfair outcomes; some need within us tells us to be fair.

ARE WE HARD-WIRED TO SEEK FAIR OUTCOMES AND TO REJECT THE UNFAIR?

In the Ultimatum Game, researchers usually tell the recipient and the proposer that they will never see each other again. They start as strangers and part as strangers. But this does not seem to affect the level of offers or of refusals. There are several theories as to why a rational being would abide by unwritten rules with unknown partners who have lives unconnected to theirs. One, developed by Martin Nowak and Karl Sigmund, pioneers of evolutionary game theory, hangs on the idea of 'indirect reciprocity'. This is the trait – which as I mentioned a few pages back, has so far been found only in humans and a very few other species – that persuades us to do a favour for someone who is not predisposed to return that favour because of kinship or proximity on the basis that in some way, not contracted or agreed in advance, they will do us a favour in the future.

Nowak and Sigmund provided evidence through various tests and games that this is not warm and fuzzy niceness based in pure altruism, but a cold calculation made by the donor that he or she will, by behaving in this way, present an image of being a valuable member of a community to the person to whom they are giving. In time, that will give them an 'Image Score' which will benefit them with greater value than they have sacrificed by being altruistic. For some reason, an image of the American electoral system comes into my mind when I think about this. Be that as it may, Nowak and Sigmund thought that this explained why people would do a favour to a stranger. More recently, a slightly different theory has replaced image scoring, which is called 'Standing Strategy' – this suggests that all human motivations towards peers are based on relative status within a community. Doing a favour to someone who already has good 'standing' in the community will affect your own standing positively, but refusing a favour for someone of bad standing will have no negative effect. For some reason, the American welfare system keeps popping into my head when I think about this.

Reputation is, of course, important in Western societies, but in Eastern societies it still plays a role so central to the sense of self that it can provoke what we in Europe and North America regard as extreme reactions. Think about the concept of losing face in Japan or China, which still to this day drives people to destroy themselves rather than appear to accept the dishonour of their own and their family's reputation. Think about the appalling violence committed in the name of family honour in some South Asian societies. In the West, until relatively recently, men fought duels over their reputations (one of my ancestors fought the last duel in the Irish province of Connaught in 1817) and were prepared to die to protect their 'good name'.

I have gone on a bit longer than I might have done about this, because it seems to me important that we try to understand why people are nice to strangers, and that the current scientific approach to it is a bit too damn data-driven. The value that our ancestors did, and some cultures still do, put on reputation suggests it is enough to motivate behaviour that brings us no obvious reward.

But there are other considerations. There is no measurable benefit to people in listening to music, standing in front of a painting or watching clouds process across a cerulean sky in the Tuscan countryside. We do it anyway. It makes us feel good.

So what is hard-wired and what is just being nice? Well, we know that we have physical and chemical impulsions to reject unfairness, because the capuchins taught us that. How does the capuchin experiment relate to Man? I suppose that, if the hand that gives out grapes in de Waal's study is translated into a human context, it is the hand of government or perhaps even of Chance, Destiny, Nature or the Law. Like the monkey, we are not in a position to combat that process; all we can do is complain loudly about the unfairness of it – the purpose of the complaint being to let the 'hand' know that its division of favour has been noted and rejected. The unspoken part of such a complaint is that if the rules are broken, neither party ought to benefit or the other will withdraw cooperation.

When it comes to more recent evolutionary history, we know higher species of ape seek to treat each other kindly and fairly in order to maintain order within their small and vulnerable communities. Bonobos and chimpanzees are heavily into making up after a row rather than breaking up, because their societies are too small to survive weakening the tribe through ostracism, except in extreme cases where dominance of the tribe is at issue. Incidentally, chimpanzees manifest their 'making up' through mutual grooming and eating each other's parasites; bonobos do so by having sex. Colour me bonobo.

We know that there are also reward areas of the brain that light up either when we are treated fairly or when we are put in a position where we treat others fairly. The UCLA team of Golnaz Tabibnia and Matthew Lieberman used the Ultimatum Game on subjects wired up to functional-MRI scanning to make the link between fairness and the *ventral striatum*, a reward area, even when the circumstances of the game were not bringing them additional rewards in cash terms. The subjects were just enjoying being treated fairly. As we saw in the Caltech study where subjects were asked to distribute finite resources in a Ugandan school, reward areas of the brain also light up when people are *being* fair, not just being fairly done by. Incidentally, other emotions, for instance envy which is linked logically to our concept of fairness, are connected to even more basic parts of our brain, specifically the limbic system.

But it remains the case that both for good and bad, fair and unfair, what exists in your brain is not a logic circuit for your reactions, but a switch. You don't have to think about it, you just feel it instantaneously. Rejecting unfairness, which has clearly been with us for tens of millions of years, is more visceral because failing to do so could have cost our distant forebears not only their lives, but their opportunity to reproduce. We know that welcoming fairness is a more recent instinct, because it is not as apparent in lesser species. We will look, in the next chapter, at recorded human history and where fairness sits in that, but it is certainly a more recent product of our evolution, one we probably learned in the same way as we learned how to live in communities and thus had to do less work individually and had slightly more leisure time to sit on our simian backsides and just relax. Might it be the case that the positive side of fairness evolved in us as we began to realise that being fairly treated was the opposite of being unfairly treated? We could relax because we worked in cooperation and had a more assured future than our ancestors if we achieved a cooperative state. We could afford to be less calculating about our altruistic behaviour and just enjoy the reward sensations of our fairness to others and theirs to us.

Prof Lixing Sun says:

> Fairness as a mental instinct and behavioural rule for solving conflicts of interest, is spawned from social living and social hierarchy. Behind it are two major selective forces, reciprocity for mutual benefit and compromise for social harmony, both of which are critical for maximising the net benefit of cooperation.[28]

Sun also describes fairness as an instinct that 'emerged through competitive interactions over evolutionary time'. This is certainly true and I would argue that the reason it emerged in that context was that competitive interactions became cooperative interactions, with the sense of fairness acting as the intermediary between one kind and another. As human history progressed, cooperation showed greater benefit to larger groups – from families to extended families to clans to tribes to peoples – as time gave us the opportunity for trial and error in the way that we lived alongside each other.

Which probably makes this a good moment to talk about history.

---

[28]Sun, L., 2013. *The Fairness Instinct: The Robin Hood mentality and our biological nature.* 1st ed. New York: Prometheus Books. Page 48

4

Fairness in History

HISTORY — A WARNING

My first memory of studying history was reading comic-book adaptations of Homer's *Iliad* when I was about four. I played with plastic toy soldiers that came in cardboard boxes which carried information about the wars in which these inhuman warriors fought. History has always sung to me. I still base all my thoughts and conclusions about the way we are today by thinking about the way we were before. So do you, but you may not think about it as consciously as I do.

I do not make an apology for the fact that this is a long part of the book.

To be fair is to be a part of one narrative of history; but it is just a small part. The bigger share of recorded human history is a story in which fairness seems to play no role, except in the poignancy of its absence. But when we look deeper, we will see that fairness has indeed played a part in the development of states of cooperation over millennia and this will help us to understand how it does and will play a part in the current and future story of mankind.

History is the peer-review of politics and philosophy. For a politician or thinker to launch ideas without comparing them to the work of politicians and thinkers past is like a scientist refusing to compare their findings with experiments done by rivals in the same field. While there is a chance that the scientist is a peerless genius such as Newton, whose work is so original that it cannot be compared with others, the chances are greater that he or she is a charlatan who fears the judgement of peers.

In the following pages, I will not so much canter as gallop headlong through thousands of years of human progress and regress, smashing the filigree of human thought with the hammer of summation. I will reduce profound lessons of centuries to a few paragraphs and cause paroxysms to specialists in a host of historical fields, all in the cause of brevity.

Sorry.

DID EARLY MAN HAVE A CONCEPT OF FAIRNESS AS THE FIRST TRADES WERE MADE?

It is not a coincidence that in developing the Ultimatum Game, a game that allowed us to measure fairness, we turned to the disposition of financial resources. Cold, hard cash. The medium of exchange.

You could make a plausible argument that the history of human progress was a history of exchange. It need not be an exchange of goods. It could be an exchange of information. Progress – in the broadest sense of the word, a sense that does not necessarily connote positive outcomes – is driven by restriction, curiosity and ambition. Restriction thwarts ambition and provokes curiosity as to how change might be achieved; ambition-unleashed removes restriction and provokes further curiosity until new boundaries are reached which impose new restrictions because of practical limitations of resources and space.

In some cases, progress can be driven by a sense that everyone should have a chance to share in the goods that lie over the horizon of the world we know. This doesn't mean some whimsical desire to set up anarcho-syndicalist collectives – though those have happened in the past if you think about the Shakers or less familiar names such as the Oneida Perfectionists, the Amana Inspirationalists, and the New Icarians. Christopher Columbus, Hernando Cortes or Francisco Pissaro could be seen as people motivated by a sense of human progress to take shares in whatever riches they found as they sailed. And nobody would call those men starry-eyed idealists, least of all the millions of indigenous Caribbean islanders, Aztecs, Olmecs, Mayans and Incas that they left dead in their wake.

But that kind of progress was unknown to our distant, prehistoric ancestors. Without the pressure of competition that we now call progress, human beings tended to settle for what they had. The norm appears to have been to move towards a cooperative rather than a competitive impetus. For almost all the history of *Homo sapiens*, when there was precious little of what we would now call progress, our ancestors were foragers. Their ancestors were foragers too, back into the times when there was nothing *sapiens* about *homo* – between 2.5 and 7 million year ago. The earliest remains classified as the species *sapiens* date from around 315,000 years ago, although this is one of many areas of dispute between palaeontologists and a stricter application of bone-reading places the first members of our family as no more than 160,000 years old. DNA studies also point to the earliest date for a common ancestor in both male and female lines of *Homo sapiens* at about 150,000 years ago. Academic arguments rage about how the species spread out around the planet, but current consensus is that it was confined to Africa originally, beginning to migrate and reach different parts of the world such as China (between 80 and 120,000 years ago), Australia (50-65K), Europe (43-45K) and the Americas (13-14K, but possibly 45K).

Sapiens appears to have been different from its older cousins because of the frequency with which it made cognitive advances, that is, sudden progress in its ways of thinking. Hundreds of thousands, even millions of years elapsed between advances in Stone Age tools and there is virtually no evidence at all of abstract thought until around 70,000 years ago. Scientists believed until recently that this was also the period at which something that we would call 'trade' developed, but in 2018, findings at a site known to be 300,000 years old in the Olorgesailie Basin, in southern Kenya, suggested that obsidian used to make weapons was being traded. This is because the closest point at which it was naturally available was thirty-five miles away.[29] There were also lumps of pigment which early man is known to have used for decoration that originated at least eighteen miles away. Even if we imagine that the people at the site travelled to places where obsidian and the so-called 'paleo-crayons' could be found, it is possible that they had at least traded information with neighbouring groups of humans as to the location of sites. Humans with such a tenuous hold on survival did not travel what, to them, were huge and perilous distances from home without motivation. Because there are no human remains at the Olorgesailie site, we cannot say if

---

[29]Boissoneault, L., 2018. *Colored Pigments and Complex Tools Suggest Humans Were Trading 100,000 Years Earlier Than Previously Believed.* Available at: https://www.smithsonianmag.com/science-nature/colored-pigments-and-complex-tools-suggest-human-trade-100000-years-earlier-previously-believed-180968499/

these sites were occupied by *Homo sapiens* or, more likely, by another more primitive member of the genus called *homo heidelbergensis*. The latter is not thought to have had language in any form, nor at that point in history did any *sapiens* ancestor, so if information was traded, it must have been with signs, not words. Perhaps this makes it more likely that the trade was in physical goods rather than information. Yet trade in information, after the development of language, is as likely to be the most common and useful early kind of trade as trade in goods. As Harari says in *Sapiens*, the trade of information cost the proposer nothing of actual value and brought with it the likelihood of reciprocal and useful information from the recipient.

Current thinking is that the great leap forward by our species began 70,000 years ago, a period known as the Cognitive Revolution, possibly prompted by a change in the anatomical nature of the *sapiens* brain which sparked the ability to formulate a range of sounds to convey meaning: language. Another theory holds that an environmental calamity, particularly a huge volcanic eruption in Indonesia, caused a years-long winter for the planet that wiped out many species and almost finished off our ancestors. Under this theory, the concentration of our DNA in perhaps as few as between 2,000 surviving individuals may have sparked an intense need to evolve rapidly just to survive, with those who did being the most capable intellectually and physically, leading to a dramatic increase in genetic predisposition to cognitive and cooperative abilities. Whatever spurred this Cognitive Revolution, it marks the beginning of what we call history.

What were these people like, the oldest animals with whom we might still be able to communicate (although not necessarily speak) were we to meet them today?

According to anthropologists who study the few remaining bands of people that still live as we believe our ancestors did at the time of the Cognitive Revolution and for some 60,000 years afterwards, they lived in small bands based on blood relationships. And they were rather bitchy.

Studies of the hunter-gatherer societies that survived intact into the twentieth century suggest that they all had one thing in common: egalitarianism. Sharing of food and even status were found in all the twenty-four different forager communities studied by Andrew Whiten and David Erdal in the late 1990s.

They are societies where the rules that mandate equal shares for those who do equal work are enforced by gossip and its positive or negative effects on reputation. Christopher Boehm, the director of the Jane Goodall Institute at the University of Southern California, has written of the pygmies of the Congo forest that:

> 'Public opinion, facilitated by gossiping, always guides the band's decision process ... and fear of gossip all by itself serves as a preemptive social deterrent because most people are so sensitive about their reputations.'[30]

In the late 1950s, the British anthropologist Colin Turnbull observed Mbuti pygmies in the Congo as they dealt with a 'deviant' member of the band named Cephu (please remember Cephu as he will crop up a few times in the rest of the story). He pursued his own course in hunts and even tried to keep back meat he had caught himself

---

[30]Johnson, E. M., 2012. *Ayn Rand vs. the Pygmies: Did human evolution favor individualists or altruists?*. Available at: https://slate.com/technology/2012/10/groups-and-gossip-drove-the-evolution-of-human-nature.html

rather than put it into the common pot. A council of elders decided to drive him out of the band, which would probably have led to his death, but he was reprieved, demonstrating a reluctance similar to our simian forebears to weaken small bands by retributive action. Cephu had broken the rules, because individualism and enterprise were not appropriate to Mbuti culture.

Obeying these rules, which are of course not written down but understood, is not a trivial responsibility. Ostracism from the band is effectively a death sentence. But you do not even need to go that far. In most hunter-gatherer societies, reputation is closely linked to attractiveness. Your chances of reproduction plummet if you are not seen as a team player.

If these groups of hunter-gatherers who are still with us are an accurate reflection of typical behaviour from our collective past – and every single one of the groups studied by Boehm's team and by Whiten and Erdal had the same elements of collectivism – then it indicates that early man had a very highly developed sense of fairness. In fact, his imposition of fairness was stricter than any society we know of today. There is restriction on the powerful – or at least on those who would be powerful, but are not allowed to be – and there is a distribution of food not on simple mathematical lines, but according to need. To attempt unfairness, to cheat the system, is to court punishment and even death.

But just because these hunter-gatherers are fair and cooperative with each other in their small bands, we should not be tempted to think that they were all sweetness and light to the rest of creation. Fossil evidence suggests that inter-tribe wars in the period of the hunter-gatherer were brutal, albeit rare and practiced on a small scale. And these little bands must have been even more aggressive and merciless with the other species of *homo* that they came across. Neanderthals in the Middle East and Europe and *homo erectus* in East Asia disappeared by about 30,000BC.

There is nothing utopian about this kind of life either. The need for equality of opportunity imposes limitations on other aspects of the human character. As Cephu and others discovered, dissent from this lifestyle is not tolerated. Dependence on one another is reduced, which can have side effects that we would not associate with paradise. In a pioneering lecture in 1981, James Woodburn of the London School of Economics said of egalitarian societies that 'they may limit the care provided for the incapacitated because of the controls on dependency'.[31] If this sounds like a euphemism for something worse, it is: elderly or sick members of a band who slowed down the nomadic move from one hunting and gathering ground to another would have lived in fear of being culled for the common good. Primitive egalitarian societies were not fair on everyone simply because they were 'fair' to all. Or to put it another way, what was fair to the whole was unfair to the euthanised individual. Boehm goes as far as to suggest that the suppression of individual interest by hunter-gatherer bands in favour of the interests of the group could explain why human evolution favoured cooperative behaviour and altruism. Evolution in the case of *sapiens* worked on a group level rather than an individual level, a refined form of how bees cohabit.

Humans are far, far less aggressive than chimpanzees and even than our mutual cousins, the docile, matriarchal bonobos. A recent book by the British anthropologist,

---

[31]Woodburn, J., 1982. Egalitarian Societies. *Royal Anthropological Institute of Great Britain and Ireland,* 17(3), pp. 431–452.

Richard Wrangham, suggests that we domesticated ourselves in the same way that we domesticated other species – by selective breeding. In part using an observation by Boehm – that hunter-gatherers could go much further than the ostracism of Cephu and actually co-operate to kill aberrant, overaggressive males – Wrangham suggests that over millennia this had the effect of 'breeding out' the most aggressive members of the species through a prototype of capital punishment which he calls 'proactive aggression' which reduced the more destructive 'reactive aggression'.[32]

Reduced reactive aggression must feature alongside intelligence, cooperation, and social learning as a key contributor to the emergence and success of our species.[33]

What this means is that, for the majority of the history of human beings, the biggest wasn't always the best. Might wasn't always right. Nice guys didn't always finish last. In fact, if they played their cards right, fairly, co-operatively, they often finished equal first.[34]

Of course, the truth is that both competition and cooperation – self-interest and group-interest – were forces shaping human evolution from millions of years

[32]Wrangham, R., 2019. *The Goodness Paradox: How Evolution Made Us Both More and Less Violent.* 1st ed. London: Profile Books Ltd. An alternative or complementary theory by Prof Melvin Kenner of Emory University is that in hunter-gatherer societies where women had more equal status than in later history, they achieved the defanging of humanity by deliberately choosing less aggressive mates; bonobos are the prototype of this.

[33]Wrangham, R., 2019. *The Goodness Paradox.*

[34]It took us an awfully long time to remember this and we are in some danger of forgetting it again.

ago. The forces themselves were in competition to drive success and eventually ran together in an unbeatable confluence. Competition between individuals rewards selfishness; cooperation within groups is rewarded because the group with a preponderance of good cooperators is likely to out-compete a group with a preponderance of not-so good cooperators. This is one of the theories as to why *sapiens* defeated Neanderthals: the latter were a bit crap at what modern management consultants call 'collaborate to compete'. (You might say we aren't that great at it ourselves now.)[35]

For our distant forebears, some idea other than equality was needed if humans were going to achieve a balance between the interests of many and the interests of one. In other words, if you want to see why fairness today is not the same as equality, but is better, look to our forager forebears.

In *Sapiens,* Harari argues that our species controls the planet because we are the only animals that cooperate both with flexibility and in very large numbers. Our ability to work with others of our species who are outside our kinship or knowledge group is key to this.

One of our skills that makes this possible is to do with stories – not just gossip this time – but the kind of stories which allow us to hold a belief in something non-corporeal. It might be a god or it might be a limited liability company or it might be a concept such as human rights. Or fairness. Taken altogether, our stories become our culture, our shared imagination of a structure of things which do not have the physical existence of a rock

[35]For more on this, see Haidt, J., 2013. *The Righteous Mind.* 1st ed. London: Penguin Chapter 6

or a tree, but hold even more importance to us in the way we bind our society together.

Harari says in a TED talk that is well worth watching at least twice:

> *A human can say, look there is a God above the clouds, and if you all believe these stories that I've invented then you will follow the same norms and laws and values [as me] and you can cooperate. This is something only humans can do.*[36]

Harari says that we live in a dual reality: an objective one like the one animals live in and a fictional one – an imagined reality – where we use our language capability to invent these shared myths that hold our communities together.

I think that fairness is part of that fictional reality, but it is founded in objective reality. On the one hand, fairness is a concept which we can write about and debate and give a name to and put at the heart of an idea like Fair Play which is an imagined reality in Harari's sense. But it is also an objective reality, in that it is part of the genetic code of our species. People who are born without a capacity to be fair or to react against unfairness are regarded as aberrant. We call people who cannot empathise sufficiently to recognise when they are being unfair, or who do not see the necessity to be fair, psychopaths or sociopaths.

So we can see fairness, in Harari's terms, as a kind of bridge between the hard reality of animals, with several species of whom we share the instinct for fairness, and the

[36]TEDGlobalLondon: *What explains the rise of humans?* Available at: https://www.ted.com/talks/yuval_noah_harari_what_explains_the_rise_of_humans/transcript?language=en

'fictive' reality of man that is based in stories and ideals of fairness. We have to assume that stories and fables played a part in the earliest incarnations of human society, because they certainly did play a part in the first civilisations we know about. Those settled civilisations, those city-states and kingdoms that emerged in the millennia following the Agricultural Revolution, were unlike hunter-gatherers because they were equipped to pass on information about their lives and their thoughts through writing and illustration. And we know they based their whole reason for being in stories. These stories are the creation myths of the first civilisations, stories that help us to understand how the first civilisations saw themselves and their own past. Writing also allowed them to conduct business, to trade and to administer polities, as we will see in the next section.

DID THE INHABITANTS OF THE FIRST SETTLEMENTS MAKE A FAIR TRADE OF THEIR FREEDOM FOR SECURITY?

The period before the advent of literacy is an enormous pool of time in which even the most brilliant researcher today can have little or no knowledge about how people related to each other. They reach all their suppositions by deduction from shards of pottery and the excavation of ruins. They know that their published claims could be turned on their head by a new find or a new ruin. It is an occupational hazard of palaeontology to be proved to be wrong by the turning of someone else's trowel. By the same token, any assumptions about the nature of fairness in such a time are dangerous. The most we can say now is that there is a strong feeling among those who have devoted their lives to the study of the period that hunter-gatherers lived in broadly equal, cooperative bands, starting small and growing bigger. They also believe that, from the point where we can begin to trace *Homo sapiens* living in settlements, where lifestyles are beginning to become sedentary rather than foraging, the earliest settlements show no signs of a break with that past. There is no archaeological evidence to show that the terms of cooperation among the first people to settle in single sites were noticeably different from the hunter-gatherers who came before. The shelters found at various sites in the Middle East, in the Indus Valley, in China, are predominantly equal in size – no palaces or mansions. The remains of goods, of food, of animals domesticated within those settlements, are not disproportionately distributed.

As we saw in the last section, equality has its downsides, but it must have taken an immense effort by our hunter-gatherer ancestors to promote it as a way of life over the desire to create and maintain hierarchies which characterised their cousins among the other great ape species and which, presumably, was a feature of the early species of *homo* as well. If hunter-gatherers were predominantly collective, it is logical to think that there must have been an evolutionary advantage to egalitarianism over hierarchy or mankind would not be here. A lot of recent historians have looked back on the period before the Agricultural Revolution – about 12,000 years ago – as a well-nourished, pleasant and productive past in which man lived in greater harmony with the rest of nature. These historians, including Harari and James C Scott, believe the next step was a negative one, and you can see why.

The thesis of *Against the Grain*, Scott's recent history of earliest urban societies, is that city-states such as those founded in the Fertile Crescent of Mesopotamia some 5,500 years ago were not seen by their inhabitants as progress nor as inevitable steps in human collectivisation. It was a trade-off of the freedoms that people enjoyed in forager and earlier agrarian societies in return for a greater degree of protection afforded by walls and multitudes. But the walls and multitudes gave its reluctant inhabitants more than security. Not everyone brought within the fold of civilisation were willing participants. The walls of the first cities such as Uruk or Jericho forced upon their citizens categorisation, servitude, insignificance, diminution of status and above all else, disease.

Evidence of this comes from the period between the beginnings of sedentary life some 12,000 years ago and the emergence of what we might recognise as civilisations about seven millennia later. The evidence comes from excavations of Neolithic villages in southern Turkey and northern Iraq, in Jordan and Israel that date to around the time of the Agricultural Revolution.

At the beginning of this period, when settlements were tiny and agriculture in its infancy, the culture of communities was more likely to resemble the egalitarian hunter-gatherers. But as they became larger and more complex in their approach to cultivation and the domestication of animals, particularly the latter, evidence emerges that some were more equal than others.

Take the site of Çatalhöyük in southern Turkey, a place that flourished for a period about as long as from the birth of the prophet Mohammed to today. The earliest traces of it can be dated to around 7100BC. At its height, several thousand people lived there. Çatalhöyük has been held up by the first people to excavate it as an example of anarcho-communism, because tools and food appear to have been shared equally and there were no houses of notably bigger size than the norm. But more recent work suggests that as levels of domestication increased over time, inequalities of wealth and status began to emerge.[37] The settlement collapsed around 5700BC.

Archaeological evidence supports the idea that the same sort of evolution, away from equality and towards a more status-conscious type of society, happened in other parts of the ancient world too. One theory to explain this is that the domestication of large animals, which not all individuals were able to share in, led to greater inequality. By around 6,500 years ago, the existence of large earthworks in central European sites, believed to be for some sort of ceremonial purposes, points to social organisation taking place in which some individuals are directing the labour of others. Not long after, burial pits showing bones with wounds caused by sharpened instruments and the presence of defensive fortifications suggest that the relatively pacific period of the hunter-gatherers had given way to a more bellicose era.

Why would people do this, permitting their way of life to be altered in a profound way that would most likely see them, as part of a majority that would be governed, disadvantaged? The sand of time has buried the reasons in individual cases, but this change happened in an era when there were a number of meteorological events that reduced the availability of food and other resources, that changed climate to an extent that people could not have coped with, that made places that had been habitable uninhabitable. At the same time, the increasing sophistication of communications and the availability of fixed food sources – cultivated fields and orchards – may well have made gathering together seem like a good plan. The huge

[37]Wright, K. I., 2014. Domestication and inequality? Households, corporate groups and food processing tools at Neolithic Çatalhöyük. *Journal of Anthropological Archaeology*, Volume 33, pp. 1–33.

advantage of language is that it allows trust to be spread among groups of people who do not know each other.

How would people deal with the emergence of these differences if, for all the time they and their oral traditions could remember, there had been nothing but some form of egalitarianism in the way they associated, with no tradition of hierarchy and stratified social orders? We know that metaphysical beliefs had been present in *Homo sapiens* society since at least 30–40,000BC. It may have been in that context that people were able to justify the change in the nature of their own relationships. If they could conceive of non-existent beings that influenced their lives, it must have been possible to believe that some *existent* beings could have a superior role. This would be especially true if bands that developed a hierarchical structure were more successful and aggressive than those that retained egalitarian lifestyles. This would have been even more the case if they began to express aggression and survival-success in the name of what Harari calls 'imagined orders'. It is not hard to imagine influential individuals and the families of such people emerging as leaders from within social groups that are under pressure from external forces – Cephus with a mission to make everyone have their defined place in the society. They could use the imagination of others and shared belief in imagined orders to create the justification to begin the process in which the quality we now call fairness became overwhelmed by pragmatic authoritarianism.

DID FAIRNESS PLAY A PART IN EARLY CIVILISATIONS AND ANCIENT EMPIRES?

The gradual conversion of mankind from a hunter-gatherer, to a settlement-dwelling pastoralist, to a citizen, took place over several thousand years between about 14,500 and 5,500 years ago. The first humans to live in what we would recognise as states were the citizens of places like Uruk, the earliest of dozens of cities of the Sumerian culture in modern Iraq and Syria. These city-states commanded areas outside their walls to a distance of between 10 and 30 kilometres. They developed two means of communication and sharing which we would also find very familiar: stories and bureaucratic records. The first writing to be recorded anywhere on the planet is the cuneiform script of Sumer, which was used for 3,000 years to record a number of different languages, including Akkadian, a tongue that was held in common by both the Assyrian and Babylonian empires. From its first use in 3200BC, cuneiform had an intensely practical application. As far as we can tell, for five centuries after its invention, this form of record-keeping was not used for anything more than keeping details of business transactions and ownership of goods or property. After that, it began to be used for more ephemeral purposes: letters between people, recorded on clay tablets, but also communications that convey, to us, familiar ideas such as recipes for food or medicine and mathematical calculations of astronomy.

But to think of the technologies that more or less continuously developed during this period is considerably to overestimate the stability and resilience of the civilisations that came into being during the last few millennia before the birth of Christ. The way in which people lived with each other, judging both from archaeological records (for the first 5-7,000 years after the Agricultural Revolution) and a combination of written and archaeological (for the next 3,500), was a series of trials and errors. Between 12,000 and 7,000 years ago, the number of humans walking the planet increased from some four million to only about five million. It was barely survival as people learned to live together in larger numbers and simultaneously domesticate both plants and animals to keep them alive.

Why did humans not thrive? We can't be certain, but considering that in the 5,000 years that followed, the population of Earth grew by 2000 per cent rather than 20, it must have been some spectacular event that is not recorded in any way we have been able to find, or it must have been spectacularly mundane and awful, but grinding. Apart from famine, war and other forms of death, the greatest obstacle to population growth was the fourth horseman – plague.

The consequence of community was disease. Hunter-gatherers had of course succumbed to illness as they do, as we all do, today. But in the first civilisations, people lived close to each other and coronavirus has taught us how friendly that can be to the spread of diseases. The houses of Çatalhöyük were so closely packed that the only way to enter each one was through holes in the roof. Those who study the period believe that child and female mortality from diseases like typhus and diphtheria were so common that the only way humans could guarantee to grow in number (which was the point of their gathering in cities, at least as far as the kings were concerned), was to breed like crazy. An arms race began between viruses and bacteria on one side and copulating humanity on the other. The creature with the bigger brain won, but not until food supplies became sufficiently reliable to allow survival of individuals more often than not. Having enough food meant having more people to grow it and farm it than were just there to eat it, or to improve the efficiency of agriculture.

The early civilisations were not much more spacious than the first settlements. The point of gathering together was security. Security meant restriction, meant walls. Housing needed to be small and densely associated so walls could be as small in circumference as possible. But security was a delegation of authority for one's own protection to another person. It was an exchange, and not a good one, for those crammed into the ordinary housing of the earliest cities – Uruk, Jericho, Ur, Babylon. In exchange for the security provided by a ruler, you had to submit to his rules. In fact, remembering how we define the difference between rules and laws, it is important to use the right terminology. To live in a society where a law-giver became a law-enforcer, you had not just to obey the *laws*, you had to pay for the privilege. This involved surrendering part of your liberty and part of your labour. If you grew crops, you had to provide surplus food to the king; if you were a maker of goods, you had to provide surplus goods or surplus money to the king. Even if you didn't have a surplus.

Hence famine. Hence disease. Hence collapse of civilisations. There were at least three occasions on which the city of Ur rose and fell again through some kind of instant or prolonged catastrophe. The sites were reoccupied because they were the best sites for the needs of human gathering. But that process showed up the fragility inherent in gathering.

There was throughout this period – you might easily say throughout all recorded history – a complex dance going on between human resilience and the resilience of natural forces, whether they were tiny microbes or staggeringly vast evolutions of climatic change.

From the time people began to huddle behind walls to get away from whatever they found the most threatening aspect of life outside, they were beginning to surrender to the vicissitudes of unhygienic and unhealthy community. But the most significant thing you were likely to surrender was your freedom. It is highly unlikely that people living in an early city-state like Uruk would have any folk-memory of the egalitarian societies of the hunter-gatherer: a past-time of small families, children spaced an average of about four years apart so that there was never a need to carry two infants. Instead, the reality of Uruk's citizens was one of continual pregnancy and childbirth, crammed small homes, filthy surroundings made toxic to human health by an absence of means to dispose of excreta and any surplus food. In some earlier 'cities', the memory of the dead, a group that quickly outnumbered the living in any new home, was kept close by actually burying relatives under the floors of houses.

Living in and among filth and smell and disease and even above death must have created a sense that life was an unwelcoming environment. It would have been hard to convince an inhabitant of 'Ur 3' that human evolution was a process of improvement. Had there been any method of preserving the memory of ancient hunter-gatherer ancestors who had survived – though not thrived – in the same Mesopotamian regions centuries and millennia before, that past-time would have appeared to be a utopia. The walls of a Garden of Eden such as described in the Book of Genesis encompassed not misery, stench and sickness, but all of the necessities and comforts man could imagine, within easy reach and secure from a perilous outside world. The word paradise comes from Old Persian and means a walled park, literally a 'wall around'. Our settled ancestors could perhaps remember dimly a time when the earth had offered everything they needed, but without the downside of stench and misery, chaos and conflict they themselves knew. The relative paradise of hunting and gathering made a comeback in creation myths.

But that was not really the story that their rulers wanted to tell. Like a modern-day Trump belittling Obama, it was necessary to depict the past as a bad place, a place without strong leadership where humans made no progress and could not ever thrive. It would not do for there to be a time in which humans were happier without than they were within city-state walls. What was needed was a layer-cake of stories that showed why authority and hierarchy were necessary to happiness. While it is fanciful to suggest that those who *created creation,* the authors of the founding myths of our species, had any better memories of pre-agricultural life than those they sought to control, it would also have been necessary to snuff out any lingering tradition that man had ever been able to live in contented bands of foragers, practising egalitarianism and recognising no rulers. Settlement-dwellers may, until comparatively recently, have been able to see living examples of this different lifestyle and the contrasts it offered: after all, we can do so ourselves if we look in the right places. If we think back to the Mbuti pygmies of the Congo, then the civilisations of Mesopotamia, of Egypt, of early China, were all places where the mentality of Cephu was now king and the elders who had forgiven him his trespasses on the rules of the jungle were expected to do as they were told. They could not expect the tolerance he had enjoyed.

Fairness was reduced to a fable.

If there was a pursuit of fairness in the ancient civilisations, it is expressed in the laws that became necessary to control the increasingly large populations of early city-states. The first we know of is the law code of

Urukagina, a Sumerian king of the twenty-fourth century BC. But the code itself does not survive, only references to it in later codes and hagiographic poems about the king. It is perhaps telling that the law code is a work of reform. It aims to outlaw bullying and corruption by officials over ordinary workers. It exempts women from taxation – although it also has a section which treats women harshly for adultery while apparently having no equivalent law for men. It is the first time that a word for freedom is used in any written language in the world, but there is no word for fairness. Nor is there in the next substantive code, that of Ur-Nammu of Ur (2112–2095 BC), but its prologue does speak of the need to protect the vulnerable from the mighty.

A similar sentiment is found in the introduction of the next substantial development of law, the *Code of Hammurabi*, a Babylonian king, which was written in 1776BC. 'In order that the mighty not wrong the weak, to provide just ways for the waif and the widow,' the epilogue says, 'I have inscribed my precious pronouncements upon my *stela*.'[38]

Unlike the law code of Ur_Nammu, which speaks only of free men and slaves, the set of rules laid down by King Hammurabi for his empire of about a million people, was based on a rigid three-tier hierarchy in which people had to know and to accept their place as either slaves, commoners or 'superior' people. Only by accepting inequality would everyone be able to get along. That was what made sense to the Babylonians in what was the first civilisation to operate at a scale we recognise as equivalent to our own nations and states.

---

[38] A stela was a stone tablet or post on which important documents were inscribed.

Over the centuries, man's efforts at 'civilisation' – living in a *civis* or city – had seen the disappearance of hunter-gather equality, the emergence of leaders who became rulers and then divinely-appointed kings, the imposition of stories to explain why one group of beings should be naturally assumed to be worth more than another, and had then introduced the idea that some should have no value at all in terms of what we would call their rights. They had only a monetary value.

Slaves play an enormously important part in the history of all ancient civilisations – and some not so ancient – but their existence also points to why, in some civilisations, mankind eventually moved away from denying equal or just treatment to a class of unfortunates and towards fairness.

FAIRNESS AND SLAVERY IN THE ANCIENT WORLD

According to current theories, the early city-states of Mesopotamia all had access to similar technology, similar resources and similar environmental conditions. As a result of these equal opportunities, what would set one apart from others was access to a single resource that could increase collective productivity: people. The competing communities of this, the advance guard of human progress, became what have been called 'population machines'. The more citizens, the more likelihood of producing surpluses of goods and food which would be used to trade for other goods not easily available such as copper and tin to make Bronze Age weapons. Add weapons to manpower and you have an army. With an army, you can take over a smaller, weaker community, adding its surpluses to your own and its manpower to your own.

Of course, the population of a smaller city might very well not want to work for the lords of a larger one and even if they did they would want something in return. Unless they were enslaved. Slaves might not be as productive because they were working unwillingly for the joint enterprise, but that didn't matter because they only cost food. Slaves freed up 'free' citizens to work in other areas or to fight in armies, leading to more conquests and more slaves. Pretty soon, you are Hammurabi and you have a million subjects producing lots of surplus goods and food (in a good year, anyway) and you can afford to differentiate between 'superior' people – the ones who enjoy or who make a trade in surpluses – ordinary people – the ones who make the surpluses – and slaves – the ones who make everything that's needed to enable the ordinary people to make the surpluses. Superior people enjoy the utility (value) of this process, ordinary ones make the utility and slaves merely have utility, which is their value in a marketplace.

Historians believe that the early city-states had relatively few slaves. Even in the Old Kingdom of Egypt, the idea that the great pyramids of Giza (constructed sometime around 2550BC) were built by an army of slave labour is too simplistic. There were a variety of different types of labour: freemen worked for themselves and for the state; slaves worked for their masters, but there were also 'debt labourers' who worked to pay off loans, criminals and what was called corvée labour, where work was done for nothing because a lower-ranked person had an obligation to a higher-ranked person. All of these relationships had rules about them, but all also engrained the idea that there was a working class and a worked-for class.

However, the empires that followed in time, such as those of the New Kingdom of Egypt, Persia, Greece and

Rome, were far more committed to slavery, to giving nothing back in return for the contributions made by a group of human beings to the society in which, against their will, they lived.

The Greeks, like the Sumerians, lived in city-states that competed with each other for power and resources, not least the resource of human labour. Consequently, slaves were in high demand and it made no sense to treat them like ordinary citizens, even if we know that some Greeks were beginning to see slavery as morally wrong. Aristotle, whose writings dominated thought on how people ought to live together, saw slaves as being like tools to be sharpened or like animals to be domesticated. Hence, the proportion of slaves in neighbouring Sparta, including the entire race of people called Helots who were condemned to working for nothing to support their Spartan overlords, may have approached 60%, although it was only 'chattel' slaves that were seen as mere property. Other classes – Helots or the similar group called *penestae* in Thessaly – could not be bought and sold. In Athens, the proportion of slaves was probably about half as much as in Sparta. A majority of the occupants of Rome at any one time were slaves.

Any discussion of fairness in these ancient civilisations has to be set against this context. If every second person you walked past on your way to the Forum had no rights at all, no claim on fair treatment, then your attitude to fairness is not based on whether or not someone is human, but whether or not they owned their own name.

Perhaps this is why there is no word in ancient Greek which translates only as 'fair'. Nor in Latin. In Greece, the goddess Themis most closely embodied the idea, but she also represented 'things that are the same as each other' – hence the English word 'theme'. In the same way, 'aequitas' is the closest Latin approximation to what we mean by fairness.

In *A History of Western Philosophy*, Bertrand Russell devotes twenty-eight chapters to Greek philosophy and only two to that of Rome. If we had as much surviving literature depicting how Sumerian or Egyptian intellectuals thought about their world as we do from the Greeks, we might have a different perspective, but we don't and the Sumerian and Egyptians used written languages that were less practical for that purpose. One thing we can say for sure is that the Greeks were less dominated by religion in their examination of how humans can live together. Although they had their pantheon of gods, thinkers such as Socrates, Plato and Aristotle paid homage to reason. Religion was part of the fabric of Greek culture as much as any ancient people, but we know it was a fabric weaved by men and women themselves more than an imposition by a separate elite of priests or 'god-appointed' kings. The role of religion was central, but not dominant. It was a convention, it was part of the rule of law, but it was a servant of man's own mind more than his master. One of the charges against Socrates, put to death by his fellow Athenians for challenging the rule of the Thirty Tyrants in 399BC, was that he did not recognise the gods that Athens recognised, rather than that he did not believe in them.

The Greeks and their different ways of ruling their city-states had evolved from earlier monarchical societies, particularly that of Mycenae, which were much closer to the cultures of Sumer and Egypt than the democracies, oligarchies and even the tyrannies of what we now think of as the familiar state of Greek culture. Disputes over land probably caused the break-up of Mycenaean civilisation, although natural disaster also played its role. War thrived in its place as the homeland of the Greeks was fractured into hundreds of competing parts. Homer made poetry of it, but the emergence of 'classical' Greece derived from bloody prose.

The legacy of that period of history may have encouraged Greek philosophers, beginning with less familiar names such as Heraclitus, Parmenides and Empedocles, to delve into the nature of life and the working of human society which did indeed make them question assumptions that, as far as we know, earlier civilisations took for granted. Social relationships and political structures were central to their sense of themselves.

I have already embarked on a series of sweeping statements about centuries of intellectual endeavour that will have close students of classical philosophy and political thought screaming with frustration, but in the context of a short book on fairness, there is not enough space to do more than outline them.

Greek political thought, the place where we should look for signs of fairness, was mostly focused on the relatively small institution of the *polis*, the city-state which, during the millennium before the beginning of the Christian era, contained between 500 and never more than 40,000 adult male citizens. What made Greeks different and still relevant to us today (think of the words politics or democracy or tyrant – all are Greek) is that they put the nature of their community and its institutions at the heart of everything they did and all that they talked about. The very idea of 'public affairs' was a new toy to mankind in this period and they wanted to know how it worked. Their opinions differed widely, from Spartan totalitarianism, as Russell called it, to Athenian cooperation, but what they were most sure about was that there was no separation of the public and the private world as we would hold today.

This was mostly because all citizens – in itself an elite category – were expected to participate in the affairs of the *polis*. That meant fighting for it, but also fighting over it. Involvement in society and how it fostered cooperation and competition was a duty that no Greek citizen would ever question. Individualism was barely considered and certainly not valued: the Greek word for citizens in a private sense was *idiotes*, from which we get a pretty clear hint.

Like the early Mesopotamian city-states, the Greek cities were close together and in constant and brutal competition. War was an essential part of their make-up. For that reason, combined with the sense of collective duty, the rights – as we would see them – of individuals and their immediate families were subordinate to the point of irrelevance. To the extent that fair treatment of people was considered, it was in relation to their place within the *polis*. The extreme subjugation of individual interest to the collective was seen in Sparta, where even the breeding of citizens' children, their education and training for war and sex were treated as matters for the state to control. While the myth of Sparta was different from the way Spartans actually lived – they were more venal and inefficient than their public image, much as the Nazis were – they were seen as the ideal Greeks by other Greeks, even Plato, though he did not want to go through the privations of the Spartan way of life. The ideal of Spartan civic organisation was in some ways closer to bees than to our modern world, but theirs was not a happy hive and it did not last as long as others with more humane principles.

For Greeks, equality was an ideal. So was freedom. But it was the equality of the privileged. It was the freedom only of those deemed free. Most humans in Greek cities were not permitted a share in the luxuries of life, such as freedom to think and participate in public life. This was because they had been born female or had been born or forced into slavery. Running through the works of Aristotle and his definitions of liberty was the idea that some groups of human beings are born to be subject to others.

For those citizens, their biggest fear was *stasis* – not as it sounds today an admirable normality, but 'civil dissent' or disagreement or even civil war that occurs because people take a stand from which they will not shift[39] – and to avoid it they sought *homonoia* – a condition in which unanimity triumphed. They did so by having fierce debates among each other, a sign of how competitive Greek society was, even if it did not recognise individual rights at all.

Of course, because decisions were taken collectively by the citizenry, disagreement was a by-product of debate. Because the duty to the *polis* was paramount, some form of positive outcome to difficult issues had to be reached. Cooperation was desirable, but if it could not be achieved, bloody competition was seen as a reasonable and, we might tentatively suggest, fair outcome. The members of the *polis* were the *polis* in a concrete way. The Greeks did not really have an abstract concept of a state or a community. If you had no abstract state against whose interests the relative sacrifice of an individual's interests could be compared, or in whose name the strong could be restrained, the preconditions of fairness as we have defined it do not exist.

If classical thought is your thing, you will by now have probably chewed through several knuckles in frustration at my summary of the thought of some of the most

[39]Rhodes, P., 2017. Stasis. *Oxford Classical Dictionary*, 07 March.

intelligent and thoughtful people ever to have breathed. Or made the less painful choice of skipping this chapter. But even I cannot entirely ignore the fact that Aristotle (or his disciples) also wrote at great length about ethics, where ideas of fairness might also be expected to pitch up. However, I think it is reasonable, ethical and even fair to say that Aristotle's ideas of the working of the human mind, or reason, of ethics, of virtue, are rather more deterministic than they should be if we are to find ideas of fairness in them. Aristotle believed that all virtues, either intellectual or moral, came from either education or the forming of good habits. He espoused a theory that goodness came from a 'golden mean' of conduct between insufficiency of that conduct e.g. wit or bravery and excess of it. There is a certain rigidity of thought here that leaves little room for the fudge of fairness. Aristotle's knuckles would be gone by now.

What have the Romans ever done for fairness? The way Romans thought about their relationship with each other was dictated principally by constantly looking over their shoulders at those who had come before them. But this sense of their own history was informed by a constant sense of crisis – that the current state of affairs had to be improved in order to conform as closely as possible to the *mos maiorum* – the mores of our ancestors. So it was easy to harness personal ambition to what might become suffocating nostalgia by having a customised interpretation of Roman history. There are echoes here of Orwell's invention of the dictum 'Who controls the past controls the future…' in *1984*.

Roman political history was a never-ending forum of conflicts between different elements of its citizenry (again excluding an enormous number of the unfree and women), such as plebs and patricians or conservative *optimates* and radical populists – all of whom belonged to an elite class.

Cicero, who is regarded as the first political thinker of republican Rome despite living in its end times rather than at its height, put two ideas at the centre of the Republic – literally *res publica* – public things: a partnership of people for a common interest and an agreement on what constituted justice. In theory at least, the competing parties of the Roman state were part of a dynamic procedure to assess continually what justice was and to ensure that people shared both the fruits of their past labour on behalf of the *societas* and in the rewards of the future cooperation of fellow Romans.

Although the realities of ancient Rome do not mark it out in modern eyes as a crucible of fairness, its ideals as expressed by the lawyer's mind of Cicero do have the elements of fairness that John Rawls offers to us. There is a combination of stability in the form of authority from the past – expressed by the law-making assemblies of the Senate and the People – and energy in the form of executive power, both of which come together in balance. Tradition and innovation. Cooperative and competitive forces. In the words of the historian Dean Hammer:

> *What is striking and distinctive in Cicero's approach to politics is the personal tone: society is neither an abstraction nor a complex arrangement of explicit laws, but a people bound together through trust, affection, recognition of service, tradition, status, and regard for need.*[40]

[40]Hammer, D., 2014. *Roman Political Thought.* 1st ed. Cambridge: Cambridge University Press.

As mentioned before, there is no single word in Latin for what we call fairness. The word most often used to convey a sense of personal morality in matters of justice and equity is *aequitas*. In his writings, Cicero uses this word to convey that quality in a person. But as we shall further explore in the next chapter, the word fair has subtly different and broader meanings than either just or equitable as conveyed in Latin. It is also the case that, for Cicero and other theorists in the development of Roman justice, *aequitas* is a quality inherent in individuals, such as a judge or an emperor, and dispensed by them, but not seen as a quality that could be inherent in a society or organisation as a whole.

If you know your Roman history, you will know that not everyone agreed with Cicero. He was one of those figures who we use today to help us envisage the history of a whole thousand years of human evolution, but he is also one of the first whose place within his society and his fate are very clear to us. As another clash of Roman dualities – the ideal and the actual – played out in the bloody end of the Republic, Cicero was murdered by political rivals in 43BC. Any ideal of careful balance between the forces that drove Roman social and political progress for the previous 700 years was swamped by the actual ambition of tyrants, sociopaths and the very occasional reformer, such as Marcus Aurelius, in the half-millennium that followed Cicero's death.

The empire itself was subsequently swamped by peoples who, while by no means as unsophisticated and uncultured as the name 'barbarians' implies, were not inclined to explore the balance of competition and cooperation in any way, at least not until their cultures had been exposed to the tempering forces of Celtic Christian belief.

It would be typical of someone born and raised in the wet, north-western outcrop archipelago of Britain to look at a subject as profound as fairness in history through eyes that focused no further than the eastern end of the Mediterranean.

There were, throughout the period when the Greeks and then the Romans thrived, as there are today, spiritual and philosophical forces at work on our human species and its view of itself in all parts of the world. Those forces operated at different paces and at different scales. All of them in their theoretical expressions aim at fairer societies, happier people and greater cooperation.

Some societies operated within more developed philosophies – from our perspective more 'enlightened' – than others. Confucian thought in China from the sixth century BC centred on the balancing of human relationships based on five qualities of conduct: benevolence (ren), righteousness (yi), ritual propriety (li), wisdom (zhi), and sagacity (sheng). While Chinese society was hierarchical, Confucius himself (b.551BC) – his name before it was westernised was Kong-zi – taught that human beings were capable of self-improvement and shaping their own destiny. They did not have to stay at a particular level in society, but it was important that they used the benefits of formal education and informal learning – Chinese education at the time counted charioteering as one of the six must-haves of the school curriculum – for public service.

Confucianism is more of a way of life than a religion, but one that demands a constant state of 'self-cultivation'.

Confucius himself was a proto-civil servant, whose moral rectitude made him deeply unpopular in the royal court of his homeland of Lu. His thinking turned towards the past in as much as he taught reverence for ancestors and custom; it turned to the future because he wanted to revitalise what he saw as the ideal philosophies of ancient China for the generations that would come after him. When he looked backwards, he saw a burning desire in people to belong to communities and to exchange information and culture; when he looked forward it was to ways in which the concepts he found in the past, such as the authority of perfect kingship fused with the ethical force of a 'Mandate of Heaven', could be applied in the future.

Confucius, or his words as conveyed by his disciples, had a political view of society where benevolent rule by a monarchy, the promotion of self-cultivation in all members of society and the practice of benevolence by all to all, creates a harmonious community. In that context, treating people with justice to promote common goals could be seen as fairness. It took place, however, within a framework of observing rituals which were rooted in the past and were seen as the only way of achieving overall social harmony. The Confucian outlook was humanistic. Religion existed within it as part of ritual. To strive to become more human and to live as part of a well-functioning society was the most pious thing a person could do.

While Confucianism placed ritual at the heart of good conduct, Buddhism was born from a rejection of it. The rituals of Hinduism had become suffocating to many and, in times of social unrest and inter-communal war, north-east India was ripe for some kind of change. The lesson of the life of the Buddha, the son of a minor princely family, was that all animal and human life is a life of suffering and it is only through self-enlightenment that a being can achieve their perfect form and pass through suffering (*samsara*) to a different realm (the process called *nirvana*). Knowledge and improvement of the self was common to Confucius and the followers of the Buddha, but in the latter case they were more focused on the individual and less on public good.

But the pure focus on the individual has been less important in modern implementations of Buddhism which concentrate more on how individuals, by improving themselves, can contribute to the communities and societies around them. In its ancient, purer form, the breakdown of all self-interest seems to me to be at odds not so much with modern definitions of fairness as with the essential nature of humans, with those immutable parts of the human mind that have sat in our genetic make-up for millions of years.

The structures of Hinduism are, in their essence, based on altruism and fair dealing with others. The Sanskrit poet, Bhartrihari, wrote in the first century BC:

> *The most noble people are those who, giving up self-interest, bring about the good of others. People that do something for the sake of others, if it is not inconsistent with their own interest, are the norm. People who through self-interest damage the good of others are demons in human form. We do not even have words to describe those who harm others' welfare for no reason.*

That is a pretty good statement of fairness and unfairness. In older Hindu writings, ethics are grounded in religion, so decent conduct is phrased in the context of the good deeds of the gods of the pantheon. More recently, in a tradition most of us would associate with Mahatma Gandhi, ethics have been cast as the foundation of religion. Some scholars, including the Nobel-prize winner Amartya Sen, have criticised the central text of Hinduism, the Bhagavad Gita, as being too focused on duties rather than an abstract sense of what is the right thing to do and defining what rights people have. Others point to a certain moral relativism, but defenders of Hinduism say that this is the result of a misplaced understanding of a religion that has sought to describe most moral struggles in terms of epic stories rather than, say, the more modest parables of Judaeo-Christian or Islamic scriptures.

As expressed in the earlier books of the Old Testament, Jewish approaches to ethics suggest a grounding in views that express obligations to practise fairness to all. The fundamental concepts of Judaism lay down that humans should aspire to reflect and reproduce the divinity of God, particularly in interpersonal relationships. Leviticus gives examples of the type of 'holiness' that God has and which mankind should imitate. It includes caring for the sick and handicapped, for those without means to support themselves and obligations both to neighbours and strangers. There is, in Deuteronomy, an emphasis on mercy, grace and righteousness as well as describing God in terms of being a person who comes to the aid of those who need it. The nature of individuals and society as a whole are inextricably melded.

Some scholars of Jewish history say that the dissolution of the state of Judea by the Romans in 135AD meant that until the establishment of Israel 1,800 years later, the echoing of divinity was encompassed more in the individual's experience than in that of a Jewish state with its own boundaries and system of practical law. This separated ethics from politics.

This of course leads us to the central question of how Jews related to the non-Jewish world in which they had to live for nearly two millennia. It is a central tension of Judaism and, of course, to this day dominates how Jews see and are seen by non-Jews. There can be no doubt that, in its teachings and at its heart, Judaism aspires to the fair treatment of all in society and the restraint of the over mighty. The same can be said of the traditions and aspirations of Christianity and of Islam, the ethical cores of which are equally concerned in providing balance between cooperation and competition.

Perhaps the most familiar practice of Muslims as observed by non-Muslims is the observance of the fast of Ramadan. Its purpose, as laid down in the Hadith, the record of the sayings of the Prophet Muhammad, is to teach people what it is like to be hungry, no matter how much food they may be able to afford for themselves. In a similar vein, charity – the giving of alms – is extolled as a type of conduct that will be rewarded in the afterlife, providing a practical exchange for believers in return for their assistance to the vulnerable of society.

History teaches us, of course, that the best intentions of men and women are often not reproduced in their conduct. Ethical teachings in any faith can be harnessed towards any political purpose. In their pure expression, almost all religions and cultures that developed in every corner of the world, and left a written record of their origins, are recipes for a planet of peace, goodwill and fairness. More or less.

But this does not chime with a history in which men and women have been killed and persecuted in vast numbers and cruel ways in the name of one godhead or another, over the interpretation of a text or a word or sometimes even a letter of religious doctrine. The forcible conversion on pain of death of entire peoples and nations by conquest of evangelical religious forces have taken place in almost every corner of the world for centuries and probably multiple millennia too. Corruption in the medieval and early modern Christian church, for example, some of which can still be found in the operations of Christianity today, is equally indicative that the fallibility of humans perverts the intentions of faith. Fairness is rarely to be found in the doctrinal, *political* expression of religion, however hard we look, because of the dominance of ideas of good and evil, right and wrong and the diminution of compromise.

Yet, at the same time, people acting in the name of religious faith have not only made some of the most beautiful creations in art, music, literature and philosophy, but in practical terms have hugely improved the lot of our species. Healthcare, education, housing and food have all been supplied in unquantifiable amounts by organisations that would not exist without faith in the divine: from the activities of social reformers such as the Quakers to the work of the Red Crescent in regions of the world ravaged by violence, forced on countries by greed of foreign powers or the schisms in faith itself.

How religion contributes to fairness on our planet is as much in the hands of mortal men and women as is the exercise of secular power.

MAGNA CARTA AND THE COMMUNITY OF THE REALM

From the death of Cicero and the fall of the Roman Republic to the English Civil War, the vast majority of the world's polities were monarchies or empires, systems that snuffed out fairness. The questions asked by Plato, Socrates and Aristotle and thinkers all over the globe – how do we live together and how are our disparate interests and ambitions to be governed? – were answered in terms of degrees of absolute power and overwhelmingly in terms of religious conduct.

Something like political thought can be found in the West as Rome fell to the Visigoths in 410AD: the *City of God*, written by St Augustine of Hippo a few years later, partly as an exculpation of Christianity as being the cause of the collapse of the Western Empire; or *Of the Twelve Abuses of the World*, the seventh century work of an anonymous Irish monk known as 'Pseudo Cyprian', which drew on Biblical texts to draw up rules for the proper conduct of men towards each other, from the top of society to the bottom; or on a smaller scale – though it is sometimes interpreted as an allegory of large-scale government – the Rule of St Benedict, a work composed in 516AD that determined how monks should live together, even when their differences outweighed their agreements and how they are rightly governed by an all-powerful abbot.

These were all overtly religious works. Every aspect of life was to be seen in relation to the duty men owed to their God and His representatives on Earth. These might be secular rulers – a whole genre of instruction books for kings and lords emerged during the early Middle Ages, books known as 'mirrors for princes' – but increasingly religious hierarchies were constructed as the 'barbarian' peoples who had invaded the Roman Empire and settled land from the Urals to Gibraltar gradually converted to Christianity.

By the middle of the seventh century AD, the last pagan king had been killed in what we now call England and by the time Charlemagne, the great king of the Franks, was crowned Holy Roman Emperor on Christmas Day 800 AD, all the important peoples of Western Europe were at least nominally Christian.

For the next nine centuries at least, the questions of how men were to live together and how they were to be governed applied at least as much to the governance of their souls as of their bodies. Charlemagne had received his imperial crown and title from the Pope, Leo III, as an unwanted gift which set the precedent that the most senior cleric in the Western Christian world got to decide who was to be top dog in the secular, political sphere. The argument for primacy would rage over the heads of ordinary people in Europe for centuries. The relative power of Pope and kings or emperors waxed and waned constantly. Ordinary people were involved only as casualties of war and religious persecution.

Meanwhile, in its damp northwest corner, England, under threat of extinction by pagan invaders, was becoming a laboratory for different experiments with the source and nature of power.

The Vikings turned from coastal raiders to serious settlers as they realised just how valuable and vulnerable the islands of Britain and Ireland were. To resist the threat and with nowhere to run to, the disparate English kingdoms unified under Alfred the Great and his descendants. To do so they had to find compromises in the way they would live and fight together. There were sufficient cultural differences between the Mercians, West Saxons, East Saxons, East Angles, Suthrige and the men of Kent that they needed to find a common voice of representation under the king. This took the form partly of Alfred's law code which consolidated the customs of the united kingdoms, but it was given human representation in the form of the *Witangemot* usually shortened to *witan*, a council of powerful men advising the king, which some historians regard as an early form of parliament. Alfred encouraged literacy among all – at least in the 'freeborn' classes of males. Many of the bureaucratic means of uniting the English – e.g. the oath of loyalty not just to the king but to the rule of law; the jury system and the tax system – were imitations of Charlemagne. But there was a uniqueness to the way in which thousands of the English king's subjects in the tenth century AD were expected to participate in common activities that enriched or strengthened the state. These were not just tax-raising measures, but also imposition of the law through *tithings* – groups of ten free men who were expected to support each other and enforce the laws and, in groups of ten tithings, put down minor rebellions.

It would be very wrong to see England at this time as a homeland to social justice that was particularly different from other nations. Through the system of *wergild* – the payment of fines for damage to the property or person of different classes of citizen – the Anglo-Saxons stratified society in a way that Hammurabi would have found familiar 2,500 years earlier. The French *ancien regime* before the revolution of 1789 would also have recognised the imposition of restraints on the freedom of the serf and slave classes of pre-Norman England. But unification in the face of the Viking threat had sowed the seeds of a sense of common purpose that would continually mark England out as different over a longer period of time. The witan was a body without comparison, apart from law-giving bodies in the far smaller Manx and Icelandic polities, in the Western world. It was a more cooperative, "fairer" nation-state than any other comparable kingdom.

In this respect, the Norman Conquest of 1066, otherwise a catastrophic interruption of Anglo-Saxon life, was just an interruption. The concepts of cooperation among the leading men of society as a restraint on the king re-emerged in 1215 with *Magna Carta* (probably the most misunderstood document in the history of fairness[41]) which protected the rights of landed classes against a monarch who countered the principles of what we would today call fairness. Kings, of course, were generally against being restrained, preferring absolute power and it was only a few decades later that the grandsons of the barons who forced King John's hand into signing *Magna Carta* held his son Henry III to account by revolting against oppressive taxes to pay for foreign wars. Their rebellion in 1258 cited the interests of what they called the *communitas regni* – the community of the realm – in a rebellion that opposed Henry's overmighty behaviour. This *communitas* was a grouping of people far wider than just the nobility. It may have been rolled out as a concept only when the powerful men of the kingdom found it convenient in their struggles with the Crown, but it reappeared later in English history – in the 1381 Peasants' Revolt or the 1450 rebellion led by Jack Cade during the Wars of the Roses – in the service of much lower-born rebels.

The energies of other European states were meanwhile spent in the fight between Church and State for supreme power over human life. The power of religion – a power derived from the exclusive right to offer the salvation of paradise or threaten an eternity in Hell – was pitted against the power of the sword. Sometimes popes, kings and emperors co-operated – the bloody monstrosity of the Crusades against undeserving populations to the east

---

[41]Magna Carta was signed at Runnymede in Surrey, one of the traditional meeting places of the *Witan*. It was meant to evoke the traditions of Anglo-Saxon oligarchy – fairness for all (above a certain income bracket).

of Europe being one example; sometimes they competed with kings assuming the role of champion of the Church in order to achieve their own unholy ambitions.

But these were battles fought in the mind as much as the melée. Theology was challenged by political thought for the first time since the collapse of the Roman Empire. The papal bull was faced with the 'mirror of princes'.

Gradually, across Europe, the secular side won practical dominance as kings turned to political theorists to establish their intellectual claim to sovereignty over the Church. While Niccolo Machiavelli's *The Prince* is the most famous of these expressions, it would not have been possible without the preparatory ideas of an earlier work, the *Defensor Pacis,* the Defender of Peace, by Marsilius of Padua. It laid out the rules for government of an enlightened ruler, based on the common good. The Defensor was also known, for those who take note of coincidence in our lives, as the 42 Propositions.

LEVELLERS, LOCKE AND THE ENGLISH AND SCOTTISH ENLIGHTENMENTS

For more than a thousand years after the fall of the Roman Empire, there was only one real question in the minds of men about power: who had it? Very few people questioned that the answer should be a single person. It might be a king or an emperor or a sultan or a khan; it might be a pope or a patriarch, or it might be a combination of the two: a caliph. In a few cases it would be a collection of people, as with the Republics of Italian city-states: Venice, Florence, Genoa. They could generate enormous wealth through trade and control foreign states as well as their own homelands. In northern Europe, dozens of cities enjoyed 'Free Imperial' status in that they were granted high degrees of autonomy by the Holy Roman Emperor (effectively the King of what we would now call Germany). No other lords intervened between their representatives and the Emperor and they could vote at the Diet, a secular council that met occasionally, but which had little real power except to choose the Emperor's successor on his death.

Elsewhere in the world, one can find examples of independent states, such as the utopian republic of the Qarmatians in eastern Arabia or the Republic of Tlaxcala in Mexico which was ruled by a council drawn from both a patrician and plebeian community, or the Haudenosaunee, the Iroquois League of north-western America, a confederacy of different tribes speaking a common language who convened a council of representatives several centuries before the white European colonists came up with a similar idea.

What all these republics had in common, with the exception of the loosely-confederated Iroquois nations, was that they controlled small areas. They all involved small populations. These were not, any more than the Greek republics had been, sophisticated devices for controlling large numbers of people spread over thousands of communities and hundreds of miles.

But in the case of Europe in the age of Reformation, they allowed a degree of independence of conduct and thought in which Protestant religious ideas could be applied to questions of how men and women should live together as well. Protestantism emphasised the individual's relationship with God and His words as expressed in the Bible. This, to use a very twenty-first century word, disintermediated the 'Church' as an idea. And by doing so it took both power and money away from the Church and the men – priests, bishops and popes – who had placed themselves in the middle of the relationship between God and man.

The single exception in terms of scale and power in these small, mostly Protestant, independent polities, is the Dutch Republic. The emergence of federation of city-states at the end of the sixteenth century led to a period in which the tiny Dutch population – never more than 1.5 million-strong, came to dominate the Western world in trade, finance, science, naval warfare and art in a way that was hugely out of scale with its size. The republic was also a beacon of free thinking and opposition to the Catholic hierarchy. The English latched on to many of its innovations after the republic was weakened by constant fighting against the Spanish and the Holy Roman Empire.

The Dutch rejected religious ritual and divinely-ordained kingship, but their society was still deeply rooted in faith and built round an ideal that they thought Jesus would have smiled on. And they still couldn't do without a single figure around whom to unite and so had the figure of the Stadtholder, a part-elected, part-dynastic figure who took command in the (frequent) moments of calamity that assailed the republic. Catholic kings in France and Spain were always trying to kill it off, partly because it showed other heretical Protestants they could thrive, but also because their skill in trade and business were deeply attractive to the larger, less effective, traditional kingdoms of Europe.

One of the Stadtholders, who took this role of being one step on from the Holy Roman Emperor as a stepping-stone from a divine right ruler to an elected secular ruler, was William of Orange (ruled 1664–1704). Through his English wife, Mary Stuart, (Protestant daughter of the Catholic King James II) William had more than a passing interest in the Crown of England. At home, his republic was struggling to repel that most absolute of Catholic monarchs, Louis XIV.

In the seventeenth century, the clash of divine right kingship and Protestant fundamentalism had become a clash of monarchy against parliamentarianism. The bad news for kings about the Reformation was that once you had experimented with disintermediating the Church from man, it was not a huge step to try the same thing with kings. If there was no reason why an institution should get in the way of our relationship with creation, then there was no reason why an institution should get in the way of our relationship with each other.

In a hideously bloody civil war – fought as the rest of Europe was coming to the end of the even more hideously bloody conflict between Protestant and Catholic cultures, the Thirty Years' War – the English had thrown off their king, Charles I, and beheaded him.

For eleven years, they tried secular rule for size. That period of history saw cooperative ideas arise that were recognisably modern in some ways. The Levellers, a sect who were purged by Oliver Cromwell as being just a bit too ahead of their time, believed in the communal sharing of all goods, land and wealth. They were against money. But even the more restrained concept of the Commonwealth, a Puritan regime that replaced kingship with parliamentary rule, banned Christmas, reintroduced capital punishment for adultery and generally prevented the English from enjoying themselves, was no more to local taste than the arbitrary, mystically-based power that Charles I had imposed on the *communitas regni*. The English welcomed back a Stuart king, Charles II, in 1660 and remained relatively happy until near the end of his life when it became clear that his Catholic brother, James II, was going to try to turn the clock back even further.

England and Scotland were, by the 1680s, deeply Protestant kingdoms with Catholic minorities. When James began to introduce laws that favoured Catholics and pandered to Louis XIV and, worse still, when his wife had a son who might therefore signal a proper 'Popish' dynasty, enough was enough.

The staunchly Anglican Mary Stuart was seen by many powerful Britons as the answer and her equally Protestant husband William was invited in 1688 to become king at her side. In a bloodless coup, England drove out James and introduced a Bill of Rights, laying out what the respective powers of the monarch and the people were to be.

The most important writing on political power anywhere in Europe at this time was by the Englishman John Locke. He was the son of a Civil War officer - a colonel of cavalry on the Parliamentary side. Like John Rawls three hundred years later, being heir to a tradition of civil strife made him think constantly about how mankind could best cohabit. Locke made major contributions to our way of thinking about society and politics – his *Second Treatise on Government* was fundamental to the Bill of Rights (and the US Constitution) and paved the way for social-contract thinking of Voltaire, Rousseau and Kant – but also on thinking about thinking. The *Essay Concerning Human Understanding* (1689) was the founding document of a movement that became known as Empiricism. It held that all human understanding comes from, and can be expanded by, experience. It challenged all religious teaching before it, based on Aristotelian methods of scholarship, that all knowledge exists already and must be dissected and analysed to discover truths. Locke built on Descartes' writing on the power of ideas to develop the belief that all answers are to be found in the human mind.

This was what allowed him to develop a 'contract' theory of social and political relationships.

We came across this in the first chapter of the book:

> *The only way whereby anyone divests himself of his Natural Liberty, and puts on the bonds of Civil Society is by agreeing with other men to joyn and unite into a Community, for their comfortable, safe and peaceable living one amongst another.*

This was not the eccentric, dogmatic and extreme idealism of the Levellers, but a developed theory that understood why humans combine in societies. Locke shared with his predecessor Thomas Hobbes the idea of a 'state of nature', the time before civilisation or a time in which there was none. But while Hobbes thought of it as an awful, violent, bloody state, Locke's conception was of a much kinder and gentler and more trusting ideal.

These two huge trends in the development of human thought – the sovereignty of ideas and the personalisation of the relationship with God – lead us back towards a relationship with the physical world that was closer to the life we lived as hunter-gatherers. Locke had neither the knowledge of palaeontology nor even the concept of evolution to know this, but we have seen that in what he would have called the 'state of nature', humans were much more likely to live cooperatively and with a tendency towards egalitarianism in order to compete against other groups and against the ever-present threat of a life that could also be solitary, poor, nasty, brutish and short.

While Hobbes used the threat of the state of nature as a reason to obey unquestioningly the rule of a lord as long as that lord could protect you, Locke saw it as an aspiration for the coming together of human beings. Our archaeological and anthropological evidence suggests that Locke was closer to being right than Hobbes.

What was missing to send this spark of humanism into full-blown reaction to the past, where fairness would begin to play a part in common interaction, was the oxygen of scientific inquiry and the final subjugation of religious ideas to the practicalities of common life. That this combination brought about not just vast wealth for Europeans through imperial conquest was inevitable. That it happened at the expense of the rest of the planet was tragic.

FAIRNESS AND EMPIRE – FAIRNESS FOR THE FAIR-SKINNED ONLY?

It is what is known as a Whig view of history to believe that societies move through stages, eternally heading towards greater progress – whatever that may mean. At the beginning of the book, I called something like it 'agathism', the idea that things tend towards the better outcome. Taking many factors into account, such as life expectancy, infant mortality, economic inequality measures, human life has been getting 'better' in the past two to three hundred years.

It would not have been as easy to make that point from the point of view of a person thinking about human progress at the beginning of the eighteenth century. The previous hundred years had, in Europe, seen a lowering of life expectancy, a huge growth in the number of people killed in wars – *per capita* the Thirty Years' War was more costly in human life than any modern conflict apart from the 1939–45 War. There was, in the second half of the seventeenth century, a serious recurrence of the plague that had been latent in the world since first appearing as the Black Death in the late 1340s. There had also been vastly disruptive wars fought elsewhere on Earth: in China (the Ming-Qing transition left at least 25 million dead), India (5 million perished in the Mughal-Maratha wars) and Korea (1 million killed during Japanese invasions). Famine and disease were the constant companions of war.

By most measures, violent death had been on a gradual decline throughout the Middle Ages in Europe, but that trend had slowed in the seventeenth century. Medicine and public health in the 1600s were not markedly different from what they had been in the fourteenth century. There was a strong sense throughout the continent that if there had been a time to be alive on Planet Earth, it was not now. Perhaps in the time of the Ancient Greeks and Romans, with their wisdom, but not 'today'.

However, up to the time we now call the Enlightenment, when science began to remove the blinkers of faith, people had not really been trying that hard to improve the lot of their fellow human beings. Even the ancients did not see the pursuit of the good in life as being something done specifically for others. It was principally aimed at individual happiness. Christian teaching from the early years of the Common Era laid great stress on the Old Testament injunction to 'love thy neighbour as thyself'. The interpretation of these words from Leviticus in the Christian era was, to be charitable, flexible: most of the societies which embraced Christianity into the early modern era were slave-owning, or practised one degree or another of serfdom or corvée labour. Love was not to be squandered on neighbours.

But two ideas began to ferment in Europe, respectively in the times we call the Reformation and the Enlightenment. First, that it was not the exclusive role of an authoritarian Church and priestly interventionists to interpret God's will; second, that human beings had inherent natural rights. It was then only a matter of time before someone suggested that maybe this ought to be the goal of a good society. If loving thy neighbour as thyself meant anything, according to the utilitarian thought of the eighteenth century, it was that we should want our neighbour to be as happy as we were. The revolutionary idea was that we should do it even if it meant sacrificing some of our own happiness. These were the truths that the Founding Fathers of America felt to be self-evident (although it does not pay to question too deeply the motives of those who staged the Boston Tea Party despite being among the most lightly taxed human beings on the planet at the time, nor those slave-owners who pronounced all men equal, although their opposition to British rule was at least partly founded on a desire to accelerate the expropriation of Native Americans that George III's ministers opposed).

The eighteenth and nineteenth centuries saw huge growth in the means of making money through Agricultural and Industrial Revolution and the equally huge growth of the means of spreading money through finance capitalism. The development of credit as an idea followed on from the Scientific Revolution that had encouraged people to question everything they thought they knew about the world, which until then had derived in great part from Plato, Aristotle and the Bible. If the answer to everything could be found in experience and in science, then economics, too, was a science and goodness could be achieved through the expansion of finance. Capitalism, as laid down by Adam Smith, was a tool for the improvement of men's common health as well as wealth. The application of ideas of capitalism – credit, trust, equity, share, bond – that were couched in the language of mutual benefit and mutual faith came at the same time as thinkers such as Voltaire and Rousseau were proposing new a new type of bond between humans – the social contract. Equality in the eyes of God was not much good for humans if their chains were put on by their fellow men. If these different types of contract, in business and politics, both signs of sophistication of the development of law since the Middle Ages, were interchangeable ideas, then what was good for man was also good for the economy and vice versa.

What was less good for man was the emergence of the idea – already old enough for Marx and Engels to identify it as an engrained evil by 1848 – that capital existed to serve growth and growth to serve capital. This was the formula that encouraged Alexis de Tocqueville to observe that Europeans acted towards other humans as humans act towards other animals. This certainly proved to be the case as imperial expansion proved that people were as quick and eager to classify others of their species as the Swedish natural philosopher Linnaeus used Latin taxonomy on the rest of the natural world. The Spanish had shown how the wealth of the world beyond the European horizon could enrich sailors as well as kings. All that was required was an ability to navigate, use a musket and be indifferent to the customs, liberty and survival of non-Europeans. On the whole, that indifference came easily.

Of course, although the Enlightenment period brought Europeans – or some of them at least – to the prioritisation of such concepts as human rights, toleration of belief, rationality and liberty, that assuredly does not make them specifically Western ideas. Amartya Sen has pointed out that concepts of social justice and rights in Indian thought, expressed through the *Bhagavad Gita* or the *Laws of Manu* long pre-dated their European expression.

But the horizons of Indian philosopher-kings such as Ashoka or Akbar were narrower than those of the white man. In the period following the Enlightenment, the race between competing imperial powers with broadly similar capacity for transporting military might across oceans led eventually to another enormous human conflict on the continent of Europe in 1914. The fallout from that war included the sense of injustice engrained in two populations – the Russian and then the German – that drove them into novel experiments with human interaction unknown before. The Russians, or at least a sufficient minority of them – tried to force scores of millions of people to share all goods in common, making the sacrifice of one's interests in favour of those of others into an involuntary act. The Germans, or at least a sufficient minority of them, imposed a doctrine of exceptionalism based on race and breeding on an entire people, then an entire continent and, if they had not been stopped, perhaps an entire species. In these ideas, in capitalism, in imperialism, in totalitarianism there may have been the germs or the remnants of ideas of fairness, but they cannot have been very strong or they would have had more power over the violently competitive instincts of those who favoured rank unfairness.

So where does the idea come from? Why is there even a word for fairness, if it skulks through history like a prototype species of mammal, hiding in the ferns, trying not to be trodden on or devoured by dinosaurs?

5

Is Fairness a Creation of the English-speaking World? (Spoiler alert: No)

IS BRITAIN DIFFERENT IN THE WAY IT TREATS ITS PEOPLE?

It is absurd to claim or believe that an emotion found deep in the recipe of human nature belongs to one small sliver of humanity. Germans are not the only people capable of feeling pleasure at the failure of others, nor are French people unique in having a capacity to act with style and poise, but only the former seems to have invented the word 'schadenfreude' and no other language has the word 'panache'. Arguably, neither of these words describes a day-to-day feeling. Of course, there are many examples of words that have been imported into usage by speakers of a different language. The English have millions of residential buildings of a single storey, but borrowed the word 'bungalow' from Hindi, perhaps originally to make the modesty of such a home sound a bit more exotic and thus positive.[42]

---

[42]The word 'bungalow' is an adaptation of 'bangla', meaning 'from or of Bengal' and was coined in the late seventeenth century to describe low-rise homes built for British settlers in that part of India.

But it seems odd not to have a word for something as frequently expressed as fairness and something that is so deep inside that human recipe. Yet, according to the linguistic experts, that is the case with every other significant language in the world than English, and in English the word has only been used in the sense we have been considering for a relatively short time, perhaps less than half of its recorded history in the tongue.

A much more likely explanation for why 'Anglo' societies keep going on and on about fairness is that they like to emphasise their difference from other nationalities and coincidentally their moral superiority. 'Modesty forbids', the British say, but it clearly doesn't. Brits and Americans have liberally rewritten the history of the English common law and Magna Carta to construct a boastful image of a nation that has been liberal and tolerant, a proto-democracy, since time immemorial.[43] Not so. Common law was at least half Norman in origin and Magna Carta almost exclusively benefitted the landed not the dispossessed.

It may also be wrong to lump all 'Anglo' societies together. In his excellent book, *Fairness and Freedom*, which is a great reference for a full study of fairness in more recent history rather than our brief foxtrot through it here, David Hackett Fischer compares New Zealand as the apogee of fairness to his native United States where the emphasis of social interaction is on freedom. He contrasts the way in which almost all Kiwi politicians for a century and a half have made 'a fair go' for its citizens central to

---

[43]In strict British legal terms, this is pretty much spot on, because 'time immemorial was defined as being the end of the reign of Richard I in 1199, only sixteen years before the signing of Magna Carta.

their manifestos, with the habit of American politicians to concentrate on liberty. It is worth saying that the Māoris of New Zealand might raise as strong an objection to the prevalence of fairness in the islands' history as the African-American or Native American populations would over the ideal of liberty in the US and the self-evidence of the 'truth' that all men were created equal. But in as much as they speak a lot about fairness and, as do Australians, have a multitude of phrases to encapsulate the idea – *fair do, fair dinkum, fair game* – then New Zealanders must spend a lot of time thinking about what fairness means to them.

As Fischer points out, that includes considering the effects of living under British hegemony and having a low opinion of British fairness. The expression 'Best of British luck!' to a New Zealander means no luck at all, because he associates the 'Mother Country' with the absence of fairness.

Fischer, who as I say is an American who spent some time on academic projects in New Zealand, concludes his comprehensive work by presenting fairness and freedom as two different, but complementary, ideas that can 'reinforce the other's virtues and corrects its vices'. He says:

> *On the subject of fairness, no nation in the world has more to teach than New Zealand; and no country has more to learn than the United States.*[44]

Others would agree that Americans prize liberty over fairness as an ideal. Theirs is, by nature, a more competitive society, hence its extraordinary success and growth. Forms of common endeavour which the British

---

[44]Hackett Fisher, D., 2012. *Fairness and Freedom*. 1st ed. New York: Oxford University Press page 493

prize, such as the National Health Service or the BBC, are viewed with deep suspicion by many Americans. US politicians are perfectly content to denounce the NHS as 'socialism' whereas a British MP who attacks the state-organised healthcare system, especially after the responses of its underpaid staff to the coronavirus pandemic, might as well resign their seat. A Briton, Australian, Canadian or New Zealander looking at some of the peculiarities of American politics – gerrymandering, voter suppression, pork-barrel legislation, governmental shutdown, a head of state who parodied standards of governance – feels a sense of smug superiority, although almost all those flaws are historical British exports.

But, objectively, it does seem that fairness for Americans still lags some way behind the absolute faith in the US Constitution as a protection of liberty. The highest form of debate that can take place in America is held in the US Supreme Court, when modern events are tested for constitutionality against a document signed in 1787 to govern a few hundred thousand people. As proved by the reverence with which it is still treated, that document, as the 'terms and conditions' of American liberty, has to be right. It does not necessarily have to be fair.

Yet whether or not the British and other English-speaking countries have any right to feel smug about the lack of fairness in others is a matter open to the most serious objection. Britain's imperial record may be slightly less awful than those of other imperial European powers, but is still stained with episodes of massacre, division, the stripping of resources, enslavement – everything, in short, that man can do to man. The ideas of toleration, liberty, decency and compromise accorded to each other, were not accorded to the Māori, to indigenous Australians, to Native Americans or to most Indian peoples. Where the British could not conquer or suppress the cultures they found when their boats kissed the sand of far-flung islands and continents, they traded with, accommodated, negotiated and manipulated them. Divide and rule was the maxim of British rule in India, of its brief domination of Chinese coastal regions, of huge tracts of Africa and North America. Alliance and betrayal drove expansion. How else could such a tiny nation wield such enormous power from the 1770s to the 1910s? Britain was and is a country of expediency. The French call us 'perfidious Albion'. They may have a point.

Other nations, including those such as Australia and New Zealand, have their own reasons to resent the British attitude to fairness. As it happens, I am writing these words on Anzac Day, when the modern citizens of those two countries remember the dead of war since 1915. It is commemorated on 25 April because on that day in that year, the Gallipoli campaign began in southern Turkey. The first major involvement of Australian and New Zealand troops is remembered bitterly as a battle in which the cream of their young manhood was squandered on the slopes of Gallipoli by uncaring British generals who had become accustomed to trading young lives for tiny tactical gains on the battlefields of the Western Front. There is an element of myth to this. The attitude of the leadership in that campaign was more or less equally callous to all the Allied soldiers – Brits and Antipodeans alike – but it reflects a deeper attitude that is fully understandable.

The British – perhaps more accurately the English – are renowned beyond their own shores, fairly or unfairly, for two things: good manners and insincerity.

Any English conversation is likely to be composed of platitudes, insincerities and gentle feelers for the other party's pliability. When a Briton asks 'how do you do?' – an increasingly rare greeting – the last thing they want you to do is tell them. It is very 'Anglo' to begin a conversation or communication with an inquiry or an expression of hope – 'I hope you are well'. In most other cultures, greetings are generalised statements of goodwill. The British, and to some extent the inhabitants of their oldest conquests, frequent a culture of commerce and negotiation, which is where they prefer to stay if possible. But, certainly in its imperial past and only by implication now, if negotiation is not possible or not necessary because of their overwhelming superiority, these are people who will, without compunction, turn to the sword.

Another Frenchman who knew the English well, Paul Cambon, ambassador to the Court of St James from 1898 to 1920, said that nothing pleased an Englishman more than to discover that his country's interests coincided with those of humanity as a whole. If such a 'confluence' did not exist, he would try his hardest to create it. It is hard to fault Cambon's view of the innate sense that Britons of that era had of their own moral superiority. (But it is worth noting that Cambon's words were expressed in French, a language that he spoke exclusively during his twenty-two years in Britain, insisting that every word of every conversation he had with anyone speaking English to him should be translated into his mother tongue. Even the word 'Yes'. The British may excel at it, but they do not have an exclusive hold on haughty self-importance.)

Perhaps it is only in the long sweep of history that we can grasp whether the British frame of mind brought about a particular attitude to fairness and whether or not that was a good thing.

Over the centuries, British representative democracy has evolved from a system originally enacted with the limited aim of achieving 'fairness' only for the wealthier strata of the population (From Magna Carta, the Provisions of Oxford in 1258 even up to the 1689 Bill of Rights) into first a system intended to provide fairness only for those who adhered to certain common principles of belief (generally Protestant Christianity), and latterly, with the development of a more secular, plural society, as a benefit to be enjoyed for all regardless of their adherence to particular moral, religious or political creed.

That is also the pattern of global social and political history. We all still share this planet with totalitarian regimes, tyrants and autarchs, but they are in the minority. More people live under democratic government (although of course this in itself is an elastic term) than at any time in mankind's history. There are global bodies that ensure cooperation in matters of health, technology, trade and food supply. There is a forum in which countries can battle out disagreements before they pick up their arms. These organisations are as flawed and ineffectual as mankind itself, but they exist at least in part because models for them were forged in a grand sweep of history; some, but by no means all, of those models trace their roots back to institutions that did not first emerge, but most durably persisted in Britain. And this, of course happened usually, and often only, with the guidance and assistance of its international friends and neighbours.

Whether all this makes *Homo sapiens* happier than we were as egalitarian hunter-gatherers can be debated. Anyone well-read could rip holes in my outline of history and its monumental generalisations, but I would stand by the idea that, today, more of us must surely be living in fairer circumstances than at any period that came between the epoch of the hunter-gatherer and the dropping of the atomic bomb.

Angela Merkel was not a happy *Mutti*. The normally domineering Chancellor of Germany even banged her fist on the negotiating table. She was standing up for her nation's rights and her emotion came flooding out of her.

'*Das is nicht* fair!' Frau Merkel exclaimed. Staring at President Barack Obama across from her and President Nicolas Sarkozy next to her, tears welled in her eyes, according to a report written by my former colleague Peter Spiegel in the *Financial Times* in 2014. His article described a dramatic night three years earlier when the German leader felt she was being bullied by her allies into sacrificing important principles of international finance. The stakes could not have been higher: the eurozone, having been ravaged by the effects of the global financial crisis three years before, was on the point of collapse. The Chancellor was being backed into a corner where she had to make a decision on behalf of her nation's central bank, but the *Bundesbank* had been independent since its foundation and she could not do as she was being pressured to do. The fact is that at this moment, the only one in her career where she came even close to crying, her mind reached for an English word to vent her frustration at a universal experience.

The Germans have been using the word fair for some time. One of the most popular political discussion programmes on the main channel of the state-owned television company ARD is called '*Hart aber* fair' – literally 'Hard but fair'.

Other languages that borrow fair include Hebrew and Slovenian, although the latter has a word which its speakers claim directly translates as fair and only as that. The truth is that if you want to get into a really profound argument with linguists, try telling them that 'there is no word for X in Language Y'. They really don't think it's right. Or fair.

However, Anna Wierzbicka did exactly that.

The Australian linguist is greatly respected as one of the outstanding experts in her field, anywhere in the world. Her mother tongue is Polish, so she has some claim to neutrality. In 2006, she published a book called *English: Culture and Meaning*. In one chapter, *Being Fair*, Wierzbicka says:

> *The ubiquity of the words fair and unfair in modern English discourse … is all the more remarkable given that these words have no equivalents in other European languages (let alone non-European ones) and are thoroughly untranslatable.*

At the risk of labouring the point, I think it's important to be absolutely clear here what is being claimed: according to Wierzbicka, there is no other major language than English that contains a single word that can be translated only as 'fair'. To put it another way, all words that are used in other languages to convey the concepts listed in our definition(s) of fairness also translate to mean something else, such as just, equitable or correct. When French people translate the English word fair they use *juste* or *equitable*; Germans tend to use *gerecht*. Wierzbicka says this is true of all major current languages and as myself someone born in one of what she calls the 'Anglo' countries – all those nation-states where English is the historic mother tongue or has been since the language adapted to its current form – it is convenient for me to agree with her (but please send her the splenetic disagreements).

Wierzbicka adds:

*[Fairness] is indeed a uniquely Anglo concept, without
an equivalent in any other language, and the question of
why Anglo culture has created this concept is an important
one… If we want to understand Anglo culture, we have to
try to understand the concept of fairness.*

I have to say that I don't think I agree with Wierzbicka
that fairness is a uniquely Anglo concept. If it were, then
monkeys wouldn't have it. Any human being recognises
unfairness and may have a different word for it in its
instinctual, intuitive form. They may use a word such as
the words we translate as unjust or inequitable, but they
mean the same as we mean by unfair.

But Wierzbicka is right to say that there is a ubiquity
about fairness in English. She demonstrates this with
reference to a database called the Cobuild 'UK Spoken'
corpus which is one of the largest collections of reported
speech online and it showed that there were 101 occurrences
of *fair* per million words, compared with thirty-three
occurrences for *just*, although that includes occurrences,
probably more common, of *not fair*.

As I said, a claim that 'there is no word for…' in any
language is a large cat thrown among flighty pigeons in the
linguists' world. Prof Wierzbicka made feathers fly. But
nobody who responded to her book seriously challenged
her until some ten years later the historian David Hackett
Fischer in *Fairness and Freedom* determined that if fairness
was unique to anything it was to a family of Northern
European languages including Old Frisian, Danish,
Norwegian and Icelandic. (We know from the written
record of a visit to the court of King Alfred in the late
ninth century by a reindeer farmer from north Norway
that speakers of Old English and Old Norway did not
need interpreters to understand each other)

But if we take for a moment as given that English-speakers – people who enjoy the luxury of fluency in what has become the world's first global language – are the only ones with a special word for fair, it might be worth asking why. It might tell us a bit more about how the word fits into the thought patterns of people today and help us look for signs of its erosion or signs of its resurgence.

The simple explanation could be that English-speakers have access to a wider vocabulary than those of other languages. Because of its mongrel heritage – part Anglo-Saxon, part French, part Latin, part Greek, part pretension – English often has multiple words meaning basically the same thing, albeit with nuances of application – think of kingly, royal and regal, which are respectively drawn from Old English, Norman French and the so-called 'dog' Latin of the Middle Ages[45]. Adverbs, beloved of some writers in English and despised by others, aptly support this idea: e.g. the adverbs available to describe something being partially of a certain nature: English-speakers can say that an idea, say, is *quite* good, *pretty* good, *reasonably* good, *moderately* good, good *enough*, or indeed *fairly* good.

I chose that example because it also speaks to a quality of at least the British, and to lesser extents Australians, New Zealanders, South Africans and Americans (I hesitate to include the Irish in the category of Anglo for fear my Irish friends never speak to me again). That quality is fudge. Compromise, moderation, consensus and agreement are key parts of the psyche in British political and social life. There are reasons why this might be the case that I will look at in a few pages, to do with the development in

[45]Tombs, R., 2015. *The English and their History.* Kindle ed. London: Penguin Books Ltd.

the eighteenth century of politeness, which, in turn, was the reaction to the shocking violence and division of the English Civil War and religious repressions of the previous two centuries.

And because of this quality of not wanting to express oneself too firmly or in too committed a fashion (a quality which is rich in my own personality and which drives my non-British wife to distraction), I think it is unlikely that the word fair emerged only because of a superfluity of words at our disposal.

Before moving on to look at ways in which 'Anglo' people treat each other and at the peculiarity of English history, it is also worth looking at some more of Wierzbicka's examination of what fairness means when she is investigating whether it has particular national characteristics.

For instance, she points out that *fairness* aligns with the concept of rules as *justice* aligns with the idea of laws. This accords with the idea that rules are things agreed between people (the dynamic between people is horizontal) while laws are designed by a superior group to be passed down on to society (the dynamic is vertical). Laws have to be accepted by those subject to them once they have been imposed, or there is a chance of rebellion, but rules have to be agreed in advance of the beginning of an enterprise. You could even boil it down to: rules are done *with* people; laws are done *to* people. The nature of rules will reappear when we look at fairness in sport (and war).

We know how laws are judged, but how do we judge rules? Well, we don't judge them in a literal sense, but we do agree them. Rules are initially accepted by consensus and if they do not work for enough people, then they are no longer acceptable and are changed by consensus.

The greatest chance of acceptance comes when there is the greatest consensus of fairness.

And this brings us back to Rawls, who wrote that:

> *The fair terms of social cooperation are to be given by an agreement entered into by those engaged in it. One reason it does this is that, given the assumption of reasonable pluralism, citizens cannot agree on any moral authority, say a sacred text or a religious institution or tradition. Nor can they agree about a moral order of values or the dictates of what some view as natural law. So what better alternative is there than an agreement between citizens themselves reached under conditions that are fair for all?*[46]

So was this pluralism, this move away from a commonly agreed 'moral authority' – i.e. religion – something that only the English and their cousins around the globe happened upon? No, but it does appear that they were probably the first to do so, certainly among Western cultures in the modern era, and that they were the first to write it all down.

In the next section, we will go back to history, briefly, to find the route down which English and Scottish political thought travelled in order to get us to a position where ethics was no longer based solely on diktat, but on reason and derived from a procedural morality rather than an absolute one.

And we will find some evidence that the English were not the only people with fairness in mind. It was also to be found just across the North Sea, in Holland, and when

---

[46]Rawls, J., 2001. *Justice as fairness: a restatement.* 2nd ed. Cambridge, MA: Belknap Press of Harvard University Press. Page 15

the two came together, there were dramatic effects on the way our world developed. Some of them were even good.

THE PECULIARITY OF ENGLISH HISTORY

Even today, big events cause big changes in our attitudes to each other and force people from top to bottom of any community to examine how they relate to each other. The disruptive effects of war, pestilence, famine and death strike societies less often today than they did in earlier centuries. The effects of coronavirus on our lives has been all the more shocking because, in recent times, we came to believe they were things of the past and we feared instead only the effects of financial, intellectual, geographical and technological disruption.

One reason for supposing that Britain might be the crucible of the concept of fairness is the way in which it reacted to the enormous disruptive pressures of big events by changing relations horizontally in society as much as vertically. By this, I mean that the normal way in which ruling classes react to vast disruptions is to enforce greater authority from top to bottom. Holding monopolies on weaponry and organised military units allowed governments on a state-, regional- and local-level to impose order on disorganised and unarmed masses.

For some reason, when the English – and in time the Scots in particular and the Welsh, then the Irish to a lesser extent – were dragooned into this approach to life, they seemed to react to massive change and threat by seeking to work together more than other nations and to reach tacit agreements of mutual assistance between peers in exchange for mutual reward when better times arrive.

They were not the only ones to do this, but it seems to be a longer skein of history in Britain than elsewhere, and to have reached an earlier point where it became the agreed and accepted norm. And this approach to unity, achieved through compromise, vagueness, the avoidance of conflict and bloody-mindedness, was born out of division.

The first example in our better-recorded history was the reaction to the coming of the Vikings. Perhaps there was a shared memory of the Anglo-Saxon invasions of the fourth to sixth centuries AD and how the violent newcomers from modern Germany and Denmark completely changed culture and life in a relatively peaceful post-Roman Britain without necessarily swamping it by force of numbers. In any case, when the equally rapacious Danes and Norse began first to raid and then conquer the north and east of England from the late eighth century onwards, the effect in the areas further from those coasts was to make disparate kingdoms come together into a united 'Englelond'. It was brought together in resistance by Alfred the Great at the end of the nineth and in the tenth century by successors such as Edward the Elder and Athelstan. But the resistance was far from consistently successful and the war bands from the North collectively known as 'Danes' frequently had the upper hand. Despite establishing an identity as kings of a nation that began to see itself as a union, there was weakness in individual kings who could not live up to the required standards as military or administrative leaders. Rather than collapse in the face of the Danish threat, though, this period saw the emergence of councils of advisers in a tradition that is also found in some other north European societies such as Iceland or the Isle of Man. We met it earlier – the witan – a gathering of older and wealthier men to advise the king on policy and inform him, sometimes reprimand him, about the state of his realm.

The Norman Conquest crushed the collective will of England's ruling classes – already weakened by the machinations of clans of nobles in the mid-eleventh century. For a century and a half, the society was subject instead to the imposition of the will of a small ruling class, which for most of the period was led by an undisputed king. Nobody argued with the autocracy of William the Conqueror, and the bureaucratic impositions of Henry I overcame challenges to his right to rule both England and Normandy. The expansion of England as just part of a miniature north-western European Empire under Henry II benefitted most of the ruling class.

But there were times when the lessons the English learned about law and order were bloody and direct, such was the anarchy that followed the very-much disputed succession to Henry I. In 1135, his cousin, Stephen of Blois, was advanced as the candidate to prevent Henry's daughter, Matilda, becoming a female ruler in opposition to all precedent (the fact that she was married to the ruler of the Normans' hated Angevin neighbours did not help her cause). These horrific times were still present in the memory of those few still alive when Henry I's great-grandson, John, began his disputed and ineffective reign in the 1190s. John's tyrannical extraction of cash from English subjects to finance an ultimately disastrous war to save Normandy from conquest by the French king, could not be tolerated. Losing that war effectively forced the barons to choose whether to be English or French. John's ineptitude, as much as his greed and arrogance, forced the English aristocracy to recognise the limitations of a single man – albeit one they accepted as having been deemed king by God's will – and band together to stop him.

But when the barons forced John's hand to sign Magna Carta in 1215, they did so in the name of something that had echoes of the witan. The venue they chose for this royal humiliation was Runnymede, just to the west of London, which was one of the traditional places where the witan gathered. This was a conscious choice by those men who believed they were acting in a tradition of common action to temper the might of kingship. The idea that the barons cited in their action against the tyrannical John was the *communitas regni* – the community of the realm that we met in the previous chapter. The concept of the *communitas regni* was to become the 'other party' in conflicts between centralised authority and the rest of England for centuries after.

As Prof Robert Tombs says in his sweeping work, *The English and Their History*, contracts between rulers and the ruled were not unknown in medieval Europe, but what was unusual about Magna Carta was the way in which it placed restraints on the Crown. That is, of course, one definition of the exercise of fairness. The course of English history made it veer towards the sort of consensual rule embodied in the *communitas regni*, Tombs says:

France provides a contrast: the succession was rarely in doubt, and so French kings did not continually have to seek the approval of their subjects as English kings did at crucial times. So English dynastic weakness nurtured an English constitutional tradition.[47]

In an interview for this book, Prof Tombs speculated that the idea of communality, which was sincerely held, but never proposed in an egalitarian spirit, may have been connected with the existence in England alone of

[47]Tombs, R., 2015. *The English and their History.* Kindle ed. London: Penguin Books Ltd. page 99.

a common law as opposed to an imposed code. Conduct was permitted under common law if it was not forbidden; codified law, such as practised by the Romans and those European kingdoms that picked up their ways in the Middle Ages, was more likely to come from the other direction.

Other English inheritances, such as jury trials, which were not unique to the country, but survived longer here, contributed to the idea of the presumption of innocence. This was cited by the writer John Mortimer, along with the herbaceous border and the full cooked breakfast, as one of the few contributions of Britain to world civilisation. As I mentioned before, there are elements of wishful thinking about the purity of this lineage of justice.

Other aspects of English history that may have been ingredients to the recipe that delivered the idea of fairness include taxation and serfdom. The first had been with us since before the Norman Conquest. In fact, William the Conqueror was delighted to discover that the English bureaucracy of the eleventh century was well developed and enabled him to tax his new subjects in a way he could not have imagined in his native Normandy. Prof Tombs suggested that the concept of paying communally in order to achieve a common national goal may date back to *Danegeld,* the tax first raised in the tenth century to pay Viking invaders to abandon English conquests. Over time, this was refined into systems that were never popular, but were usually tolerated because they were paid on value and income, so that the rich paid their fair share. This was not the case in other countries. Medieval French peasants would pay relatively far more than their masters when taxes were raised because they normally took the form of special duties on goods such as coal. The British were highly unusual in sometimes applying progressive taxes – which became increasingly common – and by the eighteenth century had become so good at it that, despite having a smaller population than France, they were consistently able to outspend them in the torturous series of wars between the two superpowers that ran from the late seventeenth to early nineteenth century.

Prof Tombs says that there was a greater willingness to trust the state in England than France or other nations, partly because taxes when raised were raised with the consent of Parliament, something that grated with weak kings and was a sham under strong ones.

Serfdom disappeared in England as much as four centuries before similar cultures in Europe. The love of liberty that grew in eighteenth century American colonies was born in England out of the sense that no man belonged to another. On both sides of the Atlantic, of course, British love of liberty did not apply to people of a different colour and much of the wealth of the British Empire was floated on the blood that slaves shed in Caribbean and American plantations.

We can also look to religion as an example of where English history diverged from its neighbours and set a pattern of consensus and compromise where other countries continued to endure absolutism. In 1558, Elizabeth I ascended the throne and confronted an inheritance of bloody religious division not by reacting with zealotry but with accommodation. Under her half-brother, Edward VI, the Catholic Mass was effectively abolished by Archbishop Thomas Cranmer's 42 Articles of faith; in reaction, their half-sister, Mary, burned Cranmer and hundreds of other Protestants. Elizabeth, on her accession in 1558, quickly produced a compromise between the traditions of both faiths that managed to hold her people together. Elizabeth's Church of England was indeed a broad church. There was persecution and execution of Catholics in Elizabethan England, but it was applied mostly to men who, often at the behest of the French or Spanish, were trying to overthrow or assassinate the Queen.

Generally, with the exception of the Civil War itself from 1642 to 1649, the English ruling classes from the accession of Elizabeth onwards tried to reach accommodation with each other on the matter of religion. It was only when religion, as it always will, edged on to the field of politics that things got bloody.

REVIVING FUDGE

English historians, like most historians, often saw themselves as the holders of a polemic pen. Through 350 years of competing narratives, of which you can still see vestiges in British national newspaper columns or indeed on Twitter, historians set out competing views of a nation that was either a champion of individual liberty or the upholder of civilisation through the benign rule of the state. In the 2020s, you could now identify the former as a Tory (conservative) point of view and the latter as an extreme form of liberalism. But for most of that time, it was the other way round – in the US the Republicans and Democrats have performed a similar ideological do-si-do – with definitions turning on how you viewed a particular polarising event.

That polarising event was the ultimate indicator of division within a polity: civil war. England fought its civil war between 1642 and 1649, long before other European nations, not least because it was not directly involved in the Thirty Years' War. Both conflicts were fought over a similar central question: who was to rule?

But the European conflict was played out in terms of the supremacy of two shades of Christian belief, Catholic and Protestant, whereas in Britain (the English Civil War was only one part of the War of the Three Kingdoms that devastated Ireland and Scotland) it was more about which shade of Protestantism would predominate. One shade was based on the rule of a body of men agreeing the terms of fair cooperation, the Parliament; the other shade was based on the rule of a single man whose right to determine the lives of the community derived from God.

As we have seen before, the Civil War divided the English into two and to some extent they remain so divided. The horror of war, though, as well as the repressive austerity that Cromwell tried to impose after Parliament's victory, repelled the English. They had tasted the compromise of Elizabeth's approach to uniting the country and the economic power that it brought. They liked it.

Hence the invitation to William of Orange and the balancing of his power with that of Parliament represented by the Bill of Rights and successive legislation, such as the power of the Commons to approve taxation, that followed it. There was radical reform too in the way the state was funded. The creation of the Bank of England in 1694 allowed Britain a superior way of funding its overseas adventurism that laid the foundations of empire, but it also established a model of national institutions that restrained the power of the Crown while spreading the responsibility for economic wellbeing to the rest of the country. The English, from 1701 and the Act of Union with Scotland, we should say the British, sought balance in their constitution. It didn't always work and it certainly wasn't always fair, but the emotions aroused by the Civil War did not die away because there were always two competing forces of political and social philosophy at work.

This was also a time of strange alliances and strange enmities. The low-church William of Orange had been supported by the Pope in his ascension to the English throne, overthrowing the Catholic James II because James was aligned with Louis XIV of France, the mortal enemy of the papacy; William's coronation was opposed, though, by the Archbishop of Canterbury who was theoretically of the same Protestant faith, because it legitimised the overthrow of a divinely-appointed monarch. The Archbishop was removed from office for refusing to crown the new king.

This tendency towards competing ideas of how men fitted together and what constituted fair answers to complex ideological problems was built on and nourished by wider philosophical thought. With Empiricism, men like John Locke laid down a view of history as progress and of man's unbounded ability to find answers to problems through his own thought, experience and endeavour. The progress of science through the Enlightenment era cemented the idea that we were a species capable of anything. Our higher instincts, expressed through religion still, were guides to our conduct, not laws. We shaped our own morality rather than having it read to us from a pulpit. The British separated religion from politics – not completely of course, but enough that one did not determine the other and left room for another type of faith, whether it be faith in liberty or in compromise or in common interests, to enter. It created a binary nation based on attitudes, from Cavalier and Roundhead to Whig and Tory to Liberal and Conservative to Leave and Remain. They were heirs to each other, but provided divided ground which the British have always wanted to unite.

As Tombs describes the Glorious Revolution:

Most of Europe moved towards confessionalisation, the identification of a state and its people with a single religion; but England became legally divided. It would never recover religious, and hence cultural and political, unity or even consensus...[48]

But something else prevailed that meant Britain did not spiral down into repeated civil conflict. Throughout the eighteenth century, Britain was seen as a beacon of liberty – Montesquieu called it the most free country in the world and Jean-Jacques Rousseau's *Social Contract* was derived at least in part from the years he spent in exile in London. The American Revolutionaries could not have had their ideas of liberty without John Locke and they cited the Magna Carta in their founding documents. I would suggest that it was the see-saw of ideas between these binary outlooks on life, neither one nor the other ever gaining predominance for very long, that powered the search for a happy medium.[49] And the abhorrence of the violence dealt out by Roundhead to Cavalier and back again, violence that killed more English people per capita

[48]Tombs, R. *The English and their History.* Page 261

[49]Compare Spain, where rigid Catholicism suppressed discussion of the human condition or social contract and produced and isolationist nation that existed on the spoils of cruel empire until that collapsed. Its political system was so cooperative that it became flabby and did not produce competitive extremes of "right" and "left" until the late 19th and early 20th centuries. Its Civil War was fought a mere 85, not 360, years ago and it was a dictatorship until Franco's death in 1975.

than the First World War did, made that search one that centred on consensus. The word we sometimes use today is 'fudge'.

Tombs again:

> To the Whigs we owe the principle – Magna Carta restated in modern form – that rulers must obey the law and that legitimate authority requires the consent of the people. From the Tories came the principle – fundamental to any political order – that people have no right to rebel against a government because they disagree with it. Combining these seemingly conflicting principles produced characteristics of English political culture: suspicion of Utopias and zealots; trust in common sense and experience; respect for tradition; preference for gradual change; and the view that 'compromise' is victory, not betrayal. These things stem from the failure both of royal absolutism and of godly republicanism: costly failures, and fruitful ones.[50]

Time and time again while writing this, I find myself in high-minded description of the big picture of history and the grand themes or patterns of human progress, as if it were a train on tracks visiting stations on the way to a terminus. In a few words, I can portray twenty or thirty lifetimes' worth of change and revolution and revelation as if they were part of a script, lines from a caption of an image of a story. But that script does not exist; there are only hours and days of lives never to be remembered or restored. And there is no grand theme, just the accident of passing time and the havoc of human habits. Where I find patterns of fairness and cooperation, I could equally

[50]Tombs, R., *The English and their History.* Kindle ed. London: Penguin Books Ltd.

find, if I looked, brutality and oppression and theft and pointless cruelty. The British, the English, the Normans, the Anglo-Saxons are not different from the other peoples of the earth. Some of them tried to live peaceable lives; others tried to grasp whatever they could from those that already had it.

The time that in one part of Britain's Empire would have showed us academics debating the nature of liberty and the proper form of education for young gentlemen, would in another part show us young men and women living in squalor in Britain without sufficient food to survive; in another part, it would show us the massacre of Indian mutineers in Delhi or the imposition of famine on Bengal (on more than one occasion), of the great and unforgivable famine imposed on Ireland which somehow the Irish, in their resignation and wisdom, have managed to forgive or at least forget, or the sanguinary subjugation of the Chinese coastal regions in the 1860s, or the enslavement and murder of millions of Africans. The British moved their own polity towards some ideal of inter-behaviour while others of their nation destroyed the polity of foreign cultures. Some of them mastered the art and business of slave-trading, massively enriching themselves, while others developed first a theory and then a fury to uphold the rights of all humans, thus bringing about the international abolition of slavery.

The British sought to practise fairness on each other while slitting the throats or breaking the bones of people they considered uncivilised and uncivilisable. In that, they were no different from a hundred, two hundred other dominant races of mankind who have imposed their view on bits of the planet. Yet, if we do not look for the good in our history, we cannot find the good in ourselves. If we do not see the bad of before, we cannot understand the bad of now. Do the British need special attention because they had an idea we call fairness? No, of course not. They need the same attention as anyone else. But that idea still needs to be seen and in being seen, preserved, because it tends towards goodness. Perhaps the most we can say is that Britain was not unique in producing people who thought about fairness, but that the nature of the polity of England, and later Britain, allowed those people a greater chance to express their thoughts and influence their fellow citizens than in any other nation. Perhaps their tendency to seek compromise, dating back to the fight against the Vikings, made them look for the good in each other. Fudge is agathistic.[51]

[51] I make no great claims for originality in this book, but I am confident that this sentence is unique.

PART II

What Does Fairness Look Like in the Modern World?

Wherever the idea of fairness comes from, and no matter how we define it, there is one tendency we can see throughout its history: the axis of fairness is horizontal, not vertical. When we look at how fairness plays out in modern life, we will find that, where it is present, it is between people who see themselves as having essentially equal shares in the outcomes of their time on Earth. Where it is absent, or not quite present, it is because the prevailing tendency is for a small group of people to tell a larger group of people what is just, equitable or right. Religion and law are examples of the latter, where the bulk of society is told what it ought to do by a group claiming expertise or an exclusive relationship with the ultimate source of justice, whether that be a divine one or a political one.

If we want to make fairness more useful to us in balancing our battling cooperative and competitive natures we need to look at the ways in which it operates in real life. How does the horizontal nature of fairness spread out among people who are cooperating to compete by following commonly agreed rules? How does that differ from the behaviour of people following a vertically-imposed imperative to obey laws? What can the actual application of fairness in sport, in business, in human relationships, in government and every other important area of society teach us about its nature and desirability?

For the rest of the book, I am going to offer my view of how fairness slots into the compartments of our complex human existence. I may be wrong.

6

Fairness in Sport (and other forms of war)

THE REGULATION OF SPORT BASED ON FAIR PLAY

I began Part I of this book by talking about Fair Play. The first expressions in English of the idea of fairness in human relationships link these two words together. Linguists even suggest that our modern idea of being fair may actually be a shortened form of 'playing fair' that has dropped the play element altogether. Perhaps play is just a rehearsal for life.

It is uniquely human to have made play a sophisticated part of our culture, to have imbued it with passion and detail and emotive language, to have used it to forge a link between our hunting instincts and our instincts for security in large groups working together, to have inescapably connected it to the parallel exchange of monetary value, to have made play a business so critical to our lives that it has to be governed by a sense of fairness. It is just that now we call play 'sport'.

That is why I want to start my exploration of fairness in the world around us by looking at how we understand it in the way we play together. By the end of this particular exploration, I suspect that you will conclude, as I have, that in sport as in life, fairness is an aspiration more than an expectation. The rewards of successful competition are so great, whether they are material or just psychological, that the temptation to discard fair cooperation can be overpowering. But the people and the organisations we remember most vividly, for the right reasons and the wrong reasons, are the ones that did or did not resist temptation. And it goes without saying that whether you think some outcome in sport was fair or not hangs on whether you take a side.

While discussing the likelihood that fairness was a British trait, Prof Robert Tombs raised with me the question of whether Britain, as an imperial force, had exported the concept of fairness alongside other ideas, particularly that of organised sport.

The British did not invent sports such as football, hockey and probably not even cricket, but they were responsible for writing rules. To no other nation did it occur first to set down regulations for boisterous activities like football – an activity that had existed since ancient times as combat between teams, sometime entire communities, where the only expectation was that it ought ideally not to end in actual armed conflict.

The rise of the British public school in the mid-nineteenth century – itself a phenomenon prompted by a perceived need to counter a rise in civil disorder among the young – brought with it a reassessment of how sport could be harnessed to higher aims. Teaching young men teamwork and leadership and making them physically fit had always been seen as a preparation for war – hence the famous remark of the Duke of Wellington (which he did not say) that the battle of Waterloo was won on the playing fields of Eton. In response to declining moral standards in society as a whole, a movement emerged in the recession-hit aftermath of the defeat of Napoleon at Waterloo to inculcate Christian values into young men. These same young men were being required to take control of the ever-growing British Empire. In other European countries, as in the US, this tendency was more directly expressed in military service or military academies such as Westpoint or Saint-Cyr in France or the many *Kriegsschule* in Germany and central Europe. English public schools were more general in nature – the term 'public' implied they were not run for private profit and were open to all to apply – but also had a martial element in their outlook. Part of the philosophy of education at this time involved so-called Muscular Christianity, which saw exercise and the discipline of physical, often very physical, games as being good for the moral development of the young (and team games were also seen as somehow an antidote to the temptations of masturbation). Fair play was an explicit part of that moral education, a mark of manly Christian endeavour that would engender respect for the spirit of the community at large and, hopefully, therefore counter the debauchery the reformers saw in society around them.

Being a game based on traditional village activities that were ubiquitous in England, football in some form was common to all of them, but the precise way in which it was played was not. When the human products of these schools went on to university, they wanted to continue playing competitive sport, but found that the different schools had developed different ways of regulating the game. Players from Rugby School, for instance, carried the ball in their hands as well as kicking it; others did not. When young men moved on from university, they still wanted to play and play against each other, so a common set of rules was needed or there could be little hope of wider competition. Eventually, the Football Association was founded in 1863 adopting the Cambridge University rules which outlawed 'hacking' – kicking the opponent – and handling the ball. Eight years later, those who preferred the Rugby version of the rules set up their own union of clubs, the Rugby Football Union.

Football set a model for the delineation of organised sport from which grew the regulation of athletics that spawned the Olympics – though the organisation of this was in the hands of the French aristocrat Pierre de Coubertin – and many of the other sports we see today.

Early on, the popular and commercial appeal of watching young men who were very good at a particular sport was obvious – cricket and horse racing had been proving that for a century and more. Thomas Lord's ground in St John's Wood, London, was a profitable venture; organised horse racing in many countries attracted huge crowds and revenues from entry tickets, food and drink sales and gambling. People would pay to watch football and the cost of organising venues, preparing pitches and kitting out a club in distinctive colours could be met from the proceeds. The glory that attached to a club or community which produced an outstanding team capable of winning national competitions meant wealthy men soon wanted to organise their own teams. Attracting the best players from outside the local area required financial inducement; nobody would expect someone from a poor social background to spend money on travel or accommodation to play for the benefit of others who were paying for and gambling on their performance.

Professionalism in sport clashed with the attitude of the wealthy young men who had formed the football unions. In response to it, they became increasingly puritanical in their non-professional outlook. Most famous in doing so was the Corinthian Casuals club, formed in 1881 as a response to professionalism.[52]

The football journalist and author, Hunter Davies, summed up the 'Corinthian spirit' thus in the *New Statesman*:

> *They were the totally amateur, public-school, Oxbridge team that put fair play and moral values above such sordid, vulgar things as winning. They never argued with the ref or entered any competition where there was a prize. If by chance the other team lost a man, either sent off or through injury, they immediately and voluntarily sent off one of their own men, just to keep things even.*[53]

The Corinthians club called its members 'missionaries of the Empire'. They and other teams that dominated early national football competitions, such as the Old Etonians and the Wanderers (whose name hinted that they were not wedded to such a vulgar, commercial idea as having their own ground), formed a connection between the idea of British sportsmanship and the spreading of other British virtues around the planet. This was, of course, a convenient cover for the exploitation of conquered or occupied lands, but from an internal point of view, it also had the effect of maintaining ties between the colonies and the 'Mother Country'. Without written rules, this would not have been possible.

[52]The citizens of Corinth in Ancient Greece were not champions of the amateur spirit. In C18th England, Corinthian was a reference to raucous hedonism for which the original Greeks were indeed known, but a century later the only part of this characterisation that survived was gathering together for a bit of fun

[53]Davies, H., 2005. *The fan - Hunter Davies yearns for the Corinthian spirit.* Available at: https://www.newstatesman.com/node/161818

Football, incidentally, was probably spread around the world by English merchants who amused themselves with a kickabout in ports such as Barcelona, Genoa or Hamburg. Le Havre had France's first professional team.[54]

Over time, and particularly as slow-motion replays of foul play or moments of genius have offered a huge television audience the chance to study what sportsmanship means at the highest level, the direction of travel for fair play has changed. While the Corinthian Casuals tried to counter what they saw as the malign effects of professionalism, if you visit a group of Sunday park footballers today, you are likely to see the downward influence of professional footballers' behaviour – arguing with the referee, feigning injury and so on. Mimicry of unfair play by children's teams grew to be such a problem in English mini football, as did mimicry of crowd trouble by parents on the touchline, that in the 2000s an organisation called Give Us Back Our Game was set up with the aim of raising the age at which children played in leagues from six to eleven. Cooperation was fighting back against (excessive) competition. It remains in existence, but the organisation has had only limited success.

It would be hard to argue that fair play had won out over professional imperatives. Unless, of course, you ask FIFA.

[54]Boniface, P., 2002. *Football as a factor (and a reflection) of International Politics.* Available at: https://www.sciencespo.fr/ceri/sites/sciencespo.fr.ceri/files/artpb.pdf

In 1987, FIFA, the governing body of world football, created a Fair Play Award, using the English phrase and helping to spread the concept around the world. Many of the winners were extremely worthy: for example, a club which demonstrated sportsmanship in the Corinthians' spirit by allowing their opponents to equalise after they had scored a goal without realising that a defender was lying injured on the pitch. In other cases of recognition of fair play, FIFA was tacitly admitting what sort of problems the world game was facing, particularly in terms of money and politics.

Barcelona, a club owned by its members rather than affluent individuals or a state-disguised-as-a-company, won the FIFA Fair Play Award in 2007 for rejecting offers of a lucrative shirt-sponsorship deal and playing a season with the logo of UNICEF on their chests instead – their president described the arrangement later as 'utopian'. However, utopia ended a couple of seasons later, when UNICEF were transferred onto the back of Barca shirts as the club signed a six-year, £123.4 million kit deal with Qatar Sports Investments, an arm of the Gulf state's government. The president said, in effect, that it was more important to compete with their Spanish footballing rivals Real Madrid than to promote the UN's children's programme. Fair enough. Business is business. Five years later, Barcelona publicly suggested that social and political conditions in Qatar, then under scrutiny for its treatment of migrant labourers, were making the Catalans consider ending their contract early. In fact, it was extended for a further season. Ethics, you might say, butter no parsnips in elite sport.

The United States and Iran won the Fair Play Award in 1998 after they met on the pitch in that year's World Cup. The game was incident-free, but otherwise unexceptional and it seems the award was made mostly because the sportsmen had managed not to recreate the virulent diplomatic war waged between the two nations since the Khomeini Revolution nineteen years earlier.

FIFA may also lack a sense of irony: in 2010 they asked the late Diego Maradona to be an ambassador of Fair Play at that year's World Cup. Only the English press were gauche enough to point out that England had been eliminated from the 1986 competition partly because this brilliant Argentine player had handled the ball into the net and even boasted about it afterwards. Other commentators pointed out that Maradona had also twice been banned for drug offences, had been sacked by his club in 1983 for an outrageous series of high-kicks into the bodies of opposing players in the final of the Spanish cup and, to complete his understanding of fair play, owed the Italian authorities about $40m in unpaid tax.

But perhaps the most undermining element of FIFA as fair play champions is its chequered history of bribery and corruption, especially around the supposed 'fixing' of the lucrative award of hosting rights to the World Cup.

Money, of course, changes everything. The early days of football were tainted by disputes over amateurism between privately-educated elites and talented working-class players; rugby split into two different codes, union and league, over payment in 1895; English cricket was divided between amateur 'gentlemen' and paid 'players' until 1963 and no player was allowed to captain the national team until 1953, a reflection of the historic British obsession of distinguishing officers from 'other ranks' in all areas of life.[55]

[55]It is ironic that among the first known rules of organised sport in England are the terms of agreement agreed before a cricket match between teams selected by two English gentlemen in 1729. This was an entirely professional affair, with

But most of this was steeped in hypocrisy. The most famous 'amateur' in the history of cricket, that sport which has fair play written into its rules, was W.G. Grace, a man who, despite being a qualified physician, earned an estimated £150,000 from a long sporting career. In 2020s terms, that haul is probably worth about £95m. Some amateur. Today, sports such as rugby face a different problem. Wage inflation has spread beyond US sports and (association) football, where astronomical figures are earned because of the entertainment value inherent in top-tier talent. Rugby, baseball, (American) football, basketball and (ice) hockey all impose salary caps – a limit on the total payroll any club can have. But the competitive spirit has also spread, from the playing field to the boardroom and clubs do their damnedest to get around these rules: at the beginning of 2020, one of the most successful clubs in recent European rugby history, Saracens, were fined heavily and thrown out of the top division of the English game for cheating the system. European Football has introduced a system which bans clubs from spending more than they earn, but this is also 'gamed' and there are plenty of top-rank teams that trade in constant debt.

Corruption of players was old when Shoeless Joe Jackson, darling of the baseball bleachers, and seven of his Chicago White Sox colleagues were expelled from the game for 'taking a dive' in the 1919 World Series.[56] And

a lot of money at stake, but these "rules" generally embrace the "Corinthian" spirit: in particular, one rule states that if a "gamester" (player) is injured and cannot continue, either a substitute will be used *or the other team will remove one of their own gamesters.*

[56]The dispute over Jackson's guilt is still alive more than a century later

let's not even mention the nobbling of horse racing and boxing.

The use of drugs has sullied the reputation of events from the lower reaches of football to the podium of successive Olympic Games. Entire countries, in the case of Russia, have been banned for cheating complex anti-doping rules. Soviet Bloc domination of athletics dissolved once those countries were opened to proper scrutiny in the post-Cold War era.

Politics is an extension of sport, or is it the other way round? We need only look at the Olympic Games, founded as an ideal to bring together the nations of the world in friendly competition. Britain used the 1908 London games to market its flagging empire and was allowed to select all the judges, with predictable accusations of bias resulting when Britain won three times as many medals as the next nation.[57] Hitler turned the 1936 Berlin event into a platform for the glories of Aryan manhood only to watch an African-American *untermensch* called Jesse Owens ridicule his crackpot theories by trouncing white athletes. There were boycotts of the Moscow Olympics by the US in 1980 to protest against the 1979 Soviet invasion of Afghanistan and by the Soviet Union of the LA Games four years later to protest against, well, the boycott of the Moscow Olympics by the US in 1980.

Football in particular is associated with off-field violence in the form of hooliganism. The English are only the most flamboyant practitioners of a 'disease' that thrives almost everywhere the game is played. Football has started wars (between El Salvador and Honduras in 1969) and more riots than there are blades of grass on a pitch.

[57]The final of the 400m saw a US athlete disqualified for obstructing the sole British entrant

What sport tells us about fairness is that it is an aspiration. Human beings will do anything for glory, that is for the admiration and status that winning brings. Throw in money and politics and it is perhaps surprising that anything like fair play survives. How and why it does survive is what we will turn to next.

THE REAL MEANING OF A LEVEL PLAYING FIELD

I don't think that Barack Obama has yet played cricket at Sheepscombe in the Slad Valley of Gloucestershire but, if he had done, he would have second thoughts about the importance of a level playing field. The former president was fond of using the metaphor, particularly in relation to trade talks, but the truth is that to ensure fairness you do not need a level playing field. At Sheepscombe, the playing area slopes away in tiers so steep that if you field out on the lowest edge there you cannot actually see the batsmen or the umpires at either end of the wicket; if the ball is struck high in the air in your direction, your teammates have to alert you to its imminent arrival by shouting. It also means that neither your teammates nor the umpires can see whether or not you make a clean catch of it, so a degree of honesty is required by the lonely long-on.

It all makes the game far more exciting. In fact, I am convinced sport is more entertaining if the ground is not level, either metaphorically or physically. Lord's, the home of cricket, slopes from one side to the other by almost 10 feet. There is an increasing use of artificial surfaces in team games; field hockey, for instance, is now almost universally played on them. In association football, they have never been accepted; in the American version of the game they are in the majority. Rugby players don't like them, claiming they cause knee injuries, but proponents say they even-out the iniquities of quirky pitches. You cannot get a more level playing field than one that is made out of plastic. But there is something about mud that appeals to the little boy or girl which sport so readily brings out in all of us.

Of course, the phrase is not meant to be literal. It means that both sides should play by the same set of rules and conditions if the game is going to be fair. For instance, in games such as football (any code) or hockey or hurling or lacrosse, it does not matter if your playing field is not level, as long as the rules insist that you change ends at half time.

The rules, then, are what matter, not the conditions. When one side or the other gets to write the rules, things go badly wrong. David Hackett Fischer points this out in *Fairness and Freedom* with the example of the America's Cup, once the most glamorous and famous yacht race in the world. Its lustre dimmed after a series of unedifying squabbles between the ultra-rich men who compete for it in boats that cost tens of millions of dollars. As Fischer points out, the Americans who control the rulebook have a habit of tweaking it so their own boat wins. In 1995, they did so to allow the US team, but not any other participant, to change boats. They still lost, but it's the thought that counts. Unsurprisingly, almost nobody takes any interest in the America's Cup any more apart from the clique of billionaires who continue to tack into foul winds, bitching about each other's unsportsmanlike behaviour.

It's when people bend the rules that things get nasty. People cheat at all sports, although of course they all deny it. Ask Brian McKechnie who is, as it happens, another New Zealander, who has been on both sides of the line. He was the man who kicked the winning penalty for the All Blacks rugby team in 1978 to beat Wales after his teammate, Andy Haden, had dived out of a line-out to con the referee into thinking he had been illegally pushed by a Welsh opponent. Three years later, McKechnie, a dual international, was the batsman who received arguably the most controversial delivery in the history of cricket. With his team needing six runs to tie the match, something that could only be achieved by hitting the ball clean over the distant boundary rope, the opposing Australian captain, Greg Chappell, ordered his bowler to roll the final ball of the match along the ground. This incident was seen as so deeply against the spirit of fair play (including by several of Chappell's teammates) that it was taken up by politicians, although it did not have quite the effect of the 1932 Bodyline series. England and Australia almost broke off diplomatic relations after the upper class manager and captain of the England team developed a tactic of having their fastest bowler – a former coalminer called Harold Larwood – bowl at the bodies of the Australians, and especially their master batsman Donald Bradman, in the hope that they would deflect the ball to one of a ring of waiting catchers around them. It was closer to blood sport than sportsmanship and is still discussed nearly ninety years later. The point of it was that 'leg theory' as the English called it, or 'bodyline' as everyone else did, was technically within the rules. It just wasn't cricket.

Some sports practise handicapping to try to make things as even as possible – horse racing for instance – while others have stringent rules about the nature, size or weight of bats and racquets and balls to prevent unfair advantage being taken. Whatever else may be uneven about the game – wealthy aristocrats playing alongside former miners, professional superstars against part-time journeymen (or journeywomen) – the only thing that two teams need to agree on for the odds to be evened out are the rules.

Is it a good thing to be even, though? Who would watch sport if, all else being equal, the best team always won? You can legislate for equality, but for fairness you have to appeal to something else: a person's sense of what is the fair thing to do. John Rawls said that the essence of a liberal democracy was that people should be free, equal and should agree on a 'fair system of cooperation.' The essence of sport is simpler; all you need is a free space to play in, opposition of roughly equal ability and a fair system of competition.

And that includes not claiming to have caught the ball at Sheepscombe when, in truth, you let it slip through your fingers. You know who you are.

HOW SPORT TAUGHT US TO BLEND COOPERATION AND COMPETITION

Do you remember Cephu? He was the Mbuti pygmy who appeared when we looked at whether early man had a concept of fairness, and who narrowly escaped a fatal ostracism from his egalitarian, hunter-gatherer tribe because he pursued his own, selfish ends during hunting expeditions. Over time, sport developed a way of dealing with Cephus. One of the most important lessons that sport can have for anyone seeking to understand why we need fairness in our lives is this: normal forms of human association tend to develop rules of cooperation that permit constructive competition while restraining the instincts of some individuals to benefit disproportionately from the collective effort or to dominate its output.

To the New Zealand 'All Blacks' rugby team, it is more simply summarised by the following rule: *No*

Dickheads. The Corinthian Casuals amateurs who rose to prominence in the early days of English football expressed it more delicately: *Brilliant but selfish players should not be tolerated*. Neither of these rules has ever been included into the constitutions of those teams, but were carved on their souls.

The All Blacks, who have been preeminent in the game of rugby for more than a century, always the team to beat, also hold a rare status in their own country where the sport has some of the qualities of a religion. In short, if the All Blacks do something, it is probably worth copying. A recent book on the culture of the team described how, after a game in which they had thrashed Wales (scoring 42 points, incidentally), two of the most senior players took responsibility for cleaning the dressing room after the post-match debrief in which the entire squad discussed how they could have scored more.[58] This policy of 'sweeping the sheds' is a manifestation of *No Dickheads* – a subordination of the individual's glory to a cooperative effort. There is nothing amateur about the All Blacks. Their revenues are the biggest in all New Zealand sport and they are among the country's best-paid employees in any field. They operate a philosophy based on the indigenous Māori culture of the country called *whānau* – literally a word meaning the extended family, but with ramifications of genealogy, tribal unity and identity. Apart from the presence of a large number of Māori and others of Polynesian or Melanesian origin in the All Blacks squad, there is also a long tradition of the Pākehā – descendants of white British colonists – borrowing Māori ideas. The Pākehā regard themselves as coming from a more dissenting, egalitarian tradition than

[58]Kerr, J., 2013. *Legacy*. 1st ed. London: Constable&Robinson Ltd.

the British society that their ancestors left in the eighteenth and nineteenth century and, although the Māori (who arrived in New Zealand in the thirteenth century AD) do not appear to have retained all the equality traditions of hunter-gatherer societies, the sense of common purpose remains strong. Treatment of the Māori by the Pākehā is no model of fairness, now or in the past. However, the country's obsession with the 'fair go' suggests that their traditions have aligned over time. That is not to say they always compete in a fair way. Opponents of the All Blacks down the years would suggest that the idea of the 'fair go' only really applies within the *whānau*. Everyone else can take their chances.

And this is how all sport has developed: groups of people coming together from potentially fractious, separate communities wishing to cooperate in order to compete on fair terms. In the eighteenth century, cricket developed as an alternative to horse racing, cock-fighting and other activities where human participation was limited to the essential business of gambling. Without the wager, no organised sport would have emerged in European society. One of the biggest threats to an ideal balance of this nature comes from the effect that money has on sport. This is a catch-22. You cannot have top quality sport without money and you cannot have money coming in unless the sport is top quality. With good luck, fairness is protected by the effort to achieve the balance I have just been speaking about. Where things get tricky is at the edges, which is where sport actually started: gambling.

The randomness of human competition is such that it makes an ideal subject for gambling. Backing one side or another in a sport goes back to days when sport was rather less wholesome (even if you could call it wholesome now). What our more recent ancestors called sports were things like cock-fighting and bull-baiting and hare-coursing, none of which would have maintained the interest if you couldn't make a few quid on the side. When sports involving the bloody death of animals became less fashionable, we turned to sports involving the bloody maiming of human beings. Fist-fighting was not quite as much of a spectacle of gore as Roman gladiators might have put on, but it was just as easy to bet on.

Gambling brought with it, of course, cheating. Competitors took bribes to lose. We know that people have it in them to bet on almost anything. And to cheat at almost anything. The laws, or rules, of the game were the solution to the dilemma that, unless controlled, cheating threatened the financial underpinning of organised sport.

From the need to wipe out cheating came the need for open and agreed rules, which could be imposed by an arbiter. The referee, umpire or marshal is there to see fair play done not just for other competitors, but for those having a flutter on the side. When the Marquis of Queensbury drew up his rules for boxing, it was as much to make the gambling fairer as to make the boxers safer.

This all shows us that the relationship between combat, sport and betting is a complex one. But in each case it speaks to our endless appetite for competition. The uncertainty of outcome, the desire to pit oneself against others for superiority, the taste of glory, the spoils of conflict. They all come from the same place: the human mind.

Other species practise violence. By which I mean in the sense of practice makes perfect. Most predatory mammals engage in play-fighting throughout their juvenile lives. The rough and tumble of lions or wolves or foxes is preparation for stalking and killing.

Similarly, when man began to organise sport, it was as an extension of their own need to practise violence. The first Olympic Games featured only sports – wrestling, boxing, running, throwing, horse-riding and *pankration* – a sort of early martial art – that were evolutions of natural skills and instincts that first allowed man to feed himself, defend himself and then to take what belonged to others. The modern Olympics added many other sports, such as 'artistic swimming', which are hardly warlike, but also some which very clearly derive from killing: archery, fencing, shooting.

With some very serious exceptions, such as doping, match-fixing and chicanery in the boardroom, we have successfully made sport more fair. The evidence is in the numbers – there has never been so much money spent by so many people on so much sporting entertainment. That would not have happened if it was all fixed or all unbalanced between competition and cooperation. An early American football league that was dominated by a single wealthy club, the Cleveland Browns, collapsed after only one season.

If we have made sport fairer, how have we done with its grandfather: war? It remains popular, but is it more fair?

EVEN WARFARE HAS A SENSE OF WHAT IS AND ISN'T FAIR

If you were a supporter of the Greens or the Blues in the Hippodrome of Byzantium in the sixth century AD, the distinction between war and sport would have been somewhat academic. Like their predecessors in Rome and Ancient Greece, the citizens of the eastern Roman empire divided themselves into *demes,* groups which had become a mixture of political factions, community groups and sporting 'ultras'. The Greens and Blues were supporters of the chariot-racing teams that wore those colours (there were Reds and Whites too, but they were also-rans, both in sporting and political terms). Not only did they cheer for their teams, but between the races that took place over a whole day they would shout slogans to signal support or opposition to policies of the emperor of the day. In January 532AD, this was Justinian, a man who had just rushed through a radical and reforming legal code, attacked corruption and generally got up the noses of the aristocrats and senior civil servants who were accustomed to running the city through their control of the law courts (fairness came at a price throughout Roman history). Those high-born people were also influential in the *demes* as Blues or Greens (Justinian himself was a Blue) and they united the two factions in opposition to the low-born emperor. After three days of rioting in which the united hooligans repeated the chant '*Nika*' – or 'Win!', with hundreds dead, they tried to crown a new emperor in the stands of the Hippodrome. However, after the leaders of the Blues were bribed by Justinian's eunuch Narses to abandon their new, hated Green allies, a large troop of imperial guards entered the arena and began a massacre of the remaining fans that may have left as many as 30,000 dead.

Relative to this example of the mixing of sport, politics and war, I realise that I have painted rather a pure, high-minded idea of sport and mostly left out the grubby bits. And they do get very grubby. As we have seen, there is a powerful argument that sport is, in any case, a form or ritualised warfare.

Violence links sport and war. While the generally accepted view is that sport evolved from warfare, there has in recent decades been a trend in the other direction, an effort to build into the practice of mass killing some of the fairness that had been inculcated in the practice of mass sweat. As we ritualised warfare to make sport, humans in the past couple of centuries have made efforts to regularise and ritualise the risk that individuals and societies run when they embark on war. Although, when you try to count the bodies that have mounted on the battlefields and in the concentration camps of history, you might think that effort has not been a triumph.

Most of us have heard of the Geneva Convention – although in fact there are four of them as well as sundry important protocols, so we should say Geneva Conventions – but did we know they were rooted in a belief in sporting activity? A group of early nineteenth century Germans, led by a man called Frierich Jahn, founded a movement which became known as the Turners from the German word *Turnvereine* meaning gymnastic unions. They set up their unions, ostensibly, as a way of introducing sport and exercise into education and social life in general. I say ostensibly because, in fact, this took place during the occupation of large swathes of German territory (Germany as a nation did not exist until 1871) by Napoleon. The hidden purpose of the Turners was to convene meetings of similarly-minded liberals to resist the French and plan how to free themselves from the yoke of the invaders. Once Napoleon had been finally defeated, the Turners became part of the liberal opposition to the conservative network of statelets that made up the German Confederation. Liberals were not popular with the authorities. Some Turners, such as Franz Lieber, left in the 1820s to avoid repeated arrests, first for more tolerant Britain; others stayed and fought in the unsuccessful Revolutions of 1848 before fleeing to America as refugees. Lieber had already arrived in the States to set up a gymnasium in the style of Jahn's model. This manifestation of sport was still a political idea and, like his fellow Turners, he became increasingly embedded in the educational, social and political development of the US. Lieber became a professor of history and economics at what became the University of South Carolina. His philosophy was summed up in a Latin motto he seems to have dreamed up for himself: *Nullum jus sine officio, nullum officium sine jure* (No right without its duties, no duty without its rights).

Lieber's particular interest to us right now is that in his opposition to the secession of the Southern states and vocal support for the Union, he came to the notice of Abraham Lincoln's administration and, in 1863, the year after the death of one of his sons fighting on the Confederate side, he helped to produce General Order 100, also known as Lieber's Code or the Code for the Government of Armies in the Field. It was the first attempt to impose some kind of order and fairness on the conduct of war and covered the treatment of prisoners, of civilians and even of property.

The following year saw the first Geneva Convention signed. This had been a separate initiative by the Swiss businessman Henry Dunant, who had been appalled at the lack of medical facilities available to the wounded at the Battle of Solferino in 1859. The convention dealt with the rights of those who had been wounded in combat.

In 1868, the Russian Tsar, Nicholas I, convened a conference which led to the Declaration of St Petersburg that tried to set the 'technical limits at which the necessities of war ought to yield to the requirements of humanity.' This particularly focused on limiting the collateral damage of war and even to seek to limit what soldiers tried to do to each other to acts of disabling rather than necessarily killing. Somewhat idealistic, it included the banning of small exploding projectiles, which we would today call 'cluster bombs' and which are also now prohibited. Later additions to this at the Hague Conventions of 1899 and 1907 included agreements to ban 'the launching of projectiles and explosives from balloons, or by other new methods of a similar nature.' Quite how successful that was would be is a debate on which the citizens of Guernica, Coventry, Dresden and Hiroshima would have strong views, but the fact that the effort was made showed a growing impulse by mankind to tame their most destructive instincts and restrain the mighty.

Of course, war crimes continued – counterinsurgencies and concentration camps set up by the British during the Boer War (1899–1902), the massacring of civilians, particularly by German and Austro-Hungarian troops in 1914, the Armenian Genocide of 1915–22, the use of gas by most belligerents in the First World War – to take just a few examples from a short period of time. The horrors revealed at the Nuremberg Trials and the fears aroused by Hiroshima and Nagasaki finally prompted the world to act, bringing about the fourth set of Geneva Conventions in 1949.

Have things changed? Yes and no. Atrocities are still committed – Srebrenica, Halabja, the use of landmines, child soldiers, mutilation, rape as weapons of war – in their scores and hundreds. But for the first time, people are being held accountable for some of those crimes in an international court. An effort to bring order to the most disorderly conduct man can practise is under way. The longest journeys begin with a single step, as Lao Tzu may well have said.

Nobody can begin to count how many people have died in warfare. Our primeval ancestors would have considered violent conflict with others as a part of the pattern of life. In early civilisations, war brought land and resources and added, by force, to the population of the victor. Skill and success in battle were highly prized qualities throughout recorded history as they must have been before it. The qualities necessary to kill and subdue humans were similar to the qualities needed to hunt and domesticate animals. Perhaps in that parallel we can see the beginnings of a concept of, if not fairness, at least restraint, in war. From the extraordinary cave paintings of bison in Altamira, northern Spain, beginning about 36,000 years ago, the hunter has always revered the prey. These earliest attempts at abstract expression were by men and women trying to portray their emotions about the great beasts that brought them life through their own death. The animal's sacrifice of its existence created a communal good for the humans.

It is not a huge leap from this to recognising that the bravery of a human enemy in battle is the necessary exchange for the glory and triumph of the soldier. In that, you can see the formulation of an idea of honour (a word, incidentally, whose origins are not known). From there, the evolution of codes of martial conduct come to us as 'what to do in war', as distinct from 'what not to do'. The codes of chivalry in medieval Europe, the ethics of the samurai warrior resisting technological change when the invention of gunpowder made the practice of sword fighting redundant, the Liber Code. They all attempt to place restraint on the excesses of the human will when unleashed as it must be in a time of war in the same way as rules of sport seek to lay down rules whereby the participants can agree, through arbitration, a fair system of cooperative competition. It may not work, but at the risk of sounding glib, it is the thought that counts.

And then you have to think about the effect of money.

7

Fairness in Business and Economics

THE LANGUAGE OF BUSINESS — TRUSTS, BONDS, CREDITS AND EXCHANGES

Looking for fairness in business has a great deal to do with looking for meaning. We try to work out what fairness itself means by looking at the way we use the word and those consonant with it. 'Fair's fair' implies that we understand what we mean by fairness; 'fair exchange' or 'fair deal' means that the process of trade is governed by an unwritten understanding of what value we place on two goods or services; 'fair trade' implies we are trying to balance the interests of a vulnerable seller against the whims of a dominant buyer by restraining the latter's pricing-power; 'fair enough' suggests that, in all cases, we recognise that fairness is not a carefully-calibrated measurement of satisfaction but a rough guide to consensual trade.

With words, it is all a question of how far back you want to go, because they do tell us a lot about how we have changed their meaning and our own understanding for our own purpose. The word bank, for instance, comes from the *banca* or benches that Florentine money lenders sat on to do business in the early Renaissance. But you do not need to know the origin of words when they have clear double meanings. Which happens all the time in the language of business.

I am drawn to the idea that the common language of trade and interaction between strangers has followed the development of humanity's understanding of how best to encourage cooperation and restrain competition. If you cast your mind back through the fog of time to when you picked up the book, you may recall the mention of creation myths. The records of the earliest peoples that laid down their thoughts in a survivable form (writing or pictures) presumably reflect the thoughts of people who came before them but did not record them. Because we can understand what the Sumerians and Egyptians were on about, it would be reasonable to assume that they could have understood what those who came before *them* were on about. The language of cooperation that we find in creation myths centres on having faith in a higher entity or entities that created our world. It requires us to have belief and faith in there being ways of living that are either decreed in a set of rules (the 42 questions of *Ma'at* in the case of the Egyptians) or made evident in stories. Most of the stories speak of a fight between chaos and order; the benefits of finding a balance between chaos and order are shown in the ability of all people (except of course slaves and probably women) to share in the good things about the planet and avoid the bad; the deficits of imbalance are shown in an unequal sharing-out of good and bad things.

Much of the vocabulary of finance and commerce is derived from words that concern stability. Credit, for instance, from the Latin *credere* – 'to believe' from the Proto-Indo-European root '*kerd-dhe*' – 'to place the heart'. Trust, as in 'investment trust', from the PIE root word (Proto-Indo-European language, the ancestor of all languages west of China and north of the Sahara) meaning firm or solid. 'Bond' is something that strongly unites (in this case the lender and the borrower). Stock derives from the same root as 'stake' and, from the early seventeenth century, was used as the word to describe the 'subscribed capital of a corporation'. A fund is the bottom, the base and foundation of the capital of a trader. 'Trade', incidentally, meant a course or path, in even older meanings it was a spoor; it was not until the eighteenth century that it got its meaning in English of exchange.

Business and finance words that aren't about stability are likely to be about sharing: equity, shares, dividend. We do business and distribute our common god of money in language that reflects our species' priorities: a belief in something greater than our own self – an arbiter of our and our community's worth – and a need to see how benefits are distributed.

Language has come to have just as vital, but a rather less subtle, importance in the way we trade with each other. At first, language in the form of signs was intended to show that an item was what it purported to be: coinage and assay marks on precious metals being the most obvious examples. Commercial signage to show where a particular good was sold appeared thousands of years ago in China, the Middle East, Rome. Street-criers were employed in medieval Europe to act as dynamic advertising hoardings.

As populations grew, as demand outstripped supply and markets opened up for multiple suppliers to compete, and quality, as a subjective measure, gained the upper hand over quantity as an indicator of value for the wealthier customer, messages became more important and more complex. Truth, the handmaiden of fairness, took a back seat. Early tobacco advertisements in the press, for instance, championed the health benefits of smoking particular types that 'not only checks disease but preserve the lungs' which make the activities of twentieth century cigarette manufacturers seem almost mild by comparison.

In today's battle for trust and trade, competing businesses learned that they have to appear in our minds through words as much as images. So they bend language to reflect what they believe to be their competitive advantage. This is an attempt to make you-the-customer think in the way they want you to think. It is an attempt to induce rather than earn your trust.

Many of the most famous slogans of the modern corporate world are either statements of belief or exhortations to act in a certain way to improve your chances of a prosperous life. It's the real thing. Just do it. Think different. Don't leave home without it. The success of these messages is inherent in the fact that I don't have to tell you which corporate entity uses them.

But perhaps we should question what a company doesn't want you to think when it flings a particular thought at you. 'It's the real thing.' It might be a fake or it might be full of artificial things which aren't good for you. 'Move fast and break things.' But don't worry about the consequences of doing so. 'Don't Be Evil.' Because when you have as much power as we do, that would be so easy. 'Be Fair' – no, nor have I.

TRUST AND TRADE AMONG OUR ANCESTORS

A fair trade is not possible if one of the two (or more) parties is holding a stone axe, dagger or revolver. The weapons do not need to be real – menace has no role in fairness. Turn that idea around and you might see that if you exchange things fairly, you don't need to hit, stab or shoot people. This is advantageous to both parties, because the unwilling party might turn out to have friends nearby who will come and shoot, stab or hit the aggressor. Trade is less risky than robbery, though it is also harder work. As with all less risky choices, it is less rewarding if it goes well. Cooperation is a bit dull compared with competition, but in the long run, everybody gets more out of it.

Yuval Noah Harari introduced to us the idea that the fictions we create, from gods to limited liability companies, produce an environment that allows us to trade using the greatest fiction of them all: money. Something we also get from trade, as a sort of free gift, is a learned ability to increase cooperation and, as a sort of buy-one-get-one-free, a learned ability to compete more efficiently. Every trade is a real Ultimatum Game, but with greater jeopardy in that you give up something of value to you to get something of equal or greater value. Trade is the gearbox of human activity and, if you buy that analogy, trust and reputation are the cogwheels and fairness the oil that keeps it all grinding smoothly.

Trade broadens the mind and the horizons. Traded goods travel further than people travel. Beads from the Middle East found in the barrow of a Celtic king in England were as likely to have passed through several pairs of hands to reach their final destination as did the smartphone-charging cable you ordered on Amazon: a manufacturer, a delivery driver, a handling agency, an airline employee, another airline employee at the other end, another handling agency and another delivery driver to an Amazon warehouse and thence to your home. You are less likely to be buried with your charging cable than the Celtic king was with his Assyrian beads, but that's progress for you.

Then, as now, trade relied on information – what to buy, where to buy, who to buy from, how to pay, how much to pay, where to sell, who to sell to, how to charge, how much to charge. It is a faster process now. We ask a search engine which answers us in seconds; The Dutch East India Company or the Hudson Bay trapper had to spend months travelling, surviving, risking. And the cost of travel, subsistence and gunpowder had to be included in the final price of the fur pelt or the bolt of silk. Anything that made that process easier would reduce the cost of trade and either increase the margin of the trader or reduce the cost to the consumer, thereby stimulating demand. The not-so-simple act of developing rules and laws for travelling and trading across vast oceans was one of the most obvious ways in which this could happen. The simultaneous development of an insurance industry, an industry as much related to gambling as to business, also reduced risk and increased appetite for both risk and the reduction of risk through agreed regulation of trade. And this spread as far as trade spread.

The political theorist, Grotius (Hugo de Groot, 1583–1645) first became interested in the concept of international cooperation and the first 'law of the sea' when his cousin, a Dutch East India Company ship's captain, became embroiled in a dispute over the cargo of a Portuguese carrack he pirated in the Indonesian archipelago in 1604. From the law of the sea came the concept of international law that allowed the emergence of today's complex global trading systems. Grotius, who went to university at the age of eleven and sounds like an unpleasantly precocious child, also developed a theory of human rights that said people 'owned' their rights and could, if they wished, trade them too. This thinking informed Thomas Hobbes, John Locke and Jean-Jacques

Rousseau as they tried to draw up various versions of a social contract between ruled and ruler. We will return to Grotius and his influences a little later.

At their root, though, what mankind was learning, at least in the European theatre, was that if you could find ways to spread risk, you could use trade to make a lot more people rich. And as a special bonus, this did not involve killing or threatening people, so you could feel good about yourself as you did business. In fact, being good became for many a prerequisite of good business practice. It didn't mean you had to be soft, but you did have to show some virtues and some sense of responsibility towards ethical behaviour in how you traded. Why? Because it improved your reputation as a trader. The Shakers, an American sect honoured for their simplicity and virtue and fairness, but sadly no longer with us because they were against breeding, used to add a pinch of grain or salt or whatever they were selling just to show they wanted to make you happy. What to an extremely competitive person would seem to be robbing yourself was in fact building a reputation for generosity that would bring more custom. This was an evolution of trust from an immediate transaction to a forward-looking transaction – 'futures' is another artifice of vocabulary that expresses how we made our business practices more involved and exploited the complex nature of human trust.

The stage was being set for a world in which trust and trade allowed for expansions of political influence and territorial acquisition as well, an imperial age, a colonial age. Depending on your point of view, this was not a good thing because it did not come with a fair valuation of the interests of the people with whom the colonists were trading. And once you begin to realise that you have a numerical or technological superiority to the people you have 'discovered' then you are, to all intents and purposes, holding a revolver over the trade. An age emerged in which the idea of a fair exchange became something of a mockery as only one side of the trade was acting without menace, without a galleon or a cannon or a musket underwriting and undermining the transaction. Fairness emerged in this era as the prerogative of the adventurer, practised among Europeans through a variety of increasingly involved financial devices, but not between Europeans and those who they voyaged for months to trade with and, as often as not, robbed blind in the process.

It is telling that we have sought to restore the idea of fair trade in recent decades and, for many people who can afford the luxury of fairness, it is an attractive part of the marketing of goods to think that the exploitation of child and bonded labour is less of a robbery than it used to be.

FAIR EXCHANGE IS NO ROBBERY

In the last three months of 2019, $22 billion of goods were sold using an electronic exchange system based on trust and reputation alone. If people were, as we often presume they are, selfish, cheating and greedy then eBay would have closed a few days after opening in September 1995. It would have been a failed website in which bad people sold counterfeit goods to bad people who paid with stolen credit cards. But it isn't and they don't. Not everything that is advertised for sale on the platform is exactly what it purports to be, nor is every payment legitimate. There are signs that some people are trying to game the system, just as bad people have always done. But there is enough honesty on the one side and enough credit on the other for a deal to be done. Millions of times over.

Winston Churchill, who had more than enough personal reasons to dislike bankers, business and the threat of bankruptcy, said: 'In finance, everything that is agreeable is unsound and everything that is sound is disagreeable.' It has a neat sound to it, but it is a statement born of weary disdain. The basis of finance is trade and trust as mitigators of risk. The basis of both trade and trust as ideas is knowledge or reputation: we trade with those we know or whose reputation we know, we trust those we know, or whose reputation we know. In both instances, knowledge or repute, we have evidence of behaviour, observed by ourselves or described by others. Either in our own eyes or in the description of third parties, what we weigh up is how the subjects of our observation behave. We will have a good look at the use of language in business shortly, but for now let us just concentrate on that one word: behave.

The Old English word 'be-habban' meant 'to contain.' *Habban* comes from a root word – *kap* in PIE – which means to hold or grasp; the prefix *be* – means 'to oneself' as in 'beget' or 'behove'. While etymologists are not totally sure of where 'behave' comes from, the preferred theory is that it evolved from 'to hold oneself' i.e. hold oneself to the idea of conduct through the idea of self-restraint.

From what is one restraining when one behaves? Well, thinking back to the ideas of Nowak and Sigmund of indirect reciprocity, we learned that restraint from selfishness by doing a good deed to others without obvious hope of reward or exchange is a way of establishing that one is of good standing in a community. When we judge someone's behaviour as good, what we are judging is their restraint from selfishness or from anti-social conduct and allowing ourselves to believe that they will be fair to us.

Psychologists say that one of the common factors shared by people trying to sell us things – snake-oil salesmen, online influencers or politicians – is what they call 'credibility-enhancing displays'. This means that in order to get us to buy, first they need to get us to try. And why would you try something new without knowing whether or not it passed the basic test of any product – that it will do no harm. So it is important for the salespeople to show the safety of the product by consuming it themselves. The snake-oil crowd drink from the bottle, demonstrate their vigour and point to a plant in the audience whose obvious health can be attributed to the elixir of life. The influencer has to show how pretty they look after use of a certain product. A politician has to live the policy they promote. But what they are selling is in each case something that at least some of their audience wants or they would not be in business.

As a result of their trading, we all gain a little bit, even if it is just the knowledge that snake-oil is useless, that we can't all look pretty in front of a camera and that politicians don't necessarily mean what they say. Trade enhances cooperation and improves society, both at the level of exchanging beads and at the level of signing multi-billion dollar agreements.

As Harari said in an interview:

> *Now, in order to have trade, you need some trust. And you can also look at the world and see how in some cases modern beliefs, like the belief in capitalism and democracy and human rights, spread far more effectively when it's done through trade and through economic relations than when it's done at the point of a bayonet.*[59]

[59]Interview with National Public Radio, Harari, Y., 2016. *Why Did Humans Become The Most Successful Species On Earth?* [Interview] (4th March 2016).

Trust is to trade what WIFI is to a smartphone. Without it, the object still works on a basic level, but you know you aren't enjoying the full benefits. You can just about trade with people you don't trust – indeed when you first do so, you probably have to do exactly that unless you know about their character and behaviour by reputation – but if you have any sense of self-preservation you will only do so for something tangible. Only a fool buys an idea from someone they do not know.

In reality, Churchill was wrong: what is sound in business can actually be very agreeable. We want to trust other people because the more trustworthy people there are in our world, the greater variety of exchanges, goods, food, information and all other tools of survival are available to us. Or, in other words, eBay.

An exchange of anything that suits both parties need not be equal, harking back to the Ultimatum Game. It only needs to be fair. On that basis, we as a species are only too keen to do business.

Of course, there is a harsh side to business. Cut-throats, robber barons, shysters and con artists haunt the market halls of history. The free market is no place for the faint hearted. You only have to remember that purist of hard-hearted capitalism, Adam Smith.

In fact, you do have to remember Adam Smith but, instead of remembering the Adam Smith of *The Wealth of Nations* (which is nowhere near the brutal manual for self-interest that some of Smith's modern proponents like to say it is), we should remember the Adam Smith of his earlier work, *The Theory of Moral Sentiments* and indeed the opening words of the book:

> *No matter how selfish you think man is, it's obvious that there are some principles in his nature that give him an*

interest in the welfare of others, and make their happiness
necessary to him, even if he gets nothing from it, but the
pleasure of seeing it.

Smith, the supposed proponent of red-in-tooth-and-claw
competition, was interested in the human capacity for
sympathy and for being fair, for our ability to *exchange*
not value but viewpoints, to put ourselves in each other's
shoes. We engage most naturally in sociable activity rather
than selfish activity. He also wrote:

> *What so great happiness as to be beloved, and to know that*
> *we deserve to be beloved? What so great misery as to be*
> *hated, and to know that we deserve to be hated?*
>
> *Man naturally desires, not only to be loved, but to be*
> *lovely; or to be that thing which is the natural and proper*
> *object of love. He naturally dreads, not only to be hated,*
> *but to be hateful; or to be that thing which is the natural*
> *and proper object of hatred.*

Through listening to flattery and through what Smith called
'self-deception' but what we might call 'confirmation bias',
we might convince ourselves we are 'lovely', he thought,
but in our private moments any sane person knows
whether or not they are truly worthy of admiration. And
you cannot be truly happy unless you feel you deserve
what you get. Adam Smith was asking his fellow men to
be honest with themselves – a philosophical device going
back to the Egyptians in all likelihood and certainly to
the ancient Greeks. The phrase γνῶθι σεαυτόν [gn-oh-thi
say-aw-ton] meaning 'know thyself' is attributed to every
thinker from Thales of Miletus to Socrates. By the time
Smith got hold of it, especially in the context of his work
as an economist, we can see this idea as being an order to

people to make a fair assessment of their own conduct. To be fair to themselves about how fair they are to others.

Although Smith wrote the *Theory* in his thirties and *Wealth* in his fifties, it would appear that the former was the closer to his heart. He spent the last weeks and months of his life trying to refine the earlier book, not the later one. The 'greed is good' Smith (who never existed anyway) was not the Smith that wanted to be remembered.

Adam Smith and his fellow Scot, David Hume, lived at a time we now call the Enlightenment when people were battling to know what kind of world they were going to live in. There were still fears that the old order that had existed since the Dark Ages would reassert itself, or whether the new age of science would predominate. Austrians and Turks were at war just five years before Adam Smith was born. Fighting dominated the European continent in the eighteenth century as it had in the centuries before.

What science and the Industrial Revolution brought to the world of business was a sense of the birth of a different type of society, an exclusively commercial society, in which every person was a participant. Before that time, commerce did not involve the vast majority of people who were to some extent self-sufficient. Employment was largely a matter of farmworkers and landowners. Barter transactions were as common as cash. Capitalism, industrialisation and the beginnings of globalisation changed all that.

It was necessary to have more rules of exchange, a sophisticated language of finance and a familiarity with the common tongue of humanity: money.

HOW THE FINANCIAL CRISIS SCREWED FAIRNESS

From the deregulation of the City of London and Reaganomics in the mid-1980s, governments focused on releasing the creativity of people working in financial services. It turns out that there are some professions where creativity is not necessarily a good thing. News reporting is one; banking is another. What began as the search for greater efficiency became, when combined with the elixir of computerisation and digital networks, a search for alchemy. Rather than turn lead into gold, the later twentieth and early twenty-first century alchemists were trying to turn money into more money.

For our ancestors, whenever people started to talk Latin to them, it was usually a good sign that they needed a lawyer because something dodgy was going on.

Before the Reformation in Europe, priests speaking Latin showed that they had, and were desperate to keep, a monopoly on the interpretation of the Bible because that way lay financial gain – a sinful laity in the grip of the fear of Hell was much more likely to spend, spend, spend on the Church to avoid eternal damnation. Yet, you will not find in either the Old Testament, nor the teachings of Jesus in the New Testament, any thinking that you had to shower the Church and its agents with money to have a hope of influencing the scales of celestial justice. This was deeply inconvenient to the Church. Hence, in the pursuit of monopoly, of turning fear to gold, the old Church took such a dim view of people trying to turn the 'word of God' into words that ordinary people could actually understand, that they tried to put them to death in the most painful way that anyone could think of at the time: burning (this method of execution also had the handy side-effect of reminding spectators of what would happen to them in Hell if they tried to do something as wicked as seeking to understand their faith; a faith, incidentally, whose central texts make no mention of the temperature to be expected in the eternal punishment that, incidentally, they don't mention either – no wonder the Church didn't want people to examine the text of the Bible.)[60]

After the Reformation, and deep into the nineteenth century, doctors spoke to each other in Latin to hide from their patients the fact that either they did not know what was wrong with them, or that they did know what was wrong with them but couldn't do anything about it, or that they were not quite sure how much they could reasonably charge the patient for the diagnosis they were about to invent. In any case, it was all bad news for the person footing the bill, so it was important that they didn't understand it. Most of all, it was important that they didn't understand that the overcomplicated systems of medicine developed during the Middle Ages and prolonged into the seventeenth century, based on concepts such as 'humours', were probably less effective at treating illness than the folk-remedies handed down from our prehistoric ancestors and their millennia of trial and error with plant-based medicines. Anyone who tells you progress is a straight line may choose to say it in Latin.

In more recent times, ordinary people were most likely to come across others using Latin in law courts; not a lot of Latin, just enough terms to make even the brightest non-lawyer lose their way in the course of tortuous argument. This could be argued to be the most dangerous form of obfuscation of the lot, more than religious charlatans and medical tricksters, because if you cannot understand the law, and the people who are paid to explain it are speaking in a language designed to stop you understanding it, who is there left to help? There is a particular irony in

[60]See Ehram, B., 2020. *Heaven & Hell: a History of the Afterlife.* 1st ed. New York: Simon & Schuster.

lawyers today using Latin, because the writing of laws in vernacular language – for precisely the reason that ordinary people needed to be able to follow them in order to obey them – greatly predates the translation of religious and medical texts.

Efforts to disguise truth in order to coerce obedience is unfair on a number of grounds: it prevents restraint of the powerful, it dissolves pretences to equal opportunity for all citizens and it undermines cooperative behaviour by privileging one group (those able to afford to avoid Hell, painful death and prison) over another.

The subject of being able to afford to escape from the bad things in life, not to mention afterlife, brings us inevitably to collateralised debt obligations (CDO).

You don't need to know what a collateralised debt obligation is. In fact, the people who invented CDOs were rather hoping that you wouldn't even ask. Nor do you need to know what a 'credit default swap' is, nor the difference between an AAA credit rating and a BBB credit rating, nor a whole host of other bits of language which, though written in vernacular language, might as well be inscribed on parchment in an unreadable court-hand and then buried under several tonnes of rock. All you need to know about 'derivatives' and 'financial instruments', as the architects of the global financial crisis hope that you still believe, is that other, better trained, better educated and certainly better paid people than you, do understand them. They know why they were so overwhelmingly profitable for some and then overwhelmingly loss-making for everyone else. They know why they all went so disastrously wrong in 2007–08 and, of course, they probably know when it will be safe to start doing the same things all over again*.

*Spoiler alert: they already are.

I am proud to say I used to be a reporter for the *Financial Times*, surrounded by incredibly clever people who did know what CDOs and CDS' were. My colleagues were also trying to warn governments and regulators about the inherent danger of bundling bad debts together and pretending that made them good debts (CDOs). And about building an insurance market on taking premiums worth twenty to thirty times the face value of debts they were insuring (CDS'). And that the credit-ratings agencies who were supposed to warn governments and regulators about such things were making money from rating CDOs and the banks that issued them, so were not that keen to voice their growing suspicion that the whole castle was built on fine-grained sand. I am not proud that I did not understand those things well myself, but I am prouder than I would be if I had been the very senior banking executive who told my colleague, Gillian Tett, in late 2007, that he did not understand half the derivatives contracts that were passed before him to be signed off. The Pope had forgotten how to read Latin.

In the pursuit of ever more wealth, financial services firms across the world played with the idea of money as it had never been played with before. They became increasingly creative and nobody stopped them. Fortunately, as we all know, when the global financial crisis hit us in 2008, when governments and central banks banded together to bail out the banks and mortgage lenders and insurance companies that had been blinded by greed, then the people who authorised all this were sent to prison and systems were introduced that would prevent it ever happening again. The banks were made to fill the financial black holes that popped up all over the planet and ordinary people did not lose vital public services that would have been cut to shreds if it were not for the financial services industry doing the right thing and paying for their misdeeds. Oh.

If there were one thing in all the pages you have read so far that I would like you to remember, it is this: that last passage was a fantasy. The single most unfair event to happen in most of our lifetimes was that the people who caused the financial crisis got away pretty much scot-free. The rest of us paid for their sins. We are still paying for them, just as the grip of coronavirus ensures that our economies will be weakened for many more years to come. Just as the passions provoked by this sense of unfairness are twisted by political charlatans into skeins of rage that strangle our efforts to be civil to each other.

> *Perhaps the most severe blow to public trust was the revelation that scores of banks operated in a 'Heads I win, tails you lose' bubble. Those banks privatised profits in the run-up to the crisis before socialising the losses when the music stopped - at a total cost of $15 trillion in public support. That unjust sharing of risk and reward contributed directly to inequality but almost as importantly has had a corrosive effect on the broader social fabric on which finance relies.*[61]

As Carney says, the people who screwed our economy still have plenty of cash in the bank. I am, as most journalists come to be, pretty jaded, cynical and resigned about the workings of finance, government and the law. However, when I come to think about the financial crisis and its after-effects, and the smug financiers I know who hope that society will never work out that they are the ones

[61]Mark Carney, *How We Get What We Value* (BBC Reith Lectures 2020 - Lecture II)

who find paradise on Earth while the rest of us pay for it, that bit of my brain lights up. You know, the bit that also prompts disgust, right in the middle, the bit where our recognition of unfairness sits and tells us that if we don't do something to protest, we may be permanently out of the game.

TO BE FAIR TO CAPITALISM

There is an argument to be made that it was fairness that caused the global financial crisis. Throughout the modern era, globalisation affected how people traded, as did shifts in technology. As that happened, there was a need to shift from the traditional ways of doing things based on trust and reputation (and, let's face it, we know from Nowak and Sigmund that this was also the *very* old way of doing things) to something that went beyond a word of honour. Trade became a matter of systems and rules. The twentieth century signs of this were the foundation of the World Trade Organisation and the Bretton Woods agreement that set the rules for the world order in finance and economics.

All well and good, but once you move away from 'my word is my bond' and you put trade on the basis of what is within a set of rules, you are tempting the human instinct to compete into overtaking the human nature to cooperate. When either of those gets the upper hand, the general sense of fairness is in peril.

Some observers see what happened next as the direct result of financial libertarianism embodied in the attitudes of Milton Friedman and the politicians he most inspired, Ronald Reagan and Margaret Thatcher. Giving greater freedom to finance to set its own boundaries led to the pre-eminence of banking and other forms of money-manufacturing over more traditional industries such as stuff-manufacturing, retailing or extraction. Within the global rules, individual cultures developed to suit the new, handcuffs-removed spirit of the age. In particular, New York meritocratics became the order of the day. That is to say, the meritocracy of the New York of Tammany Hall and the culture of the Hudson Bay fur-trapper, as my good friend Iain Dey put it to me.

Men with no track record, but a genius for numbers and invention, began to rise through the ranks of the great banks of Wall Street. Out went the men (and it was almost all men) whose main qualification for their job was that their fathers had sat in the same seat of the same oak-panelled office. Here was fairness at work, then. Take a man like Lloyd Bankfein, who was the son of a postman from the Bronx. He traded metals so successfully in the bear-pit of the commodities markets that he built a reputation based not on blood but on sweat and balls. He was unstoppable in an era where results = reputation and he became the CEO of Goldman Sachs, the toughest pit on Wall Street. And men (and it was usually men) who had fought their way to the top using the tactics of pugilism saw no special need to adopt Marquis of Queensbury Rules when they got there. Anyone who quibbled with the new ways of doing business could do so from the other side of a pink slip/P45. Many of those who came to the fore now were people whose parents and grandparents had been exploited in the early years of the twentieth century by the blue-bloods of Wall Street or ruined in the 1929 Crash. Fair was fair.

Iain Dey, former business editor and Wall Street correspondent of *The Sunday Times*, sees a parallel with post-communist Russia, where the children and grandchildren of people sent to the gulags were the ones who were fastest to exploit the fall of the Soviet Union and the deflowering of its assets and resources.

From one point of view, this was an outbreak of fairness that washed away existing laws and replaced them with the rules of the street. Not the rules of Wall Street. But, in the context of history, it did not last long, the damage it caused was profound and many of the people who had set up this new culture survived pretty happily. Lehman Bros and Bear Stearns may have fallen by the wayside, but the bulk of the industry carried on.

Economists did not really help. When perhaps the whole point of economics is to provide the 'law' by which this jungle should be restrained, economists rarely agree on anything and if they do, can often be lured by the siren beauty of a neat algebraic equation into ignoring some of the simple truths of fairness, as some of the most eminent of their own number have said.[62]

To be fair to capitalism, it has been trying to get better. All through capitalist history there have been efforts to ensure that influxes of wealth are evenly distributed. The earliest great trading bodies – the states of Venice, Genoa and Pisa, the Hanseatic League, the Dutch East India Company and its British namesake – were all set up to share the risk of far-flung international trade at times when the failure of your great venture could be proved only by the failure of your ship to return from the Indies. The way in which they were put together set this almighty risk against the mighty reward to be had if the ships did return, low in the water under cargoes of spices and silks. Elizabeth I invested large amounts of

---

[62]e.g. Paul Krugman, Nobel-prizewinning economist, in a column for the *New York Times* after the global financial crash: *How did economists get it so wrong?* 2 September 2009

money in Sir Francis Drake's 1577–80 circumnavigation of the world; when he came back the value of his trading (and the theft of large amounts of Spanish bullion) gave her a return of almost 5000 per cent. The sum could be measured in billions today. She used it pay off her entire foreign debt and still had one-seventh left over to invest in further trade ventures.

Spreading risk is the whole point of capitalism. Individuals club together to put their capital towards projects they could not afford on their own, or which they could not pull off on their own. In order for there to be value, others had to fail. If anyone could get spices or tobacco as easily as walking to the corner shop, the commodity would be worth very little. 'In economics as in evolution,' the journalist and business writer Matthew Syed has said, 'progress is driven by creative destruction.'[63]

If capitalism was more about destruction than it was about creation, then we would have put more effort into making communism work. Or indeed feudalism. But it has proved to be sufficiently balanced – so far – to be worth investing in. The risk-reward ratio has worked for us. That could be partly explained by an Adam Smith way of thinking. Some 250 years before Frans de Waal, Smith wrote:

Nature has implanted in the human breast, that consciousness of ill-desert, those terrors of merited punishment which attend upon its violation, as the great

[63]Syed, M., 2020. *A vital lesson in trust learnt long ago is being trampled by errant advisers and abitious MPs.* Available at: https://www.thetimes.co.uk/article/a-vital-lesson-in-trust-learnt-long-ago-is-being-trampled-by-errant-advisers-and-ambitious-mps-5m6fd2q2l

safe-guards of the association of mankind, to protect the
weak, to curb the violent, and to chastise the guilty.[64]

It isn't quite one of our definitions of fairness, but it is not far away.

Can we really be so hard on the world of modern business when corporations still thrive that were set up by the Quakers, with strict adherence to ethical codes in their folk-memory, and to some extent in their conduct too? In Britain, Barclays Bank may not be a role model for the business world and the principles of George Cadbury may not have survived his company's purchase by Kraft, but Unilever and John Lewis are still well regarded for their commitment to be more than just profit and loss centres.

Capitalism is making some strides towards reforming itself in the wake of the financial crisis, reforms which would have made John Pierrepoint Morgan or John P Rockefeller fall off their chairs with laughter. The Business Roundtable in America signed a pledge to champion what is known as 'stakeholder capitalism' – the idea that it is not just shareholders who should benefit from a company's activities, but their employees, their customers and the communities in which they operate. The World Economic Forum and the Council for Inclusive Capitalism are other examples of a conscience awakening in the business world.

Yet at the same time, as we will see when we look at the vexed question of what is a fair level of taxation, some of the world's biggest corporations still fail to make the simple calculation that if they can do business in a country it is because they are able to use its roads, its educated and healthy workforce, to be protected by its

[64]Smith, A., 1759. *The Theory of Moral Sentiments* II, ii, *iii*. London, page 125

police force and its army and to drink its potable water. If they can use all that, they should pay their share of its cost. The coronavirus has shown the moral nudity of some of the emperors of the new reformed capitalism too, as corporations rush to take advantage of taxpayer bail-outs while fiercely resisting any calls to restrain themselves from paying large executive bonuses or dividends and buybacks for shareholders. And the pay-cuts to which CEOs subjected themselves in the interests of sacrifice were in many cases more than made up for by improved bonus schemes.[65]

In June 2020, a professor from the Said Business School in Oxford produced a report saying that in the previous fifteen years, private equity companies – people who buy failing businesses, make them more efficient (sack lots of people), load them full of debt and then sell them again – had taken $230 billion in fees from 'investors' while providing investment returns that were very little better than putting the money in a standard tracking fund you could buy on the Internet.[66] I put 'investors' in inverted commas because it is a word that gives the impression of being impersonal – investors aren't real people, are they, but rich folk with the money to invest in things like private equity funds? Well, the truth is, you are probably an 'investor' without knowing it. I know I am. If you have a pension fund, you are most likely an investor in that sort of fund. And I am sure that you will be delighted to know

[65]Edgecliffe-Johnson, A., 2020. *Bumper CEO stock awards dwarf salary sacrifice*. Available at: https://www.ft.com/content/f6f61677-745a-4afc-b3de-3c68fd45a50e

[66]Flood, C., 2020. *Private equity barons grow rich on $230bn of performance fees*. Available at: https://www.ft.com/content/803cff77-42f7-4859-aff1-afa5c149023c

that the men who run the biggest PE funds are now not only billionaires, but billionaires several times over. They aren't really that good at making money for you, but they are world-class at making it for themselves, and you can bet your bottom dollar (if you have one left) that they employ every trick in the book to avoid paying tax at the rates you and I do. To them, fairness is a word for suckers. I am not sure why we keep letting them get away with it.

The truth is that capitalism is not a philosophy, but a force. It is like a dog that keeps having to be pulled away from smelling its own pool of vomit. You hope that one day it will overcome the instinct, but you know in your heart that it has just evolved in that way and, without the intervention of politics and government and law, it is unrealistic to expect it to jerk its own chain.

8

Fairness in Law and Taxation

FAIR USAGE, FAIR DEALING AND REASONABLE EFFORTS — CIVIL LAW

The moment you begin to write down the rules of a game, you create the need for a referee. We would have no need of lawyers if we were all able to agree on what was fair. If you want to know why there are so many lawyers, you should really ask, why are there so many laws?

The words 'fair' and 'fairness' do not appear in the US Constitution or any of its Amendments. 'Just' or 'justice' appear thirteen times and 'liberty' four times. This is not necessarily because the Founding Fathers were not interested in fairness; it is not mentioned in the British Bill of Rights of 1688 either. Perhaps the authors of these foundational documents of democracy, like most lawyers and philosophers since, took it for granted.

Fairness arises in many legal concepts, but the most important use of the idea comes in the distinction between the way justice is dispensed – *procedural fairness* – and the expectation that we have of fair treatment by the law

in both its actual and its ideal (natural) application –
substantive fairness.

This reflects a distinction which also exists in other
cultures when applied to justice. Amartya Sen points
to it in the concepts of *niti* and *nyaya* in Sanskrit texts
on ethics and law. Both words mean justice, but the
first is to do with the administration of justice and the
second describes the type of world that exists when
institutions connected with justice are functioning
well. Sen says the two ideas are reflected in the more
programmatic approaches to justice taken by the likes
of Hobbes, Rousseau, Kant and even John Rawls (*niti*)
on the one hand, and Adam Smith, the Utilitarians and
Karl Marx on the other. It might be a surprise to group
Smith and Marx, but Sen is thinking not of the *Wealth
of Nations* Smith but the Smith who wrote *The Theory
of Moral Sentiments*. It is worth noting that both Smith
and Sen are often categorised as economists or political
economists but, for both men, their work on how
societies should prioritise fairness to achieve a just state
is where they seem to feel most pride. Both consider
that justice derives from the attempt by people to put
themselves in as impartial a condition as possible when
deciding an issue. They do not require people to adopt
artificial conditions such as Rawls' 'veil of ignorance' –
imagining that you know nothing of the world in
which you will live and calculating what would be a
fair position for you to have in that world. Instead, they
seek to ask what a truly impartial observer will make of
a particular question of justice. True impartiality may
seem hard to achieve, but people who support particular
teams in a particular sport will know how different they
feel watching a contest in which they are indifferent to
all those participating. It may not be as exciting with

less emotion at stake, but it brings a deeper appreciation for the way the players operate and especially how they observe the rules and how they respect the arbiters of those rules. (And by the way, the ref is just as important in a courtroom as he or she is on the sports field; their fairness lies not in how they interpret the rules/laws but in that they do it the same way to both sides.)

Sen would take this argument out of the comfort of the harmless sports arena, though, and place it in the context, for instance, of discussing whether or not a state should abolish the death penalty. Both those who advocate for its maintenance or its return and those who wish to see it abolished or kept off the statute book should seek to imagine what an impartial observer would make of their arguments. Sen's thinking is far more detailed than this and involves concepts like 'capabilities' (by which broadly he means the opportunities for doing things) and 'functionings' (by which broadly he means outcomes or results). In essence, he seeks to find the ways in which objectively good outcomes can be achieved for as many people as possible within a society. The means by which they do so are less important to him because the differences between individuals are so great that it becomes impossible to say what equality of opportunity is: one person's chances of converting an opportunity into a good outcome could be very different to another's. Fairness – in this case procedural fairness – plays a critical role in determining how the potentialities of a good life and the opportunities to achieve it are best to be balanced.

Complex thinking of this kind underpins modern approaches to how best we should organise justice, but play less of a part in answering practical questions such as: why do I have to pay my lawyer so much?

One of the odd things about the practice of law, as opposed to its deeply-debated theory, is that it appears to defy the rather less debated law of supply and demand. No matter how many lawyers there are, on the civil side, they all seem to do very nicely and keep pretty busy. More and more of them are trained every year, presumably balanced out by more and more of them taking more permanently to the golf course at the other end of their careers. Usually, a glut of a service would depress the price of it. The opposite seems to occur with the legal profession, perhaps because the laws of supply and demand do not really apply to the creation of law either. At no point in any political manifesto I have ever read have I seen a promise to create more laws – it is implicit in various policy promises, but does not win many votes as a promise in itself. Yet, despite the apparent lack of demand, we get more and more laws with each succeeding session of parliaments and congresses. Life gets that little bit more complicated.

FAIRNESS AS JUSTICE – CRIMINAL LAW

Research cited by the 2017 Lammy Review into the outcomes of the criminal justice system in the UK for people from Black, Asian and other Minority Ethnic groups came up with one reassuring finding among a mass of worrying results: juries are fair.

Based both on a series of staged trials involving juries deliberately picked for their racial mix (and who did not know the trials were not real) and on a study of almost half a million real cases, the research showed that British juries are no more likely to convict a black or Asian defendant than a white one for the same crime. While this research is a decade old, as recently as 2018 conviction rates of white, black and South Asian defendants were respectively 85%,

83% and 81%. Left to their own deliberations and guided by the rules of the court, Britons judge their peers fairly.[67]

Magistrates, who replace juries in less serious cases, are more likely to convict members of ethnic minorities by about a quarter. Judges are more likely to jail or impose harsher sentences on non-white people no matter how fairly their juries have deliberated and returned a verdict of guilt. In 2015, 78% of offenders convicted of serious offences were white (the rough 2011 estimate is that 87% of the total UK population was white[68]), 9% were Asian (compared to roughly 5.2% of the total) and 8% were black (roughly 4%).[69] Of those convicted, blacks were sentenced to prison in 64% of cases for black defendants compared to 61% for Asians and 53% for whites.

Fairness is even more of a hit-and-miss affair in the US, even in the case of juries. According to a study conducted in 2012, juries in two Florida districts convicted black defendants 81% of the time compared to 66% of the time when the jury panels were all-white (which was the case in 40% of trials); when even one black juror was on a panel, conviction rates were almost equal. Left to their own devices, all-white juries were not fair, but mixed juries were.

[67]Uhrig, N., 2016. *Black, Asian and Minority Ethnic disproportionalty in the Criminal Justice System in England and Wales,* London: Ministry of Justice Analytical Services.

[68]Index Mundi, 2020. *United Kingdom Demographics Profile.* [Online] Available at: https://www.indexmundi.com/united_kingdom/demographics_profile.html

[69]Hopkins, K., Uhrig, N. & Colahan, M., 2015. *Associations between ethnic background and being sentenced to prison in the Crown Court in England and Wales in 2015,* London: Ministry of Justice Analytical Services.

In both Britain and the US, the real unfairness in criminal law comes before and after defendants meet their peers in court. Arrest and charging rates before a court appearance disproportionately affect non-whites in both countries (more so in America); judges sentence them more harshly too. In the US, the rate of incarceration per 100,000 of the population is about five times higher for black people than for white.[70] Federal prosecutors in some states charge blacks with possession of quantities of crack cocaine just above the point at which sentencing guidelines double the minimum sentence two and half times more often than they charge whites using those amounts.[71]

Forgive the avalanche of statistics. There are so many allegations of fairness about the criminal law that it helps to be grounded in facts. Because then we can see why it is the case that what you think about fairness in the outcome of criminal law depends on how you see the criminal justice system as a whole. How you see the criminal justice system as a whole is likely to depend on what you think about fairness in the outcome of criminal law. It is an inescapable part of human social life that some members of a community regard the criminal law system as something that is put in place to guard them from external threats, while some see it as something put in place to threaten them and keep them in place. Fairness

[70]The Economist , 2020. *Smoking-gun evidence emerges for racial bias in American courts.* [Online]
Available at: https://www.economist.com/graphic-detail/2020/01/18/smoking-gun-evidence-emerges-for-racial-bias-in-american-courts
[71]Tuttle, C., 2019. *Racial Disparities in Federal Sentencing: Evidence from Drug Mandatory Minimums.* Available at: http://econweb.umd.edu/~tuttle/files/tuttle_mandatory_minimums.pdf

in justice is in the eye of the beholder and it changes in time and place. It is not something that can be proved one way or another, but it seems quite possible that the first laws were written because people realised that they disagreed on what was or was not acceptable behaviour as a cooperator, based on how their own brains, their *anterior insulae,* reacted to a particular set of circumstances. A law is the dictate by an authority – by a king like Hammurabi, or by a group of educated and experienced people like a Senate – of what should be considered when deciding if something is right or wrong. Right or wrong how?

Well, clearly that does depend on what your society believes. For Cephu the selfish pygmy, it was entirely wrong to manufacture his own monkey-trapping net and catch food for himself rather than the whole tribe. So seriously wrong that his peers were prepared to ostracise him in what was effectively a death sentence; if I walk into a fishing-tackle shop and buy a hook or a lure or some maggots, I would not expect to be surrounded by fellow citizens eager to drive me into the wilderness. Modern Westerners regard the forcible deprivation of another person's life to be the most serious of crimes (although in many nations our fairly recent forebears would have placed treason against the Crown or the state as a higher crime); the Anglo-Saxons settled murder cases by forcing the killer to pay a *wergild* fine, the size of which varied depending on the social status of the victim; tribes like those to which Cephu belonged may have regarded what we would call the murder of an elderly member not to be a crime at all; no Spartan mother or father would have been prosecuted for leaving their supposedly-weakling child on a hillside to die of starvation; our great-grandparents' generations considered it an acceptable part of justice to execute people who procured abortions while today we call

215

them doctors; our grandparents' generation incarcerated people for having sex with their lovers when today we celebrate their same-sex marriages.

In short, justice reflects what we see as a fair way of living together – both a fair way of cooperating in our society and a fair way of competing within it.

But that on its own is not enough.

Justice has frequently, almost normally, been denied to whole groups of people in whole societies: the unfree, the poor, the female, the young, the old, the black, the brown (occasionally even the white). A system – a rule – of law can exist quite contentedly in a vacuum of fairness. But it is also true that fairness is unlikely to survive long in the absence of a system of justice.

Like most nations, America regards the legal basis of its constitution as an advertisement of the honour and nobility of its nationhood. But to an objective eye, however well the Constitution of the United States has survived 232 summers and winters, it is still a document written by men who believed slavery was a benefit to society and who deprived the basic democratic right of voting to all but 6% of the population. If the people who defined how the law of the land was to be applied did not treat their fellow humans fairly as a matter of course, could their justice be fair?

As we discovered when trying to define fairness at the beginning of the book, justice is not always fair (I put the phrase 'the law is unfair' into a search engine of English-language news publications and it returned more than 1600 entries over the last twenty years: mostly because laws were not applied equally to people of different sex, race, age or wealth) and fairness is not always just. Or, to be more precise, what is deemed by society to be fair is not always to be found in codes of law.

Anna Wierzbicka says that the two words cannot be synonymous because, in the case of justice, 'the notion implies that there are some people in the society who are in a position of power and privilege ('above other people') and whose judgements and pronouncements can have an impact on many other people's lives.'[72] The law, to reflect changing attitudes to fairness, is constantly being amended. Fairness, as a judgement between people, is equally dynamic but as a horizontal relationship not a vertical one.

Justice requires lawyers. Fairness merely requires people to wish to live in peace with each other.

PAYING YOUR FAIR SHARE — TAXATION

Tax collectors are not the most obvious candidates to put forward as the incarnation of fairness, but in a way that's what they are. The spectrum of competition and cooperation runs between those who favour individualism and minimal government and those who prefer communalism and state intervention. The issue, as I have said more than once, is how exactly do we stand in relation to each other and the taxman is the human symbol of that in the measurement that seems to matter most: money. Tax is the way we cough up our sacrifice to the society in which we choose to live. We may not choose to pay, but when we do, we are counting out our contribution to the contract we have with our fellow *Homo sapiens*.

Because of this, tax stirs the most controversy over fairness. The issue, particularly in income tax and corporation tax, is the purest mathematical expression

[72]Wierzbicka, A., 2006. *English: Meaning and Culture.* 1st ed. New York: Oxford University Press p155

of unfairness and fairness to which we are repeatedly exposed. Money-sacrifice may not be as directly harmful to physical existence as the sacrifice of liberty or even of life that some humans make in their encounters with the law, but it is an expression of fairness that we not only hold in common, but can most easily count. Even if you are not a taxpayer, that status defines how you relate to the state you call home.

The CEO of Alphabet, the parent company of Google, was in 2020 awarded a pay packet of $291million (£234 million at June 2020 prices). Unsurprisingly, a group of shareholders objected to this distribution of reward. Google is one of the world's most successful and valuable companies, with a stock-market valuation in the region of $1trillion (£805 billion). In that context, Sundar Pichai's take-home pay might seem fair and reasonable. But does the company have a similar attitude to fairness when it comes to distributing money to the people on whom it most relies?

Those people are not just its customers and its shareholders, but also its employees and the communities in which it operates to make such vast revenues and profits. The relationship with the workforce is a market-matter: Google pays very well – the average UK employee of the company earned £226,000 in 2018, around ten times the average salary in the country – but whether it is a fair distribution or not is a matter between the company and its employees. It is in the relationship with taxation where fairness applies to the relationship with the outside world: taxation is the sacrifice which nations ask 'persons' – in the legal sense, which means corporations as well as individual humans – to make in exchange for the common good. It is a price to pay in exchange for having a number of luxuries provided by the commonwealth of a particular nation which we now take for granted, but that our ancestors simply didn't have. Depending on where you live, those 'luxuries' include a health service, an education system, an infrastructure of electricity, gas, water, broadband, roads, railways, radio-spectrum etc. You may argue that some of these things are provided by private companies – although that is an argument easier to make in the US than in most other Western countries – but even then, it is the state that provides the 'protection' that allows any person to function and prosper.

In the past, this overall infrastructure might have been called something like 'the king's peace'. Today, we are more likely to call it 'public order' or some such euphemism for people living together with tolerance and decency and in the absence of intimidation and violence inflicted either by their fellow citizens or by the state. That protection does not come cheap, but because we have had seventy-five years since the end of the 1939–45 War to get used to it, we – or more accurately, those of us called upon to pay for it through taxation – have increasingly come to see it as something which we cannot be reasonably and fairly expected to keep paying for. That could be a mistake.

The coronavirus has given us a small taste of what the absence of the king's peace might mean. So did the rioting in America following the death of George Floyd. It's hard to make money from a branch of a coffee chain that has been looted. The economic wonder that is the smartphone will be restricted if the 5G masts that offer its greater potential have been burned down by idiots who have been convinced (probably by malign and false information they read on their smartphones) that this technology in some way spreads or causes the coronavirus. Advertising, which underpins the business model of social media and search engines such as Google, is lost on those too ill or too poor to receive its messages. All of those circumstances arise when a state is short of the funds to make its luxuries available to its people. The populations of countries where global commercial enterprises make money are just as much investors in those companies as the ones who merely buy shares. The sacrifice of taxpayers over centuries is the investment on which they are so frequently denied a return by companies that manipulate multinational tax systems. This is what Martin Wolf of the *Financial Times* calls 'rigged capitalism'.[73]

There is a facile argument put forward by companies that they have a duty to their shareholders not to pay too much tax. There is a more profound duty to their wider investors not to pay too little. Regulators around the world are beginning to wake up to this, although there will be a competitive market in corporate taxation rates for the foreseeable future that prevents real fairness in taxation.

Individuals who avoid tax could see themselves in the same light. The wealthy may not feel they need the mere public-funded services of education or healthcare and therefore ought not to be expected to pay for it. Yet they expect to breathe the air, drink the water, share the environment with others and they expect to live without being attacked on the street or subjected to invasion by totalitarian enemies. To seek fairness in society is to recognise that the value of life is vested in more than simply what you pay for. It is in what your fellow cooperators have paid for in cash and blood for centuries. Pay tax as a sacrifice in exchange for freedom, or what you save

[73]Wolf, M., 2020. *'Democracy will fail if we don't think as citizens' | Free to read.* [Online]
Available at: https://www.ft.com/content/36abf9a6-b838-4ca2-ba35-2836bd0b62e2

by avoiding it will be spent only on higher walls, more security guards and greater isolation from your fellow human beings.

As a business reporter for the *Financial Times* through the 2008 crisis and beyond, I have heard and seen all the justifications for tax avoidance that I have mentioned here. As a PR man since, I have heard from the inside very senior executives of global businesses with revenues in the billions not seek to defend the astronomical salaries of their leaders, but instead discuss tactics to prevent journalists from asking questions about those salaries. I have also heard the machinations of highly-paid corporate executives who want the trust of the public so that they can sell them goods and services, but do not trust the public enough to justify the amounts they pay back in tax to the communities from which they make money. Yet that public, the majority of whom in Western countries have income tax deducted from their pay packets before they receive a penny, pays its taxes with barely a murmur. Of course, when taxes rise, the discontent can topple governments, but on the whole the most taxed societies in our world – countries such as Denmark and Norway – also feature at the top of lists of human development and of happiness. If there were a fairness index – in fact, such a thing only exists in the IT industry to decide if system resources are being distributed on a network 'fairly' – I would wager those countries would be near the top of that too.

Recent data has shown very clearly who is paying the most tax and it is not corporations. In fact, on both sides of the Atlantic they are paying less, markedly so in America. Even since the financial crisis showed us just how much damage the corporate world was capable of causing to the rest of humanity, its collective share of the remedy has shrunk rapidly. According to the Organisation for Economic Co-operation and Development (OECD), in 2006, before the credit crunch and global financial crisis, tax on corporate profits in the US was 3.08% of GDP; in 2018, it was 1.06%. By contrast, tax on personal income was unchanged (9.73% vs 9.91%).[74] This is entirely the opposite of fair play in the game of money.

We all know what our fair share of debts are. Nobody wants to pay it all. We would rather get a discount on taxation, cut a corner, use an allowance, take advantage of the advice of expensive accountants, manipulate our nationality and residence so we can pretend we don't really belong to our own community. Only some of us can afford the lawyers to do all of those things, which is in itself a pretty good indication that paying less tax than a simple calculation says you ought to, is a fundamental mark that you have an unfair relationship with the rest of your species.

Things may possibly be changing. Crises bring about changes in attitude to how we should contribute to the society which, in theory, we all hold equally precious. It is normally warfare, but it could also be a reaction to the coronavirus.

As the *FT* authors said:

The American civil war made the US federal government first turn to income tax, while consumption taxes were initially tested in Europe to bankroll the first world

---

[74]OECD, 2020. *Tax on Corporate Profits*. [Online] Available at: https://data. oecd.org/tax/tax-on-corporate-profits.htm; OECD, 2020. *Tax on personal income*. Available at: https://data.oecd.org/tax/tax-on-personal-income. htm#indicator-chart

war. Tax campaigners believe the fiscal hangover of this pandemic might be another such moment.

The piece quoted the French finance minister, Bruno Le Maire, on the topic of taxing the massive (mainly US but also some European and Chinese) digital corporations that dance rings of avoidance around us and our simple-minded tax authorities

> *'It is simply a matter of fairness. We owe it to our citizens and companies, especially SMEs, who pay their fair share of taxes… Digitalisation and international tax optimisation have created, for too long, loopholes allowing some companies to escape taxes. We need to re-establish a system based on fair taxation.*[75]

Some argue that the amount of money that would be raised by re-establishing a system based on fair taxation would be less than $100 billion a year. They say it is a drop in the ocean compared to the extra costs of the coronavirus to the global economy.

Hardly worth getting out of bed for, I am sure you will agree. In which case, I can't really see why the corporate world is making such a fuss over taxation. They could just write a little cheque. To be honest, I am not holding my breath.

[75]For those still bothered about my claim that only English has a single word just meaning fair, I should point out that I checked with my former FT colleague Alex Barker who interviewed M Le Maire, and the minister spoke these words in his impeccable English.

9

Fairness in Communication and Technology

WITHOUT FEAR OR FAVOUR

Without gossip, there would be no society.
Robin Dunbar (1947-) British evolutionary
psychologist

The role played by gossip in human society is so important
that governments in free and unfree societies alike make
special efforts to ensure that it works to their advantage.

Communication was the first trade. Gossips were the
first traders. The ability of *Homo sapiens* to communicate
with speed and efficiency was what gave them dominance
over their environment and then over the species with
whom they competed to exploit it. The passage of
information between people defined the reputation of
individuals and groups. Reputation – the story of our
own behaviour and conduct within our community – can
be the determining factor in how successful individuals
and groups are in relation to the whole environment in
which they exist. Our reputation is what earns us favour
or fear within our sphere of cooperation. It can be the

difference between prosperity and poverty or, as with Cephu the hunter-gatherer, between life and death. It is, therefore, of fundamental importance that those with most power and responsibility for the making or breaking of reputations should be people who can be trusted to do so fairly. Whoops.

It is not just a cliché but an axiom that when rebels and revolutionaries want to seize power in a state, they first take control of the means of communication. Doing so determines whether they are called freedom-fighters or terrorists, whether they end up in power or a ditch. This puts enormous power in the hands of those who control the most effective and trusted channels of communication, even when there is not a coup in sight.

Until recently, those all-important channels of communication were called broadcasting or publishing, but now it can be anyone with a mobile phone and access to the Internet. In the past, whether they exercised it or not, those who controlled the means of communication were given responsibility as well as power. In the case of broadcasting, the ability to reach so many so quickly with information that affected reputation was recognised by governments to be such a revolutionary – using the word in both senses – power that it was subject to oversight and control. In free societies, that was intended – at least in theory – to ensure that communication was used to further cooperation, or in the 'public service'; in unfree societies it was to make certain that fear and favour operated on behalf of those who already had the most power. The way in which power is exercised over communication is a good indicator of how free and how fair a society is.

We call those who come between the sources of information and the audience for which that information is intended the 'media' because they mediate the message.

They have the power to mediate it in ways that can benefit either the source or the audience; ideally, in a fair media, the people who hold that power exercise it responsibly so that interests of both source and audience are balanced, so that reputations are fairly represented. The source of information gets a fair hearing. The audience has a fair understanding.

Because communication is such an important part of the way we choose our washing powder and our government, the commercial and political value of the media is immensely greater than the financial value of the businesses that produce the media. Hence the power, hence the need for responsibility, hence the central role of fairness. And hence the burning need to keep the government's hands off it.

As television was beginning to flex its muscles both commercially and in the service of politicians, those who held legislative power recognised the need to apply limits to how it could operate. In some countries, that need involved creating and sustaining a 'state-owned media' which could become a beacon of fairness and impartiality – the reputation for neutrality of the BBC, at least outside Britain, is probably the main example. In other countries, limits on television involved a 'state-controlled media' that could become a beacon of propaganda. Being able to tell the difference between the two types is not difficult: the first judges the people who license the broadcast industry; the second judges the people who watch it.

Even in America, which now has a television industry of unparalleled competitiveness where commentators can get away with any sort of bias (except, interestingly enough, in sport), there used to be limits. A code of communication was designed to prevent unequal representation of political viewpoints and to promote the broadcasting of information that imposed restraint on government. It was called the Fairness Doctrine. It was introduced just after the 1939–45 War. It was scrapped by Ronald Reagan. That turned out well, didn't it?

The publishing of news around the world has always been a scrappy affair. It says quite a lot about the nature of the press that a number of competitors in the marketplace for news actually advertise themselves on the fact that they are *not* biased. Imagine a washing powder whose advertising slogan was: 'We won't ruin your clothes!'

Historical attempts to govern the press go back to the invention of the press. Johannes Gensfleisch zur Laden zum Gutenberg was seen as a revolutionary by the authorities of his time, both secular and, more importantly, religious. They recognised after a while that his invention – more accurately his introduction of moveable-type printing to Europe – had the capacity to break their stranglehold on information. Printing smashed the hegemony of the literate elite by making it possible for people to share what they knew. Before Gutenberg, you could do that only by shouting on a street corner or whispering in the right ear. The first method was dangerous and the second inefficient. After Gutenberg, you could control a printing press and be able to tell others what you knew, something that could give you a competitive advantage in commerce, politics or faith. The instrument of Gutenberg's destruction of established power structures was the book whose exclusivity guaranteed power to the few who had read it, even though its words were supposed to define the purpose of every human life and indeed afterlife. It was Gutenberg's Bible that changed civilisation at least as much as the smartphone. Its alternative title at the time of publication was, by the way, the *42-line Bible*.

Today, in the Internet age, the power of gossip, reputation and, in some rare instances, genuinely useful information has been shared out among the people. Unfortunately, responsibility, already in scarce supply, has not. In the Facebook age, a fair hearing happens by accident and fair understanding comes about by chance. At first, anonymity was the favoured conduit of cowardice and slur. But the evolution of (anti)social media has been such that many people now feel quite comfortable to be repulsive and unfair to others with increasing confidence and transparency. Connecting everyone gave us the chance of benefitting from the wisdom of the global village. So far, it has just given an anarchic voice to the mob, manipulated by people who either should know better, or do know better.

The worst thing many people can think of to say about social media is that it makes the traditional media look quite fair.

A FAIR ASSESSMENT OF THE MEDIA ... AND OF EACH OTHER

How do we make fair judgements on politicians and on businesses, on our sporting heroes and villains, on our favourite musicians and actors, on our most despised YouTubers? They are not people we are ever likely to get to know, as our distant ancestors got to know those few people who were important to their life – through personal and intimate contact. Someone must come between us and them, must record, report and summarise their raw words, deeds and creations for our convenient understanding – imagine if you had to read all the verbal slips and stutterings of a Donald Trump or a Boris Johnson without some editing. Without someone as an intermediary, the direct communications of physically-distant politicians or business people or celebrities, to their voters, customers and fans would be hard to comprehend. It would be hard to judge if they were being honest with us and offering us a fair reflection of their real intentions and conduct? How would we know that we could trust them?

The answer is that we rely on mediation. It's called the media.

The order of battle for journalists is roughly divided into three sections, and all of them have an equal contribution to make to the fairness of the work: reporters (responsible for fair and accurate reporting); commentators (responsible for fair comment); and editors (responsible for what, when I was a schoolboy, was called fair copy – the version of your work you wanted the teacher to mark). The fairness or otherwise of journalism depends on all three. It goes without saying that fairness is in the eye of the beholder, perhaps more so in the passage of information than in any other field. We all have our own view on events as well as the causes and effects of those events that journalists bring to our attention through text, sound and pictures. But when passing our own judgment on those journalists – whose shortcomings and whose good qualities I will discuss in the next section – we should remember that without them, we would have nothing to talk about beyond what others, who are not professional intermediaries, want us to know. Of course, some media owners work hand in glove with those who govern us; in some countries and at some times, those who govern us *are* the media owners.

Where and when we are lucky enough to live in a place and time that journalists are trying to tell the truth, at least as they see it, everyone should remember one thing about the shade of gossip they are consuming: however bad you think the media is, the effect on fairness in its absence would be lethal. Because now, in the post-Gutenberg age, the age of 'social' media, we have returned to what the Danish academic Tom Pettitt calls 'secondary orality': a way of receiving information direct from other citizens in the same way as a medieval peasant did – in the form of rumour and gossip.

So, we would do well to remember the value we have, until very recently, placed on intermediation by a professional class – although as a former member I think journalism sometimes has more in common with a medieval guild than a modern profession – in the form of what is now reviled as the mainstream media. Remember that when you are looking for fairness, it is much more likely to be found in the 'mainstream', the considered and refined and fast-flowing waters of information, than in the brackish, polluted and unknowable tributaries and streams and springs of the Internet.

We ought to remember that while some commercial journalists will adopt postures and agendas and deceits, others will try simply to report or to analyse rather than just comment. And we should remember that the wisest people of our past who had most to fear and favour in journalism had mixed feelings about it too. That for every Thomas Jefferson:

If I had to decide whether we should have a government without newspapers, or newspapers without a government, I would without hesitation choose the latter.

there was a Mahatma Gandhi:

I believe in equality for everyone, except reporters and photographers.

231

We should remember that for every William Randolph Hearst, the father of the 'yellow press:

You can crush a man with journalism

there was a George Orwell:

If liberty means anything at all, it means the right to tell people what they do not want to hear

And then perhaps, when we make a fair assessment of those who try to mediate the rumour and gossip of the world, in whatever stream they swim, we might end in the same place as the French philosopher Alexis de Tocqueville, with whom, secretly, most journalists would I think agree:

In order to enjoy the inestimable benefits that the liberty of the press ensure, it is necessary to submit to the inevitable evils that it creates.

THE JUST DESERTS OF THE BRITISH PRESS

The function of the press in society is to inform, but its role in society is to make money
                                        AJ Liebling, US journalist, 1904–1963

Commercial pressures make people do things for reasons other than fair trade. As in life, so in communications, in the media.

I sat through all six months of the Leveson Inquiry, the official British government investigation into the phone-hacking scandal in 2011. There were many fascinating witnesses, the great and good of media and government in

Britain and beyond, all providing evidence to a very senior British judge as he investigated the 'culture, practice and ethics' of the press in the UK.

The Leveson inquiry was commissioned by Prime Minister David Cameron after revelations that one newspaper, the *News of the World*, had made an industry out of intercepting the mobile-phone voicemail of thousands of people, both famous and unknown. In doing so they intruded on the private lives, and often the private torments, of countless people. That number included – and this was the story that broke the dam on the whole affair – the family of a missing thirteen-year-old girl called Milly Dowler, who was later found to have been abducted and murdered by a sexual predator. The phone-hacking scandal rocked the British press and caused the closure of the *News of the World*, with the loss of hundreds of jobs. It caused Rupert Murdoch, the man at the top of a tree of senior executives who said they knew nothing about this ubiquitous practice, to appear before a committee of MPs in what he claimed was 'the most humble day of my life'.[76]

Throughout the six months of the inquiry and the evidence of 184 witnesses, there was one moment that still sticks in my memory. It was when a witness – a former tabloid editor who had been charged and subsequently cleared by a jury of phone-hacking offences – was explaining to the inquiry the process by which a story would be handled from the moment a tip-off was received by a news desk man like himself, right up to the time of publication.

---

[76]I was sitting about 10 feet from Mr Murdoch when he spoke these words. Shortly afterwards, a protester slapped a paper plate covered in shaving foam into his face and called him "a greedy billionaire". Some of the foam landed on my trouser leg, but sadly I was not able to preserve it in the scrum that followed.

He began:

You offer me a tip. I decide I'm interested in it. I then task a reporter to go and make that story work ... see if that story will work.

I have always thought that those four words were the most significant of the millions spoken about phone-hacking. The witness said: 'make that story work' and then in the same breath corrected himself, uttering a different phrasing 'see if that story will work'. Both then and later, I discussed this moment with numerous friends who worked on newspapers like the *News of the World,* indeed two of whom had been news desk executives on the paper themselves. All agreed that the phrase 'make that story work' was highly significant.

The phrase encapsulates the gulf in attitude between journalists and the rest of humanity about how real events can be described in subsequent telling and why newspapers are rarely a platform for a fair hearing. Journalists are about the only people, with the possible exception of undertakers, who think of tragedies as commodities. This is not to say that they are bad people, but that in the pursuit of 'the story', they become competitive and commercial. Information as trade in about its purest form. The phone-hacking scandal derived from the desire to keep one step ahead of the competition in the war to tell the public what they never knew they needed to know.

Some journalists working for the heavies (the serious newspapers) looked down their noses at the red-tops (the tabloid papers such as the *News of the World* whose mastheads were printed in large white fonts on red-tinted boxes). But the sensible heavies knew that the hacks on the red-tops could produce a serious newspaper in their

234

sleep, while they themselves would never be able to roll out a copy of *The Screws,* as it was known to friends and enemies. Only a gifted few know instinctively how to 'make that story work'.

If you want to be fair to people who have suffered some tragedy – the death of a loved one, survival in a train disaster, the wreck of a celebrity marriage – one should properly leave them alone. In my thirty years as a reporter, I probably only once or twice came across a member of the public who genuinely wanted someone to intrude into their grief or shame, although I did occasionally meet people who said that they found speaking to a complete stranger about some cruel twist in their own life story to be cathartic. It was unfortunately much, much more common to speak with the subject of previous media attention who felt that they had been treated unfairly, sometimes very unfairly.

On the other side of the street, in public relations, where one part of my job has been to seek fairness for my clients (alright, ideally, to seek favourable reporting of my clients, but fairness at a minimum), I became as strongly aware of journalism's imperfections as I was aware of the shortcomings of public relations when I practised journalism.

'Making the story work' boils down to using any means, fair and sometimes foul, legal and sometimes not, to write a story which accords with the version of events that the editorial management of your news organisation wishes to publish. And to publish it before anyone else does.

You will note I don't say 'broadcast' as well as publish, because, unlike their American counterparts, UK broadcasters are subject to much more serious restrictions on what they can report and generally impart less of the broadcaster's agenda than is the case with newspapers.

In fact, quite honestly, I do not know of an agenda that any broadcaster has apart from being able to sell more advertising airtime, and when it comes to news programmes, most of them have given up on that idea anyway. In Britain, news is important to presenting television channels as being complete services with a public-interest element to them, but it does not really sell cars or toothpaste.

In America, the situation is very different: there, the press tends to be more neutral, with some notable exceptions in those parts of the market and the country, particularly New York, where there is strong competition for sales. The degree to which news reporting and commentary are kept apart is unthinkable to British counterparts: in its efforts to offer fair comment, the *New York Times* has an entirely separate comment team whose editor answers to the publisher (owner); efforts to include all points of view can still falter, however, as shown when the comment editor was forced to quit in June 2020 after the paper's own staff revolted over an opinion piece by a conservative Republican senator which called for troops to be deployed against Black Lives Matter protesters.

American television news programmes, however, can make big money if they market their news as part of a wider persona for the station. Fox News is the obvious example of that, an extraordinarily partisan broadcaster which calls itself 'fair and balanced', but CNN and MSNBC are not naive about their ability to monetise a position of partiality. As people realise how much money and power is attached to partisan broadcasting, a profitability emphasised by digital journalism, even more outrageously unfair and unbalanced broadcasters have entered the ring.

The history of newspapers in particular has always been swashbuckling, their behaviour reined in much more by the restraints of law – in particular defamation – than by any self-imposed moral codes. Before the invention of the hot metal press in the middle of the nineteenth century, it didn't trouble 'scriveners' and their editors that much of what was printed might be libellous or just plain wrong. Truth was incidental to early journalism.

After newspapers became widespread and profitable, the commercial wars began and, as competition intensified and there was little more to be done in reducing prices, the main weapon of the newspaper in selling itself was what people in the industry called 'presentation' – how news stories were packaged and presented for the audiences of the different types of paper: tabloid or heavy, left-leaning or right-leaning or professedly impartial.

The need to differentiate led to the treatment of tragedy as commodity.

Matthew Engel, forty-eight-year veteran of reporting, author of a history of the tabloid press[77] and former visiting professor of media at Oxford University, says:

> *The unfairness of the press is very rarely expressed in direct lying and cheating. It is much more commonly caused by the conventions of news reporting and the way in which news reporters and editors are expected to frame news in particular ways that suit whatever the news agenda is. That leads to a loss of complexity and thus to unfairness. News has to be forced into a template and that means it is not suited to nuance and therefore not suited to fairness.*[78]

[77]Engle, M., 1996. *Tickle the Public: One Hundred Years of the Popular Press.* 2nd ed. London: Orion.

[78]Engle, M., 2020. *A Discussion of Fairness* [Interview] (10th June 2020).

Engel described an interview he had done with Desmond Hackett, a superstar sports reporter of the great tabloid era of the 1930s and 40s. Hackett's career was ruined by television which allowed others to see that his descriptions of sporting events were more to do with making the story work than accurate depiction. Engel asked him about his method. 'You'd get an idea and you'd draw the truth towards it,' Hackett said.

I would wager there are very few news or sports reporters who have worked in British papers in the past century who do not know exactly what he meant.

HOW THE BBC WAS KILLED BY FAIRNESS

If it is possible to kill with kindness, is it possible to kill with fairness? One of the many, many expressions in English involves people 'bending over backwards to be fair'. Which sounds painful and can be fatal in extreme cases.

Take the BBC.

In 2015, the year before the Brexit referendum, the Reuters Institute for the Study of Journalism (RISJ) reported that 51% of Britons who owned a smartphone had downloaded the BBC News app. In the media trade, that measure is known as 'penetration'. The institute surveyed news usage in twelve countries that year. The next greatest penetration of any news app was ABC News, which was on 16% of Australian smartphones. The BBC's website was more popular in the US than that of the Washington Post, National Public Radio or the Wall Street Journal. It was the fourth most popular news source in Ireland, a country with more reason than most not to see anything British as trustworthy. Before Brexit, the BBC was more or less the BBC of the past, the news source trusted around the world for its impartiality, the voice of dull, studied reason that never called anyone a 'terrorist', but never called anyone a 'freedom fighter' either.

By 2020, things had changed. The BBC was still trusted by more people, just, than any other news source, but it was also distrusted by a significant amount, according to the Reuters Institute research. Applying a 'net trust' analysis by deducting distrust from trust, the BBC was now in third place behind the *Financial Times* – the first time a newspaper brand had ever topped any trust chart that I have seen – and ITV News. (It was still well represented in the US, incidentally, with as many Americans citing it as a news source as the print edition of the *New York Times* in the Reuters report). Overall, trust in media brands had fallen by an average of eleven percentage points in the UK.

Reuters said, 'Even the most trusted brands like the BBC are seen by many as pushing or suppressing agendas – especially over polarising issues like Brexit and climate change.' Politically, the left were more disillusioned with the messenger than the right: trust in all news fell between 2015 and 2020 from 58% among those who self-identified as being on the right of politics to 36%, but among those who called themselves left-of-centre trust had plunged from 46% to 15%. And even though 76% of Britons told the Reuters Institute that they preferred news that at least tried to be impartial, as opposed to supporting or challenging their own views, partisan brands such as the *Daily Mail, Daily Telegraph* and *The Guardian* were cited as sourced by significant segments of the population.

What had happened to the BBC? Well, fairness happened. At a time when the rest of the nation was being split down the middle by a 52:48 vote to leave the European Union, the BBC had to stick with impartiality.

It is the law in Britain that at times of elections and during the rare referendums we hold, broadcasters have to be strictly neutral.

Neutrality does not sit well in today's media landscape. It should, but it simply doesn't. We are moving towards a different relationship with gossip/news. In the RISJ survey, across the world, while nearly two-thirds of the population said they valued the media for breaking news, only half said they valued the media for explaining it.

The problem with that is, if you are the BBC, when the world you are trying to report is encamped at extreme ends of an argument – or more accurately a range of arguments – both reporting it and explaining it brings you into contact with the whole smelly mess. You find you cannot stand back from the sewer but have to wade in and then everyone regards you with disgust.

Populists drag their critics onto their territory. They have learned to subvert the norms of political discourse so much that for others to apply logic or reportage to them is like trying to stop a tank with a shopping bag. Unless a human being is attached to the bag, the tank rolls over it. And even if a human being is attached, the tank might roll anyway.

American journalists, whose earnestness, high moral standards and respect for office have often let them down when it comes to recognising how appalling the actions of their head of state can really be, found with Trump that, for the first time in living memory, his conduct made it impossible for them to follow their normal practice of giving space to people who would defend him because he was, by any objective measure they had, indefensible.[79]

[79]Goldberg, M., 2020. *Tom Cotton's Facist Op-ed*. [Online] Available at: https://www.nytimes.com/2020/06/04/opinion/tom-cotton-op-ed-new-york-times.html

In other words, you cannot present 'both sides of an argument' when one side, the side that has become the establishment, is a roof-leak of effluent and deceit. To clean up shit, you need more than a shovel. You have to have a detergent. So-called populism drags fairness, in the sense of any effort to find an objective middle ground where some form of consensus might be reached, by the scruff of the neck and dips it in manure. Even when it has been cleaned off, fairness is still soiled, foul-smelling and forever tainted by the process it has been through. When both sides cite fairness and unfairness, often in the childlike tones that Trump used as he clung dangerously and desperately to power in January 2021, the job of the media is simply to let the audience decide which of them deserves fair play. That is the procedure.

Can the BBC ever recover its reputation for neutrality – which, for the sake of making my own position clear, I believe was always observed more in the World Service radio heard around the world than in other parts of its news output, but was still at least an aspiration in the rest? The BBC began on a slippery slope when it began to try to compete with newspapers by breaking stories in its main bulletins and flagship programmes rather than following them. Having dabbled in the commercial side of news gathering (exclusives = money in Fleet Street) while not actually having to make money from it because it is funded by compulsory public subscription, the BBC found itself in an uncomfortable straddle.

What might be the answer to this?

I asked someone far cleverer and more experienced than me: Mark Thompson, the former head of the BBC (and later President and CEO of the *New York Times*).

He says:

Many doubt whether impartiality is even possible –
isn't even the most fastidious reporting coloured by the
journalist's worldview? – while those who harbour strong
ideological beliefs often come to believe that their perspective
is the only truly 'impartial' one, and that anyone else who
claims to be impartial is probably a political enemy.

  A generation ago, [the British Conservative government
minister] Norman Tebbit talked about "the unctuous
'impartiality' of the BBC's editorialising", meaning that
the Corporation's much vaunted commitment to even-
handedness concealed a systematic liberal bias. Today this
claim by the right is louder on both sides of the Atlantic
than it's ever been, but it's matched by equal suspicion
from the ideological left that 'impartial' journalistic
institutions like the BBC and The New York Times are in
fact complacent mouth-pieces for an essentially oppressive
Establishment which always puts its own worldview – and
its own interests – first.

  The present polarisation of politics has made the
maintenance of impartiality even harder. Many young
people come into journalism with a presumption that
reporting should be a form of political campaigning in
which the authenticity of emotions – above all anger at
social injustice – is as important as the facts.

  The principle of impartiality is an increasingly lonely
and disputed path. Upholding it is one of the greatest
battles that [the] BBC will face. But it's vital that … the
Corporation stand their ground. Reality is impartial.[80]

[80]Thompson, M., 2020. *A letter to the author* [Interview] (16 July 2020).

There is another factor that has made it harder for journalists in the BBC and elsewhere to deliver a sense of fairness: politicians. Not all that long ago, British politicians were pretty content to appear in opposition to each other on the same screen or in the same studio. But once ex-Fleet Street journalists began to take charge of the 'messaging' for British political parties it became increasingly common for them to use their inside knowledge to dictate the terms of interviews on live broadcast. They began to implement strategies that had been used in American politics for decades, insisting on their ministers appearing alone, not as part of a dialogue with a political rival. Consequently, the presenter, previously a referee, had to take on the role of the opponent, posing the alternative viewpoint, advocating on behalf of the devil. That is not a tenable position for a neutral person to maintain. Moreover, the emergence of the 'personality' interviewer, imported from US television and radio, may have made broadcasting more interesting, but it meant that politicians and authority figures in general were often able to get the better of an interviewer who was not a specialist in the field and who relied more on their stance, their persona, their aggression to 'win' arguments. Their old role, of eliciting information for the rest of us to make fair judgments on the politicians, went out of the window, replaced by a performance. Journalists who become the subjects of TV reviewers' critiques have lost something indefinable about themselves, no longer an observer but a participant in the story they are supposed simply to be telling.

More than that, those who were previously judged to be neutral were being held up in the court of public opinion alongside the rest of connected-humanity, most of whom did not even know there was such a thing as impartiality, just cheering for your team, dogma or party. When the rest of the world is a sinner, you as a supposedly neutral source facing similar charges, are going to struggle to be found not guilty.

CAN WE VS SHOULD WE?

> Only with a free press could a large and populous modern country recreate the public forums of the classic city-states; only through the press could one teach the same truth at the same moment to millions of men and only through the press could men discuss it without tumult, decide calmly and give their opinion.
>
> Jacques Pierre Brissot (1754–1793)

Brissot, one of those Frenchmen who you know came to a sticky, sharp-bladed end because the year of his death is a seventeen ninety-something, marvelled at the effect that freedom of expression had on his compatriots as they shook off the yoke of the *ancien regime.*

What would he have made of the revolutionary freedom of expression we gained from the Internet, when everyone became a publisher, everyone a commentator, everyone a critic? And even more so, that everyone gained all that power while adopting none of the responsibilities.

In the twenty years since the millennium, humanity moved, without a noticeable landmark in sight, from questioning to shouting. We began the Internet era asking whether technology, in particular artificial intelligence, would affect us for good or ill. We have moved on to using that technology to abuse each other's foibles and intolerances. What we did not see was that this transition *was* the effect of artificial intelligence and it was definitely, perhaps irretrievably, for ill.

Revolutionary moments force us to ask ourselves what we are capable of. They dare us to waste the opportunity to 'move fast and break things'. In the Sumerian and other creation myths, they are the periods of chaos on which some heroic or divine figure imposes a degree of order that creates the conditions for a period of prosperity. In revolutionary periods, we ask ourselves first 'Can we?' and then 'Why can't we?' All this is good. It is how humans make progress. In more cautious and conservative times, when the chaos of nature has been regimented into herbaceous borders, we ask ourselves first 'Why shouldn't we?' and then 'Should we?' I think we are prompted to shift from 'Should we?' to 'Can we?' by the stultification of order, which fixes positions and cements iniquities; then we experiment with chaos for a while before seeking to go back again to order, impelled by the fear of the chaos we have unleashed. That is about where we are today.

The advance of communication since the millennium has had many effects that have been positive for fairness. I am with Tom Standage, the *Economist* writer who has said that while social media probably didn't cause the Arab Spring or other events that it has been credited with, it did act as an accelerant.

But in other ways, the nature of social media is a downwards movement in human relations. And while it has helped some people obtain fair treatment and given them equal access to platforms on which to have their own hearing, it has done the reverse to many, many more. The more I think about this, the more I think it is a result of anonymity. Before the arrival of hot metal printing, as Standage has pointed out media was a matter of limited-reach and limited veracity.[81]

[81]Standage, T., 2018. Social Media Retweets History. In: P. Urquhart & P. Heyer, eds. *Communication in History: Stone age symbols to social media*. Oxford: Routledge.

It was mostly pamphleteering, hyperbolic condemnation or support of political figures, or a vehicle for spreading financial information and gossip from one community to another. In other words, it was, much like digital media today, a very human, commercial activity.

The one thing about the dissemination of news and information that has changed, though, is accountability. Over time, the abuses of free speech that were the currency of news sheets and pamphlets led government authorities to license them. In Britain, licensing ended almost by accident in 1695 when Parliament bungled its attempt to renew the Licensing Act and by stealth the newspaper industry was born.

But newspapers were still, until the middle of the nineteenth century, required to pay a stamp duty that made it impossible for just anyone to wander into a print works and decide to trash the reputation of anyone they felt deserved trashing that day.

We now live in a world in which Donald Trump is not free to share his opinion morning, noon or night with the rest of his species. Respect for his office – and fear of legislative reprisal – had deterred the social media giants from muting him until he was using their platforms in genuine seditious conspiracy. Then, the debate moved on not from whether they could silence him to whether they should, which was a bit late, really. Of course, the former President of the United States is clearly only a fan of social media when it suits him. On the day that Twitter first decided to post warnings on some of his outpourings for being inflammatory or based on misleading information, he threatened the equivalent of the Licensing Act, some ill-defined presidential diktat to mark what he tweeted would be '...a Big Day for Social Media and for FAIRNESS!' Nothing happened, of course, except that the president drew attention to the reality that in the world of social media and populism, what is fair is what you agree with and vice versa. How and on what platform his relationship with social media and with his connected congregation develops we will only know in months and years to come, but it is a safe assumption that it would be harder to connect with the faithful from within a prison cell, as Hitler discovered in 1923.

The fact is that nobody, including Mark Zuckerberg, seems to have asked whether it was a good idea to 'connect the whole world'. It fell into the category of 'we can so we should'. But we have since learned that connecting the whole world is rather more complicated than presented to us and also that it is something that can be controlled and manipulated by Mr Zuckerberg and his team with tweaks of their algorithm. The same tweaks can bankrupt other media organisations – take for example the local newspaper industry – and distort the nature of public discourse.

With unlimited connection, the idea of proactive aggression, as expressed by Richard Wrangham, which has in evolutionary terms reduced violence by individuals against the interests of the community, can become the opposite, an anonymous stimulant of outrage that accelerates mob action and reduces the safety of individuals.

Facebook said it would be taking action to make sure that democracy was protected in the run-up to the 2020 US presidential election, but the point missed by most people was that no media owner has ever *had* to say that before. No media owner – and if Mr Zuckerberg is not a media owner then he is something worse, a media controller – has ever had the power to promise one way or another to make democracy safe from their own intervention in the discourse between politician and voter. No media owner has ever had to devise a project to make sure that genuine information is prioritised over, and differentiated from, misinformation and disinformation. No media owner has ever had the gall and arrogance and condescension that Facebook did to call a project to provide facts rather than propaganda 'Eat Your Veggies'. But perhaps it is appropriate that such a gutless, moronic, irresponsible response should be expressed in the language of children.

Because you can see where their power comes from. It comes from the young.

Nearly three-quarters of young people globally got their news from people who don't take any responsibility for reporting: – social media (38%) or search engines (25%) or from aggregators such as Apple News (8%). Only 16% of 'Generation Z' got news direct from the source. The rest found it through their smartphone apps or from email alerts. More than half of under-35s in Britain said they got their first news of the day via their phone rather than a newspaper, television or radio.[82] Yet the ethereal world that the young inhabit is ruled by algorithms and algorithms are by definition determined by past behaviour; the people who most count on us to look to the future dwell in an environment pre-programmed to learn from the past. I have to say that suits me, but does it really suit them?

This is one of the numerous contradictions of the information technology revolution. Another is that everyone is a publisher, but nobody knows who the publishers are. How can we therefore assess what's useful or reliable? How can we tell whether information is produced

[82]All data from. Reuters Institute, 2020. *Digital News Report 2020,* Oxford: University of Oxford.

by people with a hidden agenda when they already have a hidden identity?

As someone who made their living reporting words and deeds that harmed (or indeed helped) others, the idea that you would found an exercise to enlighten or harmonise humanity on platforms that permit participants to use anonymity to avoid responsibility has always struck me as fatuous. It is the sort of reasoning that encouraged utopian idealists to set up little slices of heaven all around the world that almost always ended up with results somewhere on a scale between discontent and mass suicide. 'Connecting people' while relying on their goodwill *and allowing them to avoid responsibility for anything they say or do* is the province of infants. Or, in our case, really, really clever computer-science students who lack any real-world experience. Those are not my words, but those of Steve Huffman, the CEO and co-founder of Reddit, speaking in June 2020 about his decision to ban a discussion group of 800,000 or more Donald Trump advocates who engaged in bullying and racism.

> *When we started Reddit 15 years ago, we didn't ban things. And it was easy, as it is for many young people, to make statements like that because, one, I had more rigid political beliefs and, two, I lacked perspective and real-world experience.*[83]

[83]Roose, K., 2020. *Reddit's C.E.O on Why He Banned 'The_Donald' Subreddit.* [Online]

Available at: https://www.nytimes.com/2020/06/30/us/politics/reddit-bans-steve-huffman.html

However, the now-experienced Mr Huffman still describes the 'mission of Reddit' as being to 'bring community and belonging to everybody in the world'.

Perhaps the most serious aspect of this is the pretence that 'connecting everyone' was an altruistic aim. The truth is, of course, that some people, notably Mr Zuckerberg, have become enormously rich by connecting everyone and the reason for that is that they have been able to commoditise emotion. In the social media industry, it is called 'engagement', but it just means emotion. The more a social media platform, or indeed any publisher, can make a person sad, happy, angry, calm, or whatever else, the longer that person stays with them and the more chance there is to sell them things. With the odd exception – the BBC being one – all media have existed for commercial reasons and all have profited from exciting emotions and selling advertising on the back of it. But before the era of social media, this was an art – albeit not a very noble one. Now it is a science, a sophisticated science that the evolution of artificial intelligence promises to make into an intensely dangerous science. And it is all driven by the need for profit. It will, followed to its logical conclusion, destroy our common bonds. Donald Trump has shown us what we *can* do with social media if the norms of truth-telling are ignored and thus also shown us what we *should not* do. Because we are not meant to deal with so many connections, so much 'engagement', so much information and rhetoric, such strong emotions, without the intercession of actual human 'connection' to help us judge it for veracity, for value, for fairness.

We *can*, for good or ill, connect everyone on the planet with everyone else and let them share their opinions and their own spin on the truth of every event that occurs during each spin of the world – and to do so anonymously, cut with venom and veiled agendas - but have we stopped for even a single spin to debate whether we *should*?

10

Fairness in Politics and Government

HAS POLITICS ABANDONED FAIRNESS?

Fairness is the business of government. In all its forms. It may be in designing and protecting a rule of law that restrains corporations and other powerful institutions (including itself) from overpowering those who cannot organise themselves for their own protection; or in distributing the benefits that come from cooperation; or deciding in what degree the interests of one group should be subsumed into the interests of another; or creating the circumstances in which there is an approximation of equal opportunity and fair competition; or holding up the rights and liberties of all, especially those who suffer from the prejudices of majorities. That is a lot of work, right there.

It is a fair exchange of responsibility for the power that the governed agree to delegate to the government. At least, that is the theory. The theory of a social contract has been with us for hundreds of years; the reality of a document to which both sides have signed their names does not yet exist. Everything about the delegation of freedom to act from the mass to the representative is taken on trust.

When Barack Obama gave his 2012 State of the Union address, which, given that his approval rating had been in negative territory for several months, might have been his last, he went all-in on fairness:

We can either settle for a country where a shrinking number of people do really well while a growing number of Americans barely get by, or we can restore an economy where everyone gets a fair shot, and everyone does their fair share, and everyone plays by the same set of rules.

These are, as was pointed out at the time, three different takes on fairness, but as we have seen there are at least five ways in which you can decide if something is fair or not and there are undoubtedly many more.

The concept of fairness plays a starring role in politics, but like all actors, it isn't exactly what it seems. In some countries, notably New Zealand as David Hackett Fischer has pointed out, it's almost as if you can't even get the attention of the people needed to put you in power unless your policies are placed within the context of how fair they are. Others, and Fischer says America is certainly one, only roll out the vocabulary of being fair when they have a special point to prove. Either way, fairness has become an arrow in the quiver of people seeking election. And nobody feels the need to define it or question what happens to it when it isn't being needed just to win votes.

In recent times, what we have seen of fairness has reminded us of the children's attitude: it's not fair! Complaints about the way in which the world is run – by elites for elites, by liberals for liberals, by the old and the wealthy for the, well you know who – are essentially all the same appeal to the wronged child in the playground: it isn't fair on you if these elite, liberal, old, wealthy people get all the baubles while you are ignored and left with nothing. But once you let the heat dissipate, it becomes pretty clear that those raising the temperature are pretty much cut from the same cloth as those they are raising rabbles against. There has been plenty in the last decade for most of us to kick against: the financial crisis being the one I tend to think of as the most heinous and fairness-destroying, but others too. Migration across continents has caused a reaction against asylum seekers and refugees so that the freedom of movement that seemed to be integral to the democratic 'projects' of both the USA and the European Union became a bad thing.

By most measures, these are far from the worst times to be living in. Inequality has been worse (though rarely as visible as it is today). Health and education may feel like squeezed services, but in Europe particularly there are significant benefits to being alive today rather than fifty or even twenty years ago. The rejection of migration is understandable when it affects employment levels, but many of the jobs taken by immigrants, legal or otherwise, were not being filled by the existing workforce. Though the quality of employment is poor in a zero-hours world, the quantity of employment is not a problem. The problem is that people who think they should have a superior claim to better jobs are being out-competed by others. And it is oh so easy to blame others.

But the real unfairness that has burst out into a lite form of revolution is the unfairness of not being listened to. Most parents know they can ignore the content of an 'it's not fair' outburst from their children, but that you start to pay more attention, or you should, if the words 'you never listen to me' form part of the dialogue. When constructing a social contract, whether it is under one roof or one sky, we undertake to seek a balance between cooperation and competition. The art of politics is to work out what people feel is a fair positioning of that balance. And to work that out, you do have to listen.

The business of government, in the executive, in the legislature and in the judiciary, is to make judgments on our behalf of how we balance our need to cooperate with our need to compete. And the modern way of doing that is not to kill people who disagree with you, but to build enough support for your way of doing things that you win the votes to put you into power. If you do that fairly, you may be able to persuade even more people to adopt your way of thinking after you have reached power. If you do it unfairly, you either have to go on cheating to survive, or you have to revert to the bad old ways of governing, which usually involve guns.

The script for doing things the fair way has been a long time in writing. Could it be unwritten? Why not? Democracy, in a meaningful sense, is very new. For some nations, it is not, and may never be, meaningful. For others, it hangs on but a different kind of script is on the shelves in the archives. A country like Spain, for instance, was following one of those other scripts forty-six years ago, for all that it is now a democratic nation. But the script that protects fairness and promotes the interests of people while maintaining their ability to alter how those interests are best served, has been under construction since human beings figured out how to rule themselves without the aid of God(s).

FAIRNESS, UTILITARIANISM AND THE FUNNY SIDE OF NUCLEAR APOCALYPSE

Until relatively recently, nobody was listening to human beings complaining because politics was so tangled up in affairs of religion. Look around the world today and you can still see plenty of states where the word of a deity is more powerful than the collective words of mankind.

Religion has been sewn into the garments of governance for as long as humans have sought to live together in great groups. It was only the emergence of an alternative way of looking at human life – through science – that the clothes began to change.

Yet even after the Enlightenment, the role of religious belief in politics and government was strong. That of course brought with it the assumptions and assertions of absolute qualities such as good and evil, or right and wrong – ideas that you may remember linguists call 'unanalysable conceptual primes'. I would hope never to belittle anyone's religious beliefs, but it is not easy to reconcile something unanalysable with something such as fairness which requires constant analysis and reconciliation with changing circumstances.

Instead, because I admit to flying over vast acres of scholarship and history like a crop-dusting aeroplane, I look for where fairness shows up in the historical roots of our current political discourse, so as to see possible routes back to it. One of the most likely places to find fairness is the great tract of mental land known as utilitarianism. This has its origins in the thought of Locke, David Hume and others who defined what enlightened thinking was. Jeremy Bentham was the first man to use the word and, together with the polymath John Stuart Mill, is seen as its originator.

Utilitarianism takes as its foundation the Greek philosophy of Hedonism, typified by the thought of Epicurus (341-270 BC), that the goal of man is to be found in the pursuit of pleasure over pain. Utilitarians then mix that with the New Testament idea that God loves all mankind equally. Epicurus thought that people owed each other justice, but did not have a duty to sacrifice their own happiness for the sake of others. Thus, by including the commandment to 'love thy neighbour as thyself', utilitarianism in its earliest form in the works of Bishop Berkeley, Joseph Priestley and Richard Cumberland, arrives at the assertion that the object of a polity is to promote the greatest happiness (or value – Bentham and Mill used the word 'utility' to mean 'pleasure and the absence of pain') for the greatest number of people. Because Mill and Bentham were not clergymen, they separated these ethical considerations from being dictates of a deity and made them duties of people to each other. They grew up in an age of enlightenment and science, so they saw the object of utilitarianism as being universal rather than being an extension of any particular religious belief. The goodness of a particular action was measured in how much 'utility' it produces. Bentham, in fact, thought you could measure happiness with a form of calculation. There were circumstances in which religious commandments – such as 'thou shalt not steal' – would be wrong because, for instance, there could be circumstances in which robbing the rich to pay the poor would produce greater happiness in balance between the two than leaving the rich man alone.

The utilitarians wanted to make ethics into science. They saw how lawyers and politicians used personal judgments and intuition to define what was good for society as a whole. They thought moral judgments could be based on empirical evidence and scientific method. But of course science cannot help you work out what happiness and fairness are. The misery of some ought not to be the price paid for the happiness of others, even if there were a lot more of them.

Such objections made sure that utilitarianism was never going to become the basis of an actual country, but elements of it still inform how we look at our societies today. It is a contribution, a framework of how we look at what a fair way of living together is, but it cannot be complete because it requires judgments which we cannot constantly make. Bentham and Mill also had problems in reconciling the sad fact that some people get pleasure in the pain of others. Can you, should you, include those people so far out on the spectrum of competitive behaviour, in a calculation of what is fair within a whole community? For the utilitarians, that became the role of government, to intervene and make decisions on behalf of all of us as to how we should best apply restraints and encouragement to gain the greatest happiness for the greatest number.

It was because the practical application of government in their own time was so unsatisfactory, packed with corruption and self-interest and irreconcilable differences between the Whigs and Tories elected by only a small proportion of the whole population, that Bentham and Mill began to see wider democracy as the answer to this. Bentham died in the same year, 1832, as the Great Reform Act was passed, beginning an eighty-year process of extending the franchise to all.

The dominant political philosophers of the nineteenth century were Germans – Kant, Hegel, Nietzsche, Marx – who were investigating the nature of man and attempting to define and control his wild side. Only the last of them spent much time looking for his cooperative nature. Collectively, we spent a lot of the nineteenth century seeking evidence of human unfairness and finding it in droves. Gradually, though, with the help of scientific discovery, we changed the terms of what we sought. Darwin opened up the way to escape the definition of human nature just in terms of right and wrong because he allowed us to see ourselves not as some superior being, but as another manifestation of natural cause and effect.

The predominant driving forces of progress remained the conservative versus the liberal. The preservation of order struggled with the chaos of liberalisation. The American Civil War was only one bloody manifestation of the fight between those who wanted to change and those who wanted to stay the same. Revolutions in France at the end of the eighteenth century and across the whole of Europe in the nineteenth century signalled the clash of old and new thinking about human power. And power through territory and trade remained as important as ever before as humanity entered the twentieth century. The scale of human viciousness between 1914 and 1989 ebbed and flowed as part of the same tide that had ruled the planet with increasing force for centuries.

Yet, finally, there were signs that people were looking to solve the moral problems of our behaviour, to restrain our worse instincts and promote our better ones, through cooperation across continents. If the Lieber Code was the first sign of an effort to 'civilise' warfare, it did not have much effect, judging from the brutality of trench warfare, genocide, the massacre of civilians, forced famine and Holocaust in the century after it. But it is possible to trace a path from the code to the Geneva and Hague Conventions, to the League of Nations and the Bretton Woods agreements and the United Nations to a time when it was possible to say that man's own destructive capabilities had become too effective to ignore any longer. Man stepped back from the brink of nuclear destruction. At least for now.

And while politicians continued on this waltz of uncertainty, philosophers and economists and behavioural psychologists were seeking ways to build on cooperation as a way of co-habitation. John Rawls is a better model for the future of mankind than Nietzsche or Marx. Nobody would die following his recipe for society and for a model of justice as fairness. A lot of people have died because we followed recipes for society as a model for unfairness.[84]

I used to spend a lot of time looking through recently declassified files in the British National Archives. Not all that long ago I found one of the earliest records, from 1952, of very senior British army officers debating what form the country's nuclear deterrent should take. It was written with cold-hearted pragmatism and made chilling reading, full of charts of bomb-blast radii and calculations of the deaths and maimings that would be needed to bring the Soviet Union to the peace table after the outbreak of the Third World War.

But at the top of every section of the Top Secret report there was a quote from *Alice in Wonderland* or *Alice Through the Looking Glass*, that repository of the absurd, each one relevant to the doom-laden discussion on the pages that followed. One of the quotes was the familiar words of the White Queen to Alice. In the mind of Lewis Carroll, whose apparent nonsense always had

[84]Rawls' theories of how to achieve a fairer, or at least a more just, society, tend to have trouble when they collide with real life, though, especially in his native land. Research by Norman Frohlich, Joe Oppenheimer and Cheryl Eavey from the Universities of Manitoba, Maryland and Florida State respectively, showed that American experimental subjects did not accept any part of Rawls' "original position" and particularly not his "maximin principle" – that people behind the "veil of ignorance" would choose to raise the floor of poverty in a hypothetical society to the maximum possible – which all 44 groups rejected. ' (Frohlich, et al., 1987))

(Other cultures are available but have yet to be tested like this, to my knowledge)

a rational double-meaning, the two are discussing faith and religion. Looking at this quote typed by an unnamed hand nearly seventy years ago, on a document of which only nine copies were ever made, I could feel the desire of these men for faith in a Looking Glass world where good results might come from evil ideas:

> 'I can't believe that!' said Alice.
> 'Can't you?' the Queen said in a pitying tone. 'Try again: draw a long breath, and shut your eyes.'
> Alice laughed. 'There's no use trying,' she said: 'one can't believe impossible things.'
> 'I daresay you haven't had much practice,' said the Queen. 'When I was your age, I always did it for half-an-hour a day. Why, sometimes I've believed as many as six impossible things before breakfast.'[85]

And I share their agathism.

FAIRNESS AND TOTALITARIANISM

In 1973, Jakob Bronowski visited Auschwitz to film part of the TV series that made him a household name in Britain, *The Ascent of Man*. One scene beyond all others questioned the title of the programme and the reason for making it.[86] In it, the philosopher was filmed walking onto a damp field, wearing a suit and tie and a pair of black leather shoes. With no soundtrack bar the muted

[85]Carroll, L., 1865. *Alice Through the Looking Glass*. 2nd ed. London: Macmillan. Chapter V.

[86]YouTube, *Ascent Of Man, episode 11- Knowledge Or Certainty*, 2011 Available at https://www.youtube.com/watch?v=ltjI3BXKBgY

whistle of birdsong, he walks to the edge of a pond so ragged and nondescript that it looks little more than a puddle, a remnant of a heavy rainstorm flooding a scruffy meadow. Behind him as he speaks, left undescribed by Bronowski, are the brick shells that are all that remain of the Auschwitz gas chambers. In a voice taut and precise, he tells the audience that into the black waters of the pond before him were flushed the ashes of the hundreds of thousands who were killed and then cremated in the concentration camp.

'That was not done by gas; it was done by arrogance, it was done by dogma, it was done by ignorance,' he says, his left hand tucked uncomfortably into the waistband of his suit trousers, his right hand, as if holding a baton vertically upright, conducting his words to the camera.

He breathes a little more deeply than before and then says:

When people believe they have absolute knowledge, with no test in reality, this is how they behave. This is what men do when they aspire to the knowledge of gods.

At this point, and without drama, Bronowski steps into the black, brackish water, which covers his city shoes and the lower few inches of his trouser leg. The incongruity of his position screams at the viewer, but Bronowski just keeps talking. He says:

We have to cure ourselves of the itch for absolute knowledge and power. We have to close the distance between the push-button order and the human act.

He bends at the waist, pulling up the legs of his trousers, as if they were not already by now sodden and soiled by the pond, so rich in a solution of the wretched of Auschwitz.

We have to touch people.

And with his right hand, he scoops up a dripping clod of mud and grass and human DNA. The power of that moment has lived with me since the first moment I saw it as a child. The genius who ruined his shoes to tell me about empathy.

There is no fairness in believing oneself to be right to the exclusion – and destruction – of others. To be right so that not only do others have to admit their own error, but they must be made to pay for it and be seen to pay for it. Cooperation with the aim of destroying others rather than merely competing with them sets back the course of the human journey. There is little to say about Hitler or Stalin or Mao. Or the counterfeit tyrants who have sought to replicate their ill-built castles of doctrine since. We cannot speak of fairness in the same breath as we speak of absolutism. One wipes out the other.

On every definition of fairness, the imposition of the rule of one person or one entity, without restraints and with a single definition of the common interest, is unfair. In modern, secular, times, such regimes have only emerged from chaos as one way of reimposing order. In the twentieth century, they arose in places where alternatives – what we would call democratic alternatives – were young and not wholly trusted. In Germany, the state itself was only forty-seven years old when the ignominious peace of Versailles was imposed on it; in Russia, revolution came against a background of attempts to reform but, as in Louis XVI's France 130 years earlier those attempts were too late and too inadequate to stem the tide of rage. Intention to change was overtaken by national humiliation on the battlefield as foreign invasion and the loss of great power status threatened. China's story was similar, driven by war, famine and decades of loss of face to the fascistic activities of the Japanese military state. Where states had powerful corporate organisations – the *zaibatsu* in Japan, the likes of I.G. Farben and Gustav Krupp who bailed out the bankrupt Nazi party in 1932 – nationalists rallied round slogans of intense private interest; where no such industrial base existed, rebellion focused on the creation of a state-mandated economy. The triumph of unalloyed capitalist competition on one hand and of unfettered cooperation on the other. But both had ulterior motives.

Why did the end of the 1939–45 War not produce a replica of the end of the 1914–18 War? Largely because, for their own reasons no doubt, the victorious alliance decided not to rub the noses of the losers in a national humiliation, but specified the blame for the war's outbreak on a group that did not represent the whole people. That was a fair judgement. Those villains who had survived the end of war were put on trial openly and fairly, made to answer charges brought under a new global system of justice that could trace its heredity to the Lieber Code. The nation was not put on trial, just those who had diverted its historical course; not the people, but persons. You cannot exercise fair judgement, the world was saying, on a whole nation, only on its representatives. Nations were better working together towards order than towards chaos. Their common similarities trumped their surface differences.

In the twenty-first century, we may once again be turning human beings into the problem rather than the solution. It is, of course, usually systems that are the problem. Humans, more often than not, follow what they are taught is the path to order.

Human beings have good reason to believe in miracle cures for whatever diseases history and nature throw at us. So it will always be. But instead, we have to look inside ourselves, into our nature, to find the cures. The cures are found in others, in trusting others, in letting others trust us. We have, as Bronowski said, to touch people.

FAIRNESS AND DEMOCRACY

It is clear then that the best partnership in a state is the
one which operates through the middle people, and also
that those states in which the middle element is large,
and stronger if possible than the other two together,
or at any rate stronger than either of them alone, have
every chance of having a well-run constitution.

Aristotle, *Politics*

Fairness between people, in the way that John Locke and John Rawls among many others imagined, revolved around the central question of how to organise the delegation of authority from individuals to an executive that administers a larger collective enterprise. If anyone has the answer, could they please let me know? Efforts to date have had limited success.

Let us look at the elements of the central question, though. How do we organise delegation of authority? Modern democracies have agreed that we organise it through elections and plebiscites – of which more later – and give a 'mandate' to a group of people to administer the collective enterprise on our behalf. If you are delegating to a parish council or a dogcatcher, the authority is very limited, but so is the need for administration. It is quite possible for the administration to be done by the exact people you have elected rather than employees of the collective enterprise. Your elected councillors can organise litter collection or sweep the streets or catch the dogs. You can help them as volunteers. Even in a community as large the 17,000-strong town of Frome in Somerset, experiments in involving voters in solving the issues that make them cross or happy enough to vote about have proved successful in making the place more egalitarian.[87] But usually, a population much larger than a couple of thousand requires a few employees to administer their delegated authority.

The civil service in democracies are our employees (technically our politicians are too as we actually pay them, though it sometimes seems hard to imagine why). Bureaucrats take a lot of stick, but over the centuries they have achieved a lot. Look at societies with limited or no civil service and you can make the comparison for yourself. Afghanistan, through little fault of its own, for instance, is far closer to a medieval European state than it is to a modern one. However, in recent years, one of the clearest manifestations of the damage to fairness in the West has been the anger directed at the normal functioning of politics. Unsurprisingly, politicians would rather not accept that the financial crisis and its aftermath were their fault, so today's 'populist' leaders – the closest I can come to a definition of the word 'populist' is that is someone who champions the 'people' against the 'elite' – when they become politicians

[87]Purdy, L., 2019. *Revolution in Frome: Flatpack Democracy.* [Online] Available at: https://www.positive.news/society/revolution-in-frome-flatpack-democracy/

themselves, find it convenient to blame others for their continuing failure to bring about utopia. These 'enemies of the people' vary from place to place and time to time. Donald Trump likes to finger journalists who report on his competence and veracity; Boris Johnson – who was a member of the elite of the elite until he discovered it was more electorally convenient not to be – has allowed civil servants to become the scapegoats for failure; every populist must have an enemy to champion the people against. The populist leaders of Hungary and Poland made the judiciary the target.

It is fair for leaders with a mandate to change things to try to change things, although it is a sure sign of unfairness if the first things they attack are those which traditionally place restraint on their own exercise of power. Over many centuries of ups and downs, democracy as we know it has developed a series of what Americans call 'checks and balances'. It happened in the US to prevent a recurrence of the tyranny exercised by George III and his Redcoats and bureaucrats on a group of wealthy Americans to prevent them avoiding paying tax and enslaving and expropriating and disenfranchising ethnic minorities and women. Did I get that right? It may have had something to do with 'liberty' and 'the people', but the exact wording is fuzzy. Things were different then.

In Britain, Parliament itself evolved as a check and balance on the monarchy. Under it evolved a bureaucracy of such extraordinary efficiency that, in the nineteenth century, it administered an empire as large as any that has ever existed with a total workforce in the 1860s of about 13,000 in the UK and the same sort of number scattered through its immense geography of conquests. The population of the Empire at the time was more than 400 million at its peak. The bureaucrats were normally chosen as 'good all-rounders' rather than experts in particular subjects. As late as 1963, there were only nineteen trained economists in Her Majesty's Treasury. Today, there are 450,000 civil servants for a population of 68 million. That might seem to make the case for reform, but the peak in the 1970s was getting on for 800,000 and the total public-sector workforce is now around 16% of all employment compared with about 22% in 2009. Reform has been going on for some time.

If a nation is delegating authority, including in the case of nuclear powers like the US, UK or France, to a very few individuals – or one very stable genius in the case of America – surely it is only fair that there should be impartial and unpolitical people advising them, even curbing them, if they are about to do something stupid or destructive? In a fair society, we recognise the need to delegate authority, but not to abrogate it. And to maintain both restraint of power and to ensure that our delegates govern in the interests of all of us, not just those of us who voted for them and will tear up norms and tear down buildings in their name, it should be a matter of nuanced, not absolute, delegation.

That is why referendums are not very good for fairness. There is nothing balanced and fair about a Yes/No question, one which contains no nuance on how to apply the 'will of the people'. There is also nothing fair or balanced about inviting people to make such absolute choices and then try to undermine their choice or overturn it. Democracy, like black and white photography, is not really black and white but shades of grey, so never trust anyone who tells you there is a simple answer to your problems. And why seek monochrome when you can enjoy the spectrum of colour?

When was the last time you voted? Was it at an election? For a member of parliament or a mayor or a president? Or perhaps in a referendum on the voting system itself? Or did you participate in an online survey about the popularity of a government policy? Or did you respond to a council email asking for your views on reducing the speed limit in your area? Or did you click on a poll in a Facebook post or 'like' a tweet by a favourite politician?

In 2020, we have more opportunities to influence external factors on our way of life than at any time probably since our 1000x great-grandparents lived in egalitarian bands on savannahs or in forests or jungles or migrated between cave systems.

Does that mean we have greater...greater what? Freedom? Opportunity? Wealth? Health? Security? Knowledge? Happiness? What does it mean to live in a democracy? Are democracies inherently fair? Lot of questions. Not much space.

Let's start by trying to remember what it is we mean by fairness. In an earlier chapter I offered five definitions of fairness[88] while simultaneously claiming that fairness could not be defined. This paradox occurs because I am a fallible human being and I am writing the book and therefore get to make up the rules.

But if we are, in all seriousness, to work out whether democracy, the currently fashionable system of government, is indeed a fair system of government, maybe we should hold it up against those five definitions.

To be fair:

[88]See page XXX Chapter 2 Section B Why being fair is different from being equal or just or...

Democracy must a) create a state where individuals or groups trust each other enough to agree trade-offs in their welfare so one may benefit at the expense of another. It is pretty clear to me that democracy is meant to do that, making it possible for us to accept that not everyone has to benefit equally from the common resources of our state, or any other entity to which we belong and contribute. However, when democracy is seen to offer consistently more benefit to one group than others, irrespective of merit, it becomes unfair. Those who abuse welfare benefits which others suppose to be exceptional measures rather than a way of life are likely to tip democracy into unfairness. Those who abuse taxation systems (as I argued in an earlier chapter) so that they end up contributing less to society than what is defined in law as their fair share, will do the same. Both these groups of people behave unfairly and breach an important definition of democracy as fairness.

Democracy must b) provide restraints on the powerful to prevent the weakening of others who have less power. Generally, democracies achieve that by laying down laws, but an important adjunct to it is that they also agree to rules of cooperation which are not written down. Perhaps the most important of these rules is that if you win a majority in a legislature, you must govern not just for those who gave you that majority, but for all those who took part in the process. And you must not try to destroy your polity because you lose an election.

Democracy must c) create the circumstances in which all those cooperating within a social entity should have an equal or appropriate chance at success in their endeavours, or at least not create the circumstances in which groups that are part of the cooperation are prevented from having such a chance. Democracy must strengthen and support, and be strengthened and supported by, impartial and independent institutions of legislation and judgement.

Democracy must d) allow and encourage those cooperating within a communal entity to lay aside prejudices and judgments of others' conduct in favour of finding and tolerating the rights and liberties associated with human prosperity so that the interests of a plural society are reflected as far as possible in common goals.

Democracy must e) allow and encourage cooperators to suspend the pursuit of absolute ideas of 'right and wrong' in favour of achieving consensus on what constitutes the highest common factors of happiness for a plural society.

There are plenty of other things that democracy has to do: defend, educate, police, maintain, house, and cure its members for a start. But if it is set up to move towards the aims in those five definitions of fairness, then it will at least tend towards fairness and fairness to all. Each member of each democracy has to make up their own mind as to whether it is or not and then apply their X in the ballot paper, or write a placard, or stand for election themselves. Moaning about fairness on social media platforms from behind the cowardice of anonymity is neither fair nor sufficiently cooperative to justify being counted as a member of a cooperative group. Whipping up hatred against others because you disagree with them is fine, as long as you do it openly, in your own name and are prepared to answer before the law for harassment, menace or defamation.

Churchill said:

The whole history of the world is summed up in the fact that when nations are strong they are not always just, and when they wish to be just, they are often no longer strong.

You might say something similar about people, collectively. When they are strong, they are not always interested in voting and when they are interested in voting, they are not always strong. It is in the nature of contentment for us to become blasé about what our forebears saw as rights so essential that they were prepared to die for them. In some countries, the turnout at elections is almost 90%; in others, particularly it seems those that claim to be champions of democracy, fewer than 60 people in 100 exercise their right to complain about the state of their lives or champion those they believe will give them a better deal. (Belgium 87% in 2014; USA 56% in 2016)

What is undeniable is that, in countries where governments are little influenced by popular opinion, political debate is stifled, so nobody really knows what others think. Where governments bend to the popular will, political debate is lively to the point of hysteria. In between those points, there are usually stable democracies in which gentle swings on the democratic pendulum push political action between narrow lines of policy change. At least, that was the pattern for much of the last thirty years, since the end of the Cold War.

Perhaps politics became too easy.

It certainly seems to many people that politics, that the practice of democracy, became too much like show business. And that, much like a show, the players on stage have come to believe they are protected by a 'fourth wall' that means their audience has no real power of restraint on them. This is surely part of the reason why we now have 'populists' in power in many countries. Those politicians are the ones who break down the fourth wall and speak, as it were, directly to the audience. That conduct is no greater an act of fairness, though, unless you are taking actions that promote fairness. And so far in the twenty-first century, it would be hard to point to populist leaders who are genuinely interested in fairness for society as a whole as opposed merely to fairness for those who put them on their stage. Populists govern for their base. Fair politicians govern for all.[89]

Yet democracy is rooted in building allegiance with enough people to get on the stage. And to quote James Baldwin:

> Allegiance, after all, has to work two ways; and one can grow weary of an allegiance which is not reciprocal.

What is damaged by one-way allegiance is not the concept of allegiance, but the concept of governance that transforms allegiance into power. In the past, that concept has been religious or it has been autocratic before we gave it a chance to be indirectly democratic. In its latest form, it has become more directly democratic, with appeals by populists to the 'will of the people'. But that latest movement is not progress as much as regress. It is going back towards the idea that one way of thinking, sometimes even embodied in one person, has attractions that permit them to absorb the interests of the commonwealth into their own interests. They want us to believe in the myth that their ideas are the only ones that count and that anything they do in pursuit of the 'will of the people' is justifiable. Eventually, its failures need not be explained or excused or even admitted. They are just the myth and their proponents depend on the idea that they will be accepted by all who understand the new reality.

---

[89]For anyone who comes across this category in real life, I can be contacted at @ benfenton on Twitter to help release the breaking news.

As Harari argues, we make up myths to be able to comprehend how things that do not exist, including societies, can function. Even if we hold fairness to be a myth – and the evidence of science is that it is far more real than Harari's imagined realities – it is no more of a myth than those conjured up by strongmen leaders seeking to regress our politics, and it has the advantage that nobody gets imprisoned or 'disappeared' in the quest for greater fairness.

Of course, the dismal failure of populists to confront the coronavirus – a disease less susceptible to bluster and self-belief than to competence and organisation – ought to have removed the blinkers from voters. But it seems that this was not the cause of Donald Trump's defeat in November 2020 as much as the effect the virus had on the economy. In some places, some things never change.

FAIRNESS AND THE VIRUS

Things fall apart; the centre cannot hold;
Mere anarchy is loosed upon the world,
The blood-dimmed tide is loosed, and everywhere
The ceremony of innocence is drowned;
The best lack all conviction, while the worst
Are full of passionate intensity.
— William Butler Yeats, 'The Second Coming'

When the coronavirus became an obvious threat to the ordinary functioning of societies across the world, some political leaders who had come to power on the promise of liberating the downtrodden suddenly found themselves having to reduce the liberty of those people in unprecedented ways. Some, of course, like Brazil's Jair Bolsonaro, refused to behave as the medical community urged him to. While we still do not know how many people died in Brazil from the Covid-19 pandemic, it was many thousands more than needed to. One thing we learned for certain is that people do not have much patience with the concept of 'excess deaths' – we never want to contemplate the 'normal' rate of mortality in our fellow citizens or ourselves – but they do understand what it means to be top of a Covid league table.

States with populist regimes such as Donald Trump's US, Boris Johnson's Britain, the Italy of Matteo Salvini or Bolsonaro's Brazil all vied for the unhappy crown. Those with more traditional and cautious administrations: Germany under Angela Merkel or Moon Jae-in's South Korea were, to their population's relief, near the foot of the table. The home of fairness, New Zealand, contained the virus so successfully that there were only twenty-one recorded deaths from the disease by the beginning of December 2020; Britain, with a population fourteen times greater than its former colony, had 2,240 times as many deaths; America, with sixty-seven times the number of people, had more than 10,000 times the number of victims as New Zealand.

The media in the US and UK – even some of those that normally showed doglike devotion to them on other issues – rounded on the incompetence of Johnson and Trump in their response to the disaster. In the case of Bolsonaro, it was his stubborn refusal to accept that the seclusion of the population was necessary that observers blamed for the disproportionately high death toll, though the poverty and social inequality of the country must have had some influence too. Leaders who took power on the back of inflammatory rhetoric found that words do not kill germs.

Globalisation is not everybody's cup of tea. The ease of international travel certainly assisted coronavirus on its world tour. But a world that operated in concert did better at producing early vaccines and treatments for the disease than was predicted at the beginning of the pandemic.

Writing as Covid-19 began to take a heavy toll on lives in dozens of countries, Philip Stephens of the *Financial Times* said:

> *The state is back. Long live globalisation. Coronavirus is remaking democratic politics. The paths out of the crisis will present liberal democracies with a choice between authoritarian nationalism and an open global order founded on cooperation between states.*
>
> *The eventual bill for the defeat of coronavirus will be colossal. At some point the debts will have to be repaid. With luck, however, the context will be a rational discussion and rebalancing of the respective responsibilities of government, private business and citizens.*[90]

Stephens pointed to a parallel with the last major disaster that had united humankind in their response.

> *The financial crash of 2008 proved a lost opportunity for change. The result was rising public discontent and the spread of angry populisms of right and left. Coronavirus leaves no room for a second hesitation. Voters across most advanced democracies are paying a price in weak healthcare systems for ideological devotion to small-state, low-tax economics. Liberal markets have a long-term future only if they rest on political consent.*

[90]Stephens, P., 2020. *How coronavirus is remaking democratic politics.* Available at: https://www.ft.com/content/0e83be62-6e98-11ea-89df-41bea055720b

The disease offered us a chance to reassess how we relate to each other in any number of ways.

By entering into lockdown and volunteering to risk the effects of massive economic damage, we essentially said we were prepared to sacrifice enormously in order to protect those most vulnerable to the disease. As this has proved to be the elderly, those already suffering from serious illnesses and the clinically obese, a less generous worldview would be to say that those people had had their chance at life, may not have survived long anyway, or should have known better than to ignore the warnings about the threat to their health of poor diet. That the world chose not to do so suggests that our sense of fairness puts life beyond financial value. Or perhaps future historians will see it as a sign of softness and decadence. How long we remember this remains to be seen; the taste of the most delicious meal can be hard to remember when the size of the restaurant bill adds to one's overdraft.

Yet there is a much more significant reminder inherent in the coronavirus, a monumentally useful tool for us if we choose to look at it. We are a very dim species, for all our cleverness. Every so often, we think we have transcended the physical, chemical and biological reality of where and what we are. By harnessing cooperation and competition, machinery grinding together oiled by the lubricant of fairness, we have achieved things that our ancestors were incapable of imagining. We do the impossible because we can, not because we should and as a result we no longer see ourselves as restricted by anything, as if the rules of the great competition of life don't apply to us anymore.

We have begun to think that only we count. In the past, religion was a reminder to us that there was something bigger than us: nature (although of course, humans being humans, they had to make up stories about it and give it human form as a god or gods). But because we now understand nature, because we have the laws (that we have written down and often amended) of physics and chemistry and biology, we don't think nature applies to us. As hunter-gatherers, we existed as units against other units and then began to cooperate with the others; as city-states we existed as units against other units and then began to cooperate with the others; as nation-states, the same. We haven't found the competition beyond this point (although we are still very willing to compete with the others), but that is the problem. We have forgotten that there is always a bigger threat than just 'others'. It is the same threat that others face – it is all the other species on our planet. We have killed or tamed almost all the physical threats – sabre-toothed tigers and bears and crocodiles are not a menace to us at a species level – and we have used chemistry to tame many of the biological threats. But not all of them.

Coronavirus is a reminder that there is something bigger than us, even if it is much smaller. It is also a reminder that the reason we have developed an aversion to unfairness and a reward system for acting fairly is that it is an ally in the only fight for survival that counts, which is the need to compete as we cooperate with the rest of existence. And just as the need to remember and recognise our true enemies has not gone away, we need to remember and recognise our allies as well.

Or, as Dr David Nabarro, the World Health Organisation's special rapporteur on the coronavirus, says:

> I hope we remember from this that we can succeed in difficult moments only if we work together, if we collaborate not if we compete.

11

Fairness in Human Relationships

*I just want equality, equality for all of us. At the
moment, the scales are unfairly balanced and I just want
things to be fair for my children and my grandchildren.*

Patrick Hutchison, Black Lives Matter protester,
asked why he rescued a far-right counter-protester
who was in danger of being beaten to death at a
demonstration in London, June, 2020

FAIRNESS AND OTHERS

At the beginning of this book, I suggested that the most
important thing we can know about ourselves is where
we stand in relation to others. Not only do we depend on
others to whom we are tied by blood and genes for our
survival, but, for all but a few thousand humans still living
as our hunter-gatherer ancestors did, we depend on others
who together form a collective body or state. We may not
like the state. There are a lot of people who don't like the
state and quite a lot of those that don't like states don't
like anyone else either, even their own families. But, sadly

for them or any of us, disliking a state does not reduce our dependence on it. And because we are dependent on the state we have to hold the state to account for its fairness towards us and towards other people upon whom we depend more directly. That smaller group may just be relatives, but it could also mean groups we depend on for reasons apart from love, finance and finding the car keys. It is my view, though I claim no originality in it, that when our relationship changes with the micro and macro, the family and the state, then these intermediate relationships become more important. This is one of the reasons why we live in unprecedented times: we can rely on more people who share our views, hobbies or sexual inclinations because they are easier to identify and easier to rally to our cause. But the corollary to this embrace of the like-minded is a distancing from the unlike-minded. Fairness requires us to consider the interests of others. However, after a long period of doing so, we seem now to be heading in the other direction.[91]

There are many other 'others' and there always have been. The cautious nature of our species – of all species when it comes to 'others' – demands of us that we suspect others until they prove themselves not to be hostile. Reactions to others range from welcoming suspicion – as the Mayflower Pilgrims experienced from the Pokanoket people of Cape Cod in 1620 – to the outright hostility displayed to anyone who comes near their shores by the violently unfriendly inhabitants of North Sentinel Island in the Indian Ocean, who have killed or injured pretty much everyone who has come within range of their Stone Age weapons for as long as anyone can remember.

[91]Let's stop.

As mankind becomes increasingly mobile, we share the state-relationship with people with whom we cannot hope to have much in common by way of experience shared: culture – whatever we mean by that – religious faith; political belief; norms of behaviour within families or communities or societies; sporting loyalties; artistic preferences; taste in food or music or soft furnishings. All of these are likely to be different in a state where people come from dozens of different ethnic backgrounds. But shared experience is not the only measure of what people have in common. For instance, we all have an anterior insula. We all have a sense of unfairness. We all have the regions of the brain where fairness is felt too. If it is a common factor of human beings, then any group of humans shares it as much as they share a similar number of fingers or toes. Or do they?

A study by American psychologists in 2015 suggests that there are national or cultural differences particularly when it comes to being fair (as opposed to unfair). They tested children from Canada, India, Mexico, Peru, Senegal, Uganda and the US with experiments similar to the Ultimatum Game. The starting age at which children objected to unfair deals – 'disadvantageous inequity' to give it the jargon name – varied between four and fifteen years-old. However, in Canada, the US and Uganda, older children also had a reaction against 'advantageous inequity', refusing offers of deals which gave them more sweets than their partner in the experiment. The scientists, perhaps fearing for the frailty of the ice on which they walked, declined to offer explanations for why there might be differences between countries.

But that is just science. What about our guts? That is where more often than not we feel unfairness and increasingly, it seems, we feel it for others as much as we do for ourselves. Younger people, in particular, see matters through the lens of justice and fairness and are increasingly taking that attitude with them into the workplace. I have lost count of the number of senior journalism figures I have spoken to who say they are both thrilled and terrified at the passion which younger journalists fling into their work.

The editor of one of Britain's biggest regional papers told me last year:

> *They don't have a separation of their private and public positions on issues like climate or race. They see the world in terms of right and wrong, not right and left.*

The Black Lives Matters movement was simmering before the death of George Floyd brought it to the rolling boil. Just like the coronavirus, all governments in the democratic nations of the world are now having to think hard about the implications for policies that might have a racial ingredient to them. Even the past is seen as a threat to order by the new generation of protester. History is not safe from revision and the future will be written as it happens by generations who do not wish to be detained by detail and increasingly seem to see things without shades of grey.

Is this a good or bad thing for those of us who champion fairness and want to drag the world back to a path where discourse without disgust is possible? Do we need journalists who can leave their prejudices and ideologies behind when they step into their role as fact-checkers and fact-writers, when facts themselves are in dispute? Perhaps it depends on the issues. Racial discrimination is the refined essence of unfairness, especially when it is institutional and unquestioned or, worse, backed by pseudo-science like eugenics. You cannot hope to find fairness in a mind which assigns to others a state of mind, or that presumes bad intent from others, based on how they look or what groups they belong to. At the shoulder of prejudice stands ignorance and hatred and behind them stands violence. Behind them all are the really bad people who stir the minds of those they push in front to do the violence, seeking to benefit from the ruins of order. To the architects of chaos, fair-minded people are the enemy. So anything that pushes racial discrimination back is going to be on the side of fairness.

Yet the point of being fair, one to the other, is to find ways of cooperation (and co-habitation) as well as competition, not to tell groups of others that they are wrong (or indeed that they are right, if we do not think they really are). Promoting fairness is not a way of defeating the unfair as much as reaching for common ground. The actions that most move us are those that show the point where ideologies or cultures meet and, instead of clashing, speak. Think of 'Flower Power,' the Pulitzer-prize nominated photograph of an anti-Vietnam War protester putting a flower in the barrel of an National Guardsman's M-14 rifle; think of Martin McGuinness, IRA gunman and Sinn Fein activist, sharing his love of cricket with the Rev Ian Paisley, the bigoted backer of Ulster loyalist terrorism, when both men became members of the elected Northern Ireland Assembly; think of the lone protester near Tiananmen Square stopping a line of tanks with his shopping bags; think of the photograph of Patrick Hutchison, the man quoted at the top of this section, carrying a far-right activist to safety in the middle of a race riot in central London last summer.

Fairness lives where antagonism becomes tolerance. Fairness dwells in others.

Happy families are all alike; every unhappy family is unhappy in its own way.

Leo Tolstoy, *Anna Karenina*

The opening lines of Anna Karenina are among the most quoted in world literature. Yet it seems odd that people pay so much more attention to the bit after the semi-colon than the bit before it. Coming from a newspaper background, I know of course that bad news sells papers better than good and the same is obviously true of novels.

But if for a moment we ignore commercial considerations and think about 'happy families are all alike', why would it be so? What are the dynamics of happiness that conform to a single pattern?

Not for the first time, it would be immensely helpful if we knew how our species had evolved from its first appearance up to the point where we know in detail how it behaved. Not all anthropologists regard it as useful to study existing hunter-gatherer tribes and extrapolate all human history from their conduct. However, there are some common factors even in the different environments that are home to groups such as the San tribes of the Namibian desert or the indigenous peoples of the Australian bush or the Ciri Khonome Pumé people of the sub-tropical savanna in Venezuela. The commonality of those factors means that they are likely to predate the individual arrival of those people where they are found today (Pumé probably 10-15,000 years ago; indigenous Australians ca. 65,000 years ago and the San 27-30,000 years ago).

These common factors are the existence of multiple bands of small family units which operate together in hunting and gathering (in more populous areas, these could come together in larger groups such as clans – those who claimed descent from a single male or female figure – or aggregations of clans); a bias towards favouring one or other sex as the one from which heredity and descent are claimed for reasons of both breeding – avoidance of incest – and inheritance – of territory (e.g. the San are more 'matrilineal'; indigenous Australian peoples tend to be patrilineal); a division of labour between sexes, almost always verging towards women's involvement in gathering food closer to settlements and childcare (often a communal activity) and men's in hunting and scavenging meat over longer distances. Although obviously controversial, there is a strong school of thought that it was the specialisation that emerged from a division of labour that gave *Homo sapiens* an edge over other species of *homo*, including Neanderthals.

If, and it is a big if, all our ancestors tended towards an egalitarian outlook, then each of these common factors would suggest that they also tended towards a fair allocation of duties, rights and heredity rather than towards strict equality. While there is evidence that some clans or even families would pass on property or territory to descendants meaning that status-differences could emerge over time, if that did happen, it was within small ranges of 'wealth' or position. The most important relationships – breeding and feeding – seem to have remained essentially equal in distribution and nature among our remote ancestors.

In short, there are signs that for the 95% of our species-history in which we acted in this apparently egalitarian manner (a period during which we acted presumably closer to the even older nature of earlier hominins than to our current forms of relationship), we found ways of balancing the obvious binary nature of our species: between holders of two X chromosomes and X,Y chromosomes; between the interests of those who were capable of fathering many offspring and those capable of mothering only a relatively small number.

In the millennia between then and now, humans imposed on themselves a variety of rituals, beliefs and laws that gradually eroded that balance of interests, almost always in favour of the male. Cooperation became more sophisticated and so did competition, but within families, cooperation became subject to external pressures. Only during the last few generations have ideas emerged that individual humans enjoyed rights – which we could see as a throwback to that hunter-gatherer egalitarianism instinct. But once that happened, it was only a matter of time before those rights began to apply to people in their choice of partners and their choice of how they contributed to both their mating partnerships and the broader 'clans' of their time. Simultaneously, we have increasingly, though not universally, broken down the idea that relationships should be governed by external pressures (e.g. marriage, heterosexuality) at the expense of internal ones (e.g. love). In each case we have edged towards fair application of our freedom to choose and away from ideas of right and wrong.

The speed with which this has happened in some Western societies is staggering. In Ireland, for instance, the control of social regulation by the Catholic church was broken in the space of four years with big majority votes to allow gay marriage (2015), repeal an anti-abortion clause in the country's constitution (2018) and liberalise laws on divorce (2019) which had been legalised only in 1995. Such a swing in attitudes merely reflected the pressure built up behind a dam of restriction by a powerful institution. Even the Archbishop of Dublin described the 2015 vote as a sign of 'social revolution'.

But it is emblematic of rapid change in our attitudes to each other. These multiple changes may be happening too fast not only for the conservative-minded, but for our instincts to catch up with. So while we should celebrate the fairness inherent in allowing everyone to express their personal conscience, liberty and love as they wish, should we also consider those whose instincts remain connected to our remoter past? Does fairness extend also to those who are still comfortable with the approach to human relationships developed over hundreds of years? There is a growing feeling in countries such as the UK and US that it does not, including a pressure on all society to adapt the use of language to describe gender in order to avoid offence to some members of society. This is an area where consensus and reasoned discourse are in painfully short supply. Would not appeals to empathy rather than efforts to censor language be the more human approach? The key here is surely tolerance, a close-knit cousin of fairness. If this 'social revolution' is to mean anything, it must mean trying to find a balance of tolerance and understanding of those who have lived within a stricter definition of personal freedom and not make them feel as though their beliefs have in the blink of a generation, become 'wrong'. It is fair to expect people to fall in with a revolution in thinking only if there is enough convincing education and communication to explain why it *should* be so.

It should not be necessary to say that fairness applies to everyone however they think of themselves and nobody should be victimised because of their sex, or their sexuality or their expression of it. In this too, we are probably closer to our hunter-gatherer ancestors than to those who have lived since the Agricultural Revolution 12,500 years ago: we have no way of knowing how our prehistoric ancestors behaved towards each other, but oppression of one sex by the other would not be consistent with what we do know of their essentially egalitarian way of life. Nor would it have been sensible.

The balance of fairness is critical to human relationships, from the general to the intimate, which are prone to go wrong if there is an excess of love on one side and a deficiency on the other, or a deficiency on both sides. They are weakened when one person contributes too much and another too little, whether financially, emotionally, sexually. They fail when one member of a family hides truths from the others (or sometimes when they show too much honesty without using tact). In the spectrum of happiness, things go wrong when they fall out of balance. People may try too hard or not hard enough. They may be so loyal as to suffocate a partner or a child, or not loyal enough so as to make others feel insecure and vulnerable. Many children are extraordinarily sensitive to the amount and nature of kindness or unkindness and attention offered by their parents, sufficient to damage or strengthen their psyches throughout their lives. Without the difficulty of finding the mean in life, psychologists would be out of work.

Families are also factories. Their output is measured in terms of housing, happiness, health, humour and a million other products. Their input is mostly measured in hours. I don't suppose anyone has ever tried to measure the ratio of happy to unhappy families, not least because the definition of happiness varies from case to case. But it must be admitted that it is odd to concentrate on what makes people unhappy in relationships when we might learn just as much, maybe even more, by studying what makes them happy.

Martin Seligman, the former head of the American Psychological Association who first posited this idea about health, asked: Why should we study sick people instead of studying well people? Part of what makes people healthy is optimism, Seligman found. Optimists tend to have more friends, healthier immune systems and much lower stress levels. A medieval physician would have found much in common with Seligman's diagnosis of happiness. For our ancestors, a healthy happy individual was one in whom there was balance between the 'humours' which they believed dominated our physiology. As we have seen, being treated fairly is more likely to make us happy, unfairly the reverse.

Families may have a similar nature to that which the medieval mind identified in individuals. A balance between practicality and levity, between masculinity and femininity, between childishness and maturity, between prudence and extravagance, between fun and ambition incline them to happiness. Most of all, relationships between people need a balance of self and other.

Where families may differ from other aspects of our human lives, at least as directed by the need to seek a harmony between competing forces, is in the balance of competition and cooperation. While it must be both natural and necessary for younger generations to compete with older – the fundamental lessons of Egyptian creation myths are about the necessity to balance the energy of youth with the wisdom of age – competition between partners is usually unhealthy. It may be that we are conditioned by our genetic inheritance, when it comes to the relationships that involve the passing on of our own genes, to consider the family unit as being more important *as a unit* than the individual. That would mean that the balance of cooperation and competition needs to be found in our relationships with the world outside our walls rather than within them.

But that is to ignore the continuing debate in modern societies, particularly in the West, about the fairness in the division of labour between couples. How do we balance responsibilities and powers to act when only one sex is capable of the act of labour and delivery at birth? Employment rights legislation has made it easier for couples to share opportunities and duties in their roles as parents. But there remains a need for us to work out how we reconcile fairly the division between us as humans that nature applied when it split us, on blurred lines, between sexes.

FAIRNESS IN FAITH

The present life of man upon earth, O King, seems to
me in comparison with that time which is unknown
to us like the swift flight of a sparrow through the
mead-hall where you sit at supper in winter, with your
Ealdormen and thanes, while the fire blazes in the midst
and the hall is warmed, but the wintry storms of rain
or snow are raging abroad. The sparrow, flying in at
one door and immediately out at another, whilst he is
within, is safe from the wintry tempest, but after a short
space of fair weather, he immediately vanishes out of
your sight, passing from winter to winter again. So this
life of man appears for a little while, but of what is to
follow or what went before we know nothing at all.
– The Venerable Bede, *The Ecclesiastical History of the English People*

For a monk who spends his days glorifying the Christian vision, Bede offers us a fairly gloomy image of what life is and what we can expect from it. The unknown before and the unknown after. Though, as the novelist Julian Barnes pointed out, any self-respecting sparrow would settle on the rafters of the mead-hall for as long as possible. Maybe that is what we do. Perch in the warm, enjoying the sights and smells around us until we are chased away.

Religion is meant to offer a variety of incentives to behave in certain ways. There are variations between how the different faiths want us to behave (to 'restrain ourselves'), but in the end organised religions pretty much all want us to do as we are told. Occasionally a doctrine pops up that suggests that people should work out for themselves what their relation is with the eternal, but generally, some rules are laid down and some kind of intervention is obligatory.

As we saw before, faiths of different kinds offer glimpses of fairness. All are in favour of doing the right thing, though the details of what that right thing might be are not so universal. The problem is that human interpretation of good, big ideas has a habit of getting in the way of the goodness while rather bigging up the bigness. Christianity and Islam have, as good, big ideas always do, become intertwined with politics. Looking at that large swathe of the world today which owes tradition and heritage to these two faiths, it is hard to find a place where the practice of the big idea is separated from the practice of government. That is not to say that there are a lot of theocracies, because there aren't. But much of how we see ourselves is couched in the language of belief. It is only recently, for instance, that countries such as Spain or Italy or Ireland have loosened the hold of the Catholic church on their exercise of certain freedoms. It is only fifty-three years since it became legal in Britain, one of the more liberal polities of the world, for two men to have sex with each other. Would you bet against it being only another fifty-three years before some other republic decides, in a fit of moral fervour, to make it illegal again? Can we look at the way in which religion is used as a tool of politics in the US, say, and be certain that could not happen?[92] The one thing we can learn from history is that what seems fair to us did not necessarily seem fair to our forebears; what was fairness in their eyes seems like unfairness in ours. Think of human rights today and slavery before.

As I was growing up in Britain in the 1970s and 80s, the one thing I thought I could take for granted was that I would always be living in an increasingly secular country. Today, I am not so sure. It is less Christian, but not necessarily less interested in faith. Once, I would have thought the same of the US, which I first visited in 1989, but the ease with which the fairground barkers of American politics picked up the seeds of the country's radical past – intolerant religion and an obsession with playing at soldiers – makes me doubt that now. Americans are, in many ways, the fairest people on the planet, except when you talk to them about their God or their nation[93], when concession and cooperation seem to vaporise.

Martin Amis, the British author, wrote after his father Kingsley died in 1995:

The intercessionary figure, the father, the man who stands between the son and death, is no longer here; and it will no longer be the same.

---

[92]The politicisation – I prefer to call it the 'opinionisation' - of justice in the US has made it possible if not likely that the right to abortion will cease to be a right, perhaps even before you read this book.

[93]Or their guns.

Religion has played that father role for humans for thousands of years. It offers to intercede between people and their end, to remove the utter blankness of oblivion and replace it with a promise of something, of anything but nothing. To keep bad people good, it threatens eternal punishment; to keep the good people good, it offers eternal reward. Faith is a monument to marketing. As I mentioned earlier, the concepts of Purgatory and Hell do not appear in the teachings of Christ, except as a metaphor for the destruction of the body, not the soul. Marketing eternity may be a fairer exchange than many, but it still does not qualify as fairness. The fair approach to life is to ensure that everyone has the best chance of enjoying it, not enduring it, and in this religion can play an essential role for many people. But fairness also involves limiting the insistence that things or ideas or even words are either good or bad. Everything from light to colour to transmitting radio signals to human conduct to the working of the human brain is on a spectrum. What is visible, brilliant, effective, beneficial, productive, tends to be found in the middle, not on the extremes. Our beliefs, especially those shaped for us by our intercessionaries, look to the worst and the best that might happen to us when our most likely fate sits with all the rest of the sparrows, up there on the rafters.

FAIRNESS IN OUR EXPECTATIONS OF LIFE

We are all fair game to death. Some of us live for minutes and some for more than a century, yet we see the differences between each other not in the quantity of life as much as in its quality. Somehow, life expectancy, a measure of quantity, has become a way for different nations to gauge their own success. It has been rising in almost all countries since the end of the Second World War. In 1950, the global average of life expectancy was forty-seven years; only seventy years later it is slightly more than seventy-three. That is the addition of almost an entire generation's extra life within one human lifetime. There are of course huge differences: a male child in the Central African Republic today can expect to live to see his fifty-second birthday; a girl born in Hong Kong her eighty-eighth.

In most countries, quantity of life has been growing. But not in all. The average of lifespans in the US began to shorten in 2015.[94] Having risen from 69.9 years in 1959 to 78.9 in 2016, US life expectancy it fell to 78.6 in 2017. The fall has been blamed on increased mortality in American adults between twenty-five and sixty-four, the most productive group of any human society, caused by a combination of factors including drug overdose, abuse of alcohol, suicide and organ system diseases such as diabetes. Forgetting the reduction in quantity of life, none of these causes speak to higher quality of life either.

The author of the study reporting these findings, when asked for reasons, instantly pointed at the underlying relationship between the family and the wider state. Dr. Steven Woolf, director emeritus of the Center on Society and Health at Virginia Commonwealth University, said that 'in other countries there are more support systems for people who fall on hard times. In America, families are left to their own devices to try to get by.'

However, there were also signs in the previous decade that even societies which do have support systems for the vulnerable do not necessarily do better. In 2010, the UK embarked on a period of 'austerity' to repair the economic damage done by the global financial crisis. If ever there

[94]Woolf, S. & Schoomaker, H., 2019. Life Expectancy and Mortality Rates in the United States, 1959–2017.. *JAMA*, 322(20).

were a stark statistic by which to measure the unfairness of the response, it was this one: the definitive study of life expectancy in Britain showed in 2020 that in the ten poorest areas of England, life expectancy for women had actually fallen by 0.3 years between 2010 and 2019; in the ten wealthiest areas it had risen by half a year. The author, Professor Sir Michael Marmot, said in an interview:

> *From the beginning of the 20th century, England experienced continuous improvements in life expectancy, but from 2011 these improvements slowed dramatically, almost grinding to a halt.*
>
> *If health has stopped improving, that means society has stopped improving and if health inequalities continue and in fact increase, that means inequalities in society have been increasing.*[95]

As for the quality of life, it is almost by definition hard to quantify, but the measure most often cited is probably the UN's Human Development Index, created by Amartya Sen and the Pakistani economist Mahbub ul Haq. It combines statistics on life expectancy, education and per capita income. The country at the top, Norway, scored .954, two and a half times the level of the country at the bottom, Niger, on .377.[96] The historical version of

[95]Sky News; Marmot, Michael, 2020. *Women's life expectancy falls in England's poorest areas while the North-South health gap grows*. [Online] Available at: https://news.sky.com/story/womens-life-expectancy-falls-in-englands-poorest-areas-while-the-north-south-health-gap-grows-11942639

[96]82. UNDP, 2019. *2019 Human Development Index Ranking*. [Online] Available at: http://hdr.undp.org/en/content/2019-human-development-index-ranking

this index gives a slightly different perspective. In 1960, Norway scored 0.500, which by 2019 had risen 47 per cent. But Niger's index score in 1960 was only .040 so its development had increased by 852 per cent.[97] These metrics may be too crude to reflect reality, but the direction of travel is surely clear. There is some equalisation of health, wealth and education, even if the world's poorer countries start from an incredibly low base and there are of course still huge disparities.

Those are some of the quantities, but what about the qualities of our expectations of life? What, after all this, can we say about the way in which *Homo sapiens* behave and how it might become better for all? How do we instinctively feel in relation to others and their conduct towards us?

If you cast your mind back to when we looked at the definitions and the psychology of fairness, you may remember that I was particularly eager to show that fairness is not the same as equality.[98]

To do that, I leaned a lot on the work of Prof Christina Starmans and her team at Yale University's department of psychology. Their position was that previous research pointing to an 'inequality aversion' had failed to detect that the subjects of previous sharing-game experiments with children and adults were not averse to economic

[97]Our World In Data, 2016. *Historical Index of Human Development, 1870 to 2015*. [Online]

Available at: https://ourworldindata.org/grapher/human-development-index-escosura

[98]Chapter 2 Section B and Chapter 3 Section C in Starmans, C., Sheskin, M. & Bloom, P., 2017. Why people prefer unequal societies. *Nature Human Behaviour*, 07 April.

inequality but to economic unfairness. A simple lab experiment fails to introduce real situations in which people have different instincts that lead them to make different judgments. So, for instance, if you ask a six-year-old child to distribute six sweets to two children as a reward for tidying up their rooms, almost all the subjects will give the two children three sweets each and will reject any option to give four to one child or two to the other. However, if you introduce nuance of detail to the scenario, things change. If you tell the donor child that one of the two recipients worked for a lot longer than the other, then most of the donors are content to choose an unequal split. They judge instinctively that it is fair to reward someone who has put more work into the same project. If you tell the donor that one of the recipients has not had any sweets for some time, they will also reward perceived 'need' with an unequal distribution. A human instinct to favour someone who behaves altruistically or punish non-cooperators is detectable in even younger children, Starmans found. Using puppets, researchers elicited responses from children as young as three that showed less generosity towards a character who was violent towards another character than to one who acted benvolently.

People of all ages are also prepared to treat a completely uneven distribution of resources, in which one person gets nothing, if a random choice is introduced, such as tossing a coin to determine who gets a piece of chocolate or a £50 note, because the introduction of fair chance makes the whole process fair. Inequality is tolerable to most people if they believe that there is a fair opportunity for everyone to get the same outcomes, but the moment they realise there is no such fairness, they begin to reject the whole proposition in front of them.

Fairness is critical in evolutionary terms to our ability to cooperate and allows us to avoid passing judgments on others that might makes us seem partisan in a group that is trying to be cooperative. It allows us to solve the problems brought about by the Cephus of the world. We instinctively shun the selfish and include and reward the cooperative, but we have to balance the fact that over-cooperative people will be exploited by Cephus. Starmans says that favouring fairness over equality means that you can distribute the fruits of cooperative production proportionately.

I would say that this doesn't quite get the essential quality of fairness, because it suggests that the 'level' of productivity is what matters, whereas I think the key is the *nature* of productivity. Measuring contributions to a society or a group or a team in mere quantity terms is, to use a baseball term, moneyball: relying on past performance to predict future value. As any sports fan will tell you the quality of a player comes through in far more than numbers and scores. A crow can count. A monkey or an ape can determine whether something is edible by its smell. Anyone can distinguish quantity or quality for their own survival purposes, but determining the quality of something or someone in a fair exchange, of the value of fairness in the round, is a distinctly human capability. Ask Jackie Robinson.

JACKIE ROBINSON AND ROY FRANCIS

But as I write these words now I cannot stand and
sing the National Anthem. I have learned that
I remain a black in a white world.

Jackie Robinson, baseball player

If any sphere of human activity should advance the cause of treating people fairly, it is sport, because fair cooperation with an agreed set of rules is what makes competition possible on the field. I have already written about fairness in sport, but because we are dealing with fairness in human relationships, because the way we relate to others seems to find its most telling expression in competitive cooperation and because my interest in fairness was sparked by an interest in sport, I wanted to end on it too. End on sport and race and the will to work together and the will to win.

In 1944, a young US Army lieutenant was court-martialled for refusing a direct order. The order was that he, a black man, should sit in the back of an army bus with other black people, even though the official policy of the service was that such buses were not segregated. The lieutenant was acquitted, though his military career ended soon after. Instead, he earned a place in history as a professional sportsman. Jackie Robinson was already a celebrity when he joined the army in 1942, having excelled in the American code of football and at athletics when he was a student at UCLA. He forced his way into officer-training – again something that was theoretically open to black candidates, but in practice was closed to them – after teaming up with another black superstar, Joe Louis, the reigning world heavyweight boxing champion, who was at the same base camp as Robinson.

After the war, Robinson became the beacon of a long-running campaign to desegregate baseball which left-wing journalists, union activists and civil-rights campaigners had been driving since the early 1930s. He was signed by the owner of the Brooklyn Dodgers, Branch Rickey, who saw both an opportunity to do something he believed in and to sell more tickets to the growing class of wealthier African-Americans moving to New York. After a torrid first season where he faced verbal and physical abuse, as well as threatened boycotts from white opponents, Robinson's on-field talent made him impossible to ignore. His breakthrough allowed a trickle of other black players to join the Dodgers, who became the dominant team of baseball in the 1950s. There was never any likelihood that American sport would be resegregated because white players could not face the accusation that they were afraid to face the best competition, regardless of race. By appealing first to the competitive natures of sport, and then to its cooperative nature, sport arrived in a place where it is now unthinkable that black or other non-white players could be excluded from the opportunity to dominate. This was the lesson learned by Adolf Hitler in 1936 when Jesse Owens mastered his own hand-picked Aryan supermen athletes at the Berlin Olympics. Once you have lost to a person you disdain, you can never again refuse to compete against them.

That is not to say that black players had or have an easy time in sport since. Recent experience shows the degree that they still battle racism daily. But they are at least able to compete and to show their capabilities. The latest figures show that 42% of Major League Baseball players in 2018 were people of colour, with many more being Latino (32%) than black (8%); in basketball, 81% of players are non-white and in the National Football League, 70%. Yet behind the scenes, in managerial and coaching jobs, numbers are far smaller. For instance, only 9% of the NFL's own management staff were non-white in 2018, down from 14% in 1996. There are only a handful of Latino or black owners of US professional sports clubs. Jackie Robinson forced open part of the door and thousands of others joined him, but there are other doors that remain difficult or impossible for people with the 'wrong' skin colour to pass through.

To many British people who visit America – and I speak as one who lived there for four years and saw it at its best and worst – race is the defining issue of the USA. Americans like to say that freedom is the defining characteristic of their country, but as Brad Pitt's character says in the film *Fight Club*: 'How's that working out for you?'

Prioritising freedom over fairness is not working for the generality of Americans. In particular, it is not working for Americans of colour. Freedom means different things to different Americans.

The *de facto* segregation of many American cities is shocking to Europeans who come across it. There are echoes of it in every major European city, but in few or any have there been laws directing where people should live based on their race. One of the things I found most alien about living in Washington DC was the discovery that wealthy African-Americans were less likely to live in the wealthiest parts of the city than they were to live in the wealthiest *black* parts of the city. Real estate agents played a part in this back-door segregation. Maybe they still do.

America's Civil War gave 'freedom' to black Americans and it made them citizens. But to look at the 166 years since its end, emancipation never delivered fairness to black Americans, merely replaced slavery with segregation, statutory discrimination with a deliberate turning of blind eyes to the economic and social plight of the most downtrodden in society.[99] Freedom is not meaningful if

[99]In the interests of balance, I should point out that 166 years after England's Civil War, there was a rebellion by Catholic supporters of the Stuart kings, the Habeas Corpus act was suspended and the last battle was fought on English soil at Preston

you can still be subject to laws that prevent you enjoying the same opportunities and rights as your fellow citizens. Jim Crow laws – local restrictions on the liberty of African-Americans that were enacted mostly but not exclusively in the US states that took up arms in 1861 for their right to keep other humans as chattels – were manifestly unfair but, shockingly to European eyes, they pertained until more than a century after the end of the Civil War.

The current power of the Black Lives Matter movement is eloquent testimony to the fact that fairness is still a long way off for black people in the US not only in criminal justice, but in every walk of life. Powerful forces are seeking to divide Americans in ways that are unfair on everyone in that society – and this is not exclusive to the US. Many American commentators argue that the success of Donald Trump among poorer white voters is linked to the idea that he opposes any limitations on their 'freedom' to live as they wish. The emphasis is always on their freedom; when Trump speaks of unfairness, it is usually in the context of how unfair the media, or opposition politicians, or vote-counting machines, or life in general, are to him personally, not to his voters.

He seems willing to trade the freedom of those loyal to him for the 'fair' outcome he feels, or pretends to feel, is his due; until now, a devoted core of them have been willing to participate in that hard bargain. So is valuing freedom working out well for *white* Americans at least? They are more likely to be free to eat what they want, vote as they want, work where and when they want and it is rare for a white American to come up against boundaries to their social mobility based on the pigmentation of their skin. But in other ways, poor America has been badly served by a different kind of freedom, the freedom of rich America to do what *it* wants. As we saw in the last section, the lives of poor white Americans are marred by obesity, by opioid-addiction (fuelled by the corporate malpractice of doctors and pharmaceutical companies) and by mental health problems. These are conditions of poverty rather than race.

And by the way, you don't need to surrender a grain of freedom in order to make fairness a priority. Returning to the story of Jackie Robinson, whose status in America was symbolic of the battle against segregation and unfairness in the country, you might think that Britain would be more advanced. But in sporting terms, not really. It might be thought that Britain, with its traditions of fair play and its less engrained, less legalised attitudes to racial division would have given it a head start. After all, the attitudes to non-whites were not enshrined in discriminatory 'Jim Crow' or apartheid laws as they were in the US or South Africa.

But the story of the great Roy Francis would make you think again. Roy who? I can hear people asking. Roy Francis was arguably the greatest rugby player of his generation and almost certainly the greatest and most innovative coach of the twentieth century. The fact that many readers will still be scratching their heads as to who I am talking about speaks to the fact that rugby league, the code of football predominant in northern England and the first part of the game to embrace professionalism, is often ignored by the noisier and more influential crowd that supports the previously amateur code of rugby union. Roy Francis scored tries at a faster rate than almost any other player in rugby league history and would have played many more times for England and Great Britain were it not for having been black. He was born in 1919, five years after Jackie Robinson, in Tiger Bay, Cardiff's ethnically diverse dock area, and struggled to get any games for his local rugby union teams despite his prodigious talent. He was poached by a professional coach from Wigan and started an extraordinary career, interrupted by the Second World War. After retiring with 229 tries from 356 games, Francis went on to become one of the most successful coaches in the sport's history, winning two Challenge Cups and one league title with Hull, Leeds and Bradford Northern in the 1960s and 70s. He introduced the concepts of sports psychology and nutrition to British sport twenty years before anyone else and was revered by his peers and players.

Barely anyone not associated with those clubs he played for or coached has heard of Roy Francis. Or the other black Welsh players who followed him such as Billy Boston or Clive Sullivan, the first black man to captain any British representative sporting team in 1971, twenty-two years before football appointed a black captain and thirty-two years before the English Rugby Union did.

In some ways, you might argue that Britain was worse than America in this respect, precisely because it did not have Jim Crow laws. There was no historical excuse, just intrinsic snobbery and prejudice, to deter non-white athletes from rising to the top of British sport.

Today, we take that for granted: many of the greatest sporting stars of recent times have been men and women who would not have been allowed to play under the bigotry of the past: Pelé, Serena Williams, Usain Bolt, Michael Jordan, Lewis Hamilton. The captain of the South African side that won the last Rugby World Cup, leading a country that in the 1960s and 70s preferred to be ostracised from the sport rather than take to the field of competition against someone they considered to be of an inferior race, was a black man: Siya Kolisi.

Do they owe it all to Jackie Robinson? No, not all. They also owe it to the people who realised that they preferred sport to prejudice and that in competition and cooperation what matters is not who you are but what you do and why you do it. In every country in the Western world, white and non-white athletes compete and cooperate under the same colour of shirt.

It is a habit of American sports teams to pay tribute to their greatest stars by 'retiring' the number of the shirt they wore (this is only possible because they have such huge squads). This would, of course, not work beyond the team for which the star played, because no other team will want to celebrate their victories. But it did happen just once in baseball. In 1997, in recognition of Robinson's symbolism and courage, the entire professional game agreed that nobody would again wear the number he wore for the Brooklyn Dodgers. Except on one day. Every April 15, Jackie Robinson Day, all baseball players wear the same number on their shirt, to show solidarity, to offer support for a man who made sport recognise that it could be free of the worst aspects of human unfairness when it sought to make fair play all that counted.

Pretty much every American, even if they are not keen followers of sport, knows what that number is. And having reached this stage of this book, I imagine you have a pretty fair idea too.

It is 42.

42

Is Fair Play the Answer to the Ultimate Question?

HOW CLOSE CAN WE COME TO A FAIR WORLD?

Fairness is innate. Our reaction to unfair treatment, like the monkey in Frans de Waal's cage, is not learned, but felt. While unfairness may sit deeper in the brain, the sense of fairness done to others occupies the reward centre of our minds for a reason: to be fair is to win. It is linked to other actions we associate with the highest notes reached by humanity – altruism, generosity, kindness.[100]

Fairness helps us understand how we stand in relation to other people, which is the most important thing we can know about ourselves. To know how we mesh with the other cogs of the increasingly complex machine of human existence is a necessity to shape our behaviour. Fairness intercedes for us, it lubricates the machine of human progress through time and permits a balance between our instinct to work with other humans and our need to strive against them. It teaches us our duty as well as our entitlement, our responsibility as well as our power.

[100]See Nowak, M. A. & Highfield, R., 2011. *SuperCooperators* Reprint Ed ed. s.l.:Free Press.

The absence of fairness between people throws out the balance of competition and cooperation and makes all parties feel there is something wrong in their lives.

Fairness is a procedure, a process of reaching consensus and doing a deal with the rest of the world. We cannot lose faith in the idea of fairness because it is too much a part of our nature, so instead, when fairness seems to fail, we blame the procedure.

If a procedural approach to our survival is letting us down, there is only one way to turn and that is to follow the path of absolute, not asking what is fair, but only what is right. Not asking what we might do with others, but what we can do to them.

Not only does this kind of thinking go against the genetic inheritance of millions of years, but it also runs counter to the intellectual and moral direction we have been following since the end of the 1939–45 War.

And we all know that the bad, dark side of technological change has been acting as an accelerant on the smouldering loss, first of certainty – in the wake of 9/11 – and then of fairness, in the reckoning that followed the global financial crisis.

Simultaneously, we have seen an urgent clamour for fairness between people. It has been mixed up in these same currents of human change that caused fairness between the hierarchies of mankind to get out of kilter. But the clamour is there and getting louder: the #MeToo movement, Black Lives Matter, the rise of 'identity politics' are just some of the manifestations of how people want to change the way they receive fairness or unfairness from their peers and from the institutions to which they delegated their authority.

All in all, we are significantly, perhaps even dangerously, out of balance between competition and cooperation.

The former is strong, the latter as little in evidence now as at any time in my life. People are out for themselves and less interested in reaching accord with others. Greed and disproportion occupy Wall Street and the City of London. Those who struggle look at those growing immeasurably wealthy and detached with increasing feelings of 'otherness'. Restraint withers away. As the mass of people begin to lose faith in the order and reason of the past seventy-five years, their cynical political leaders are driving them harder down that path, sending them to the barricades on a diet of deceit, all inadvertently corralled by the algorithms of social media. I fear that the recent crop of authoritarians, egotists and so-called populists are not the disease, but the symptoms of the disease. Those that come after them, gorging on the disappointment and frustration of those whose aspirations to be heard and aspirations to be counted were milked but not met by Trump or Brexit, are the ones to fear.

Covid favoured the wealthy and disadvantaged the poor, as disasters usually do. Because viruses don't have minds, they don't care about our petty struggles for eminence. But it is possible to learn from that, not least that cooperation in the face of a common threat is a more effective response than competition or diktat.

History shows us that we always make progress. We change and we move closer to fairness over time, having gradually lost it when we first banded together in larger and larger numbers. We can restore the balance that fairness tells us to seek and there are at least two ways of doing it. The first is to destroy everything, tear up the nature of cooperation and competition, of collective, social action and of market-driven capitalistic action and we can start again from some point. Perhaps a computer program can help us restart; it seems more likely that one will make us destroy. Artificial intelligence deals in 1s and 0s, true and false, yes and no, binary choices that do not allow for interpretation, consensus or fairness. It often feels as if even the humans, the Silicon Valley geniuses that shape our momentum, have the same binary functions. And if restarting sounds painful, something that might work for a laptop but not for a society, that is because it would be painful; there is no guarantee we would ever get back to a moment where we feel that the path of progress ahead of us is taking us towards a common good.

But we could choose another path. We can use our innate sense of what is and isn't fair to help us get back to where we were heading at the beginning of this last, digital, revolution. We can and we should change the balance of our search for a better society.

If that means that we are seeking fairness, and everything I know tells me that we have no choice but to do so, then it is immediately and forcefully time for us to stop trying to be right and start trying to be fair.

Afterword and Further Reading

I am a reporter. My value, if I have any, is to bring to your attention things that have happened, words that have been written. To the extent that I have any originality to offer, it is in combining facts, theories and observations in a stream. It is not in my nature to create a polemic, but because I care a lot about this subject, that is what my stream seems to have become.

And my stream has sources.

While I have included quite a lot of references, there are some of those sources which I especially want to recommend as further reading on different aspects of fairness.

On the science of fairness, Lixing Sun's *The Fairness Instinct – The Robin Hood Mentality And Our Biological Nature* (Prometheus Books, New York, 2013) is a comprehensive and readable study that has more detail on the structure of the brain than I could include. I am not sure that a historian would share his fascination with the character of Robin Hood who, before Walter Scott and then Hollywood got hold of him, was a somewhat morally ambiguous character. In fact, he was a bit of a villain, even in myth, till he was romanticised in the 19th century.

Speaking of historians, the first history of fairness, by his own account and I would not demur, was *Fairness and Freedom: A History of Two Open Societies: New Zealand and the United States* (OUP, 2011) by David Hackett Fischer. In the opening of the book he deals a lot with questions about our understanding of fairness and its linguistic origins. In his appendix, on p.500–501 he refers to the same idea as mine about the balance of competition and cooperation:

> *Ideas of fair play might be understood as a cooperative way to promote competition and vice versa: a competitive way to promote cooperation. One might take the inquiry to another level by hypothesising that it is not competition or cooperation alone that is the key here but their dynamic interaction. This may help us to understand why ideas of fairness become more important as systems become more complex.*

Although I had not read Fischer before I began writing this book, I hope I have taken the inquiry on in the way he suggests and expands on the thoughts he expresses here.

In fact, Fischer was at this point in his appendix also exploring the work of others as it affected his comparative history of New Zealand and the US. His particular focus here was the work of the Harvard mathematical biologist Martin Nowak (who I have also cited several times) and his argument in SuperCooperators: Altruism, Evolution, and Why We Need Each Other to Succeed (Free Press, 2011), which he wrote with my former Daily Telegraph colleague Roger Highfield, a man who has done as much to make science explicable as anyone. As Fischer says, Nowak and

Highfield do not dwell on fairness, but they have much to say on competition and cooperation. They argue, inter alia, that morality is an offshoot of evolution's path towards more and more complex types of cooperation between social species such as Homo sapiens. So are cognition and language. There are huge controversies about some of the premises of Nowak, and indeed about the nature of evolution as a whole. It is my luxury as a polemical reporter to leave them to others.

Among those others are the scientific writers recently satisfying an understandable appetite among the bemused citizens of the disrupted world for reassurance that people are not all bad, mad and dangerous to misjudge. They include: Michael McCullough: The Kindness of Strangers: How A Selfish Ape Invented a New Moral Code (Oneworld, 2020); Richard Wrangham: The Goodness Paradox: How Evolution Made Us Both More and Less Violent (Profile Books, 2019); Brian Hare and Vanessa Woods: Survival of the Friendliest: Understanding Our Origins and Rediscovering Our Common Humanity (Oneworld, 2020); Rutger Bregman: Humankind: A Hopeful History (Bloomsbury 2020).

Other books which you may find interesting to pursue particular tributaries to this stream are:

LINGUISTICS

Anna Wierzbicka: *English: Meaning and culture* (OUP 2006)

HISTORY OF THE ENGLISH

Robert Tombs: *The English and Their History* (Penguin 2014)

PHILOSOPHY

John Rawls: *A Theory of Justice* (Harvard University Press, 1971)
John Rawls: *Justice as Fairness* (Harvard 2001)
Christopher McMahon: *Reasonableness and Fairness* (Cambridge University Press 2016)

MEDIA

Matthew Engel: *Tickle the Public: One Hundred Years of the Popular Press* (Gollancz 1996)

Acknowledgements

This book began as a rant. Then it turned into a proposal for founding a new social movement to restore fairness. Then the one and only Richard Charkin got hold of the idea and it became what you see now. Thank you.

I owe my sanity and any sense I make to Miranda Vaughan Jones, my patient and brilliant editor. Thank you.

People who played a part in contributing ideas and guidance, even if they don't realise it, include Matthew Engel, Helle Thorning-Schmidt, Iain Dey, Simon Olswang, Adrian Martin, Emran Mian, Robert Tombs, Nick Humphrey, Mark Thompson, James Kirkup and Diane Coyle. Thank you.

Those who have consistently taken the piss out of me for my obsession with fairness and so kept my feet on the ground include my children, Alex, Sophie and Julius. Thank you.

Leading me always towards being a fairer thinker, reporter and human being is my wife, Lila. Thank you is nowhere near enough.

A Note on the Author

Ben Fenton was a newspaper reporter for thirty years before becoming a media consultant. He worked in some forty countries on five continents covering wars, injustices, triumphs and disasters, Olympic Games and presidential elections.

Having seen humanity at its cooperative best and cut-throat worst, Fenton became fascinated by the idea that fair play, the innate process of deciding how we live with each other in competition and in social harmony, might be the ultimate answer to our increasingly troubled times.

Fenton is married with three children and lives in London.

A Note on the Type

A Note on the Type

The text of this book is set Adobe Garamond. It is one of several versions of Garamond based on the designs of Claude Garamond. It is thought that Garamond based his font on Bembo, cut in 1495 by Francesco Griffo in collaboration with the Italian printer Aldus Manutius. Garamond types were first used in books printed in Paris around 1532. Many of the present-day versions of this type are based on the *Typi Academiae* of Jean Jannon cut in Sedan in 1615.

Claude Garamond was born in Paris in 1480. He learned how to cut type from his father and by the age of fifteen he was able to fashion steel punches the size of a pica with great precision. At the age of sixty he was commissioned by King Francis I to design a Greek alphabet, and for this he was given the honourable title of royal type founder. He died in 1561.